My Version of the Facts

My Version of the Facts

Carla Pekelis

Translated from the Italian by George Hochfield

T**M**P

The Marlboro Press / Northwestern
Northwestern University Press
Evanston, Illinois

The Marlboro Press/Northwestern
Northwestern University Press
Evanston, Illinois 60208-4170

English translation copyright © 2004 by Northwestern University Press. Published 2005
by the Marlboro Press/Northwestern. Originally published in Italian as *La mia versione
dei fatti*. All rights reserved.

Printed in the United States of America
10 9 8 7 6 5 4 3 2 1

ISBN 0-8101-6086-2 (cloth)
ISBN 0-8101-6087-0 (paper)

Library of Congress Cataloging-in-Publication Data

Pekelis, Carla, 1907–1985.
    [Mia versione dei fatti. English]
    My version of the facts / Carla Pekelis ; translated from the Italian by George
Hochfield.
       p. cm.
    Originally written in two parts in a mixture of English and French.
    ISBN 0-8101-6086-2 — ISBN 0-8101-6087-0
    1. Pekelis, Carla, 1907–1985. 2 Jews—Italy—Biography. 3. Holocaust, Jewish
(1939–1945)—Italy—Personal narratives. 4. Holocaust survivors—Biography.
5. Italy—Biography. I. Title.
DS135.18 P45713 2002
305.892'4045'092—dc21

                                       2002002401

Contents

Introduction
The Antidote to Fascism

In their search for a common definition of "fascism," historians and political philosophers have sometimes adopted the metaphor of disease. Fascism, they write, was a virus, a virulent malady, a political affliction, a moral disorder, an ethical sickness. It attacked all that was healthy in European civilization (the Enlightenment tradition, rationality, humanitarianism, and all the freedoms associated with classical liberalism) and ended with the rotting corpses of Benito Mussolini and Adolf Hitler.

As with other forms of totalitarianism, fascism sought to strip away the private sphere from the individual and turn it over to the state. On another front, it inflated language to its own ends so that the rhetoric of a rabid nationalism and distorted history became the common tongue of empire.

For many, the antidote to the bombastic, inflated rhetoric of fascism was the seemingly plain and simple language of American literature; it was no coincidence that the anti-Fascist writer Cesare Pavese and others spent the 1930s translating Whitman, Melville, Thoreau, Anderson, and the other great American writers of the nineteenth and early-twentieth centuries.

In the face of the grandiose (and often ridiculous) claims of Fascist rhetoric, writers and others took refuge in the simple pleasures of the quotidian. To combat the attempt of the Fascist state to seize control of the family through social legislation (preventing abortions and contraception, taxing bachelors, granting stipends to large families), some writers fell back to the familial and domestic scenes of the hearth.

One such writer was Natalia Ginzburg, best known for her *Lessico famigliare* (1963), translated into English as *Family Sayings* (1967). American readers now have an opportunity to compare Carla Pekelis to Ginzburg. The similarities are striking: both born into bourgeois, cosmopolitan Jewish families; married to intellectuals exiled from Odessa (Leone Ginzburg, a noted anti-Fascist, was captured by the Gestapo, tortured, and killed; Alexander [Sandro] Pekelis fled on the last ship out of Odessa in November 1917 and died in a 1946 plane crash); their writing focuses on family, friends, and memory; their canvas is small, awash in colors but occasionally tinted by the shadows of history and nostalgia. There are a detached, ironic sense of humor, a profound sensitivity, and an ever-present doubt manifest in a self-irony that were a welcome relief from the absolutes of the Fascist state.

Although both Ginzburg and Pekelis deal with the small miracles of daily life, Pekelis also wrote of the larger world. This was an imperative of her years of exile in France, Spain, Portugal, and the United States. But it was also an obligation to the times in which she lived. We can afford the luxury of the quotidian pleasures only when the world is at peace; in Pekelis's lifetime, the world was often at war. Pekelis's status as an "outsider," whether as a woman, a Jew, or a writer, has rendered in her writing a poignancy that survives even in translation. She arrived at this status as an outsider only after resisting it for many years; it was Sandro who taught her the value of such a position and that it often confers a privileged perspective of the world. After having dismantled and reconstructed her life a number of times, Pekelis comes to recognize those things that are transient and those that are permanent.

The reader should note that the first half of *My Version of the Facts* was written by Pekelis when she was already in her late sixties, almost a lifetime after the events occurred. Though based on a detailed diary she kept at the time, the story is filtered through the eyes of a woman near the end of her life, thus imparting a note of nostalgia and wistfulness. The second half of the book, beginning in 1947, was written almost contemporaneously with the events themselves. In 1946, Sandro, who had survived the Russian Revolution, Mussolini's Racial Laws, and Hitler's Europe, died. As he was returning from a meeting of the World Zionist Congress in Switzerland where he was the American Labor delegate, his plane went down outside Shannon, Ireland. After this devastating loss, Pekelis returned to Italy in 1947, but the return was full of a subtle pain for an Italy that seemed to have already forgotten—only two years after the war—what fascism had meant.

Carla Pekelis (1907–85) was born in Rome to Dante Coen and Ada Ascoli. In 1924, the family moved to Florence, where her father took over a jewelry shop on the Ponte Vecchio, and seven years later, Carla Coen married Alexander Pekelis. Sandro Pekelis is an animated and charismatic presence in these pages. When he arrived in the United States, he had to go to law school all over again. With his quintessentially cosmopolitan view of the world and his talent of quickly being able to understand different disciplines, he excelled at Columbia Law School, becoming the first foreign-born editor of its law review. The next year the school appointed him to the extraordinary post of Graduate Editor, which was created for him. For the short time he was in the States, he was also on the faculty of the "University in Exile," part of the New School for Social Research. "He believed," wrote Max Ascoli, another exiled anti-Fascist at the University in Exile, "that the limit of man's power should be his willingness to pay a fair price for the attainment of his ambitions."[1] With the passage of the anti-Semitic Racial Laws in 1938, Sandro and Carla left Italy, first for Paris, then, during the fall of France in June 1940, for Lisbon. From Por-

1. Max Ascoli, "Alexander H. Pekelis, 1902–1946," *Social Research,* 14, 1 (March 1947): 2.

tugal they eventually managed to make their way to the United States, where Carla Pekelis taught Italian language and literature at Sarah Lawrence College. Until the end of her life she managed—with an indomitable spirit—to keep an extended family together and write numerous short stories.

From the very first page, Pekelis is clear that this is an ambiguous memoir; she is honest not only that memory is a tricky ally at best but also that her fondest memories are tinged with fear, embarrassment, and unease.[2]

And like a silken thread, there is the subterranean but ever-present dilemma of being a Jew in twentieth-century Italy. Although Pekelis claims early on that, during her childhood, being Jewish meant "nothing, absolutely nothing!" and that it was "more a question of things that I did not do than things I had to do," clearly there is more here than meets the eye. For, as Lynne Gunzberg in the United States and Michele Sarfatti in Italy have made clear, there was undoubtedly a strain of anti-Semitism in early-twentieth-century Italy.[3] As Pekelis discovers during her 1947 trip back to Italy, Jewish names had been "purged" from the telephone books and Jewish Italians still had not been added to the postwar books.

But most impressive here is the doubt and self-irony that Pekelis allows to permeate each page. For fascism permitted neither doubt

2. This is a common motif in some other outstanding Jewish memoirs. In English see Dan Vittorio Segre, *Memoirs of a Fortunate Jew* (Bethesda, MD: Adler & Adler, 1987); Giacomo Debenedetti, *16 October 1943/Eight Jews* (Notre Dame, IN: University of Notre Dame Press, 2001); Maria Luisa Fargion, *Besides Still Waters* (Ashfield, MA: Paideaia Publishers, 1992); Fabio Della Seta, *The Tiber Afire* (Marlboro, VT: Marlboro Press, 1991). For a Christian perspective, see Rosetta Loy, *First Words: A Childhood in Fascist Italy* (New York: Metropolitan Books, 2000); first published in Italy as *La parola ebreo* (Turin: Einaudi, 1997).

3. Lynne Gunzberg, *Strangers at Home: Jews in the Italian Literary Imagination* (Berkeley: University of California Press, 1992; Michele Sarfatti, *Gli ebrei nell'Italia Fascista: vicende, identità, persecuzione* (Turin: Einaudi, 2000).

nor irony. Pekelis's doubt and irony do not sink to nihilism: there is still a core of deeply held beliefs and consciousness: "Although believing firmly in the right of every individual to his own personal version of the facts, I have always been inclined to place particular trust in my own." If the Fascist regime sought to eliminate any doubts and impose a single truth, Pekelis was not susceptible: "'Truth' was a complex word, its destiny inevitably at the mercy of a thousand circumstances, a thousand interpreters."

Although the socialist deputy Matteotti had been killed as early as 1924, it was the assassinations of the Rosselli brothers in 1937—a full fifteen years after Mussolini's rise to power—that signaled "the beginning of a period of acute awareness . . . only now did we come to realize that people would first have to suffer a great deal [for the fall of fascism]." And the Rosselli brothers were killed because of their antifascism, not because they were Jewish.[4]

A year later the regime published its "Racial Manifesto" and this time there could be no confusion. Fascist Italy was following Nazi Germany in implementing policies to create a "racially pure" state. Now there was a "feeble awareness that our world was coming to an end." Thus began the peregrinations of the Pekelis family, their desperate attempt to seek shelter, their anxious waiting for visas, their nights huddled over the radio, the shadowy world of refugees and their "escorts." The depiction of grand and epic events such as the fall of France or the London blitz are counterposed by quiet domestic and interior scenes rendered masterful by a deep sensitivity, acute psychological insight, a sharp eye, and an awareness that their destiny could be transformed overnight by a trick of fate. Pekelis is confronted by an almost unimaginable and indelible reality of poverty in Spain after the civil war, and the spectacle of Madrid bombed so that it suggested "the idea of a fantas-

4. For more on the charismatic Carlo and the historian Nello, see Stanislao G. Pugliese, *Carlo Rosselli: Socialist Heretic and Antifascist Exile* (Cambridge, MA: Harvard University Press, 1999).

tic parade of gigantic skeletons staring fixedly at the sun. They didn't speak of war any longer, the cause we knew of so well; they didn't appeal to our faith, or our convictions. They bore witness to only one truth, death." Indeed amid this destruction and despair she is touched by grace when she writes "we Jews, exiles . . . we were still privileged."

Part Two, which traces Pekelis's life in the eight months of the immediate postwar period, is tinged with melancholy and sadness. It begins with the death of Alexander Pekelis in an airline crash and continues with a profound psychological acumen: "Each of us has to give a name to our own unhappiness, to tell ourselves: if it weren't for this, I would be happy. And to think that somewhere there's a remedy, a sort of magic formula to cure our own particular condition."

When returning to Italy on a cruise ship with other exiles, she realizes how deceptive memory and nostalgia can be. "For these people, . . . Italy has become, through distance and imagination, something miraculous, infinitely sweet, familiar, and protective." For Pekelis herself, the return to Italy is both painful and joyous. Facing the ruins of her beloved Florence (the Nazis had, among other atrocities, blown up Ammannati and Michelangelo's *Ponte della Trinità*), she writes that "if some message must come to humanity by means of war and about war from Florence, it must come through its ruins." When someone asks her why she has returned to Italy, Pekelis responds, "To see how things stand, to make a new beginning without the burden of memories." But the burden of memories is not one that she or we can lightly toss aside. And in some deeper way, Pekelis is conscious of this, for many of her sentences begin "I remember. . . ."

We continue to remember and continue to want to remember because, as Pekelis frankly admits, "desire and regret burn stronger than reason."

Stanislao G. Pugliese

My Version of the Facts

Part One
1907 to 1941

1 Like Nothing, Nothing at All

People in search of their past must begin, I imagine, by recalling their earliest memories of childhood and allowing the rest to flow from there. I would like to be free to do the same. I would love to dig in my memory and find, let's say, the dark broom closet in the house where I was born in Rome in the first decade of the century, or the incredibly white hair of my great-grandmother and her imposing double chin, or the dark velvet lining of the glass showcases in my father's jewelry store in Corso Umberto. To bring those things back to life, however, might prove to be a mixed blessing, since the mere mention of them makes me aware that I was frightened by the broom closet, made uneasy by the double chin, and in some way embarrassed by the fact that my father was not really the proprietor of the jewelry store but worked for a rich uncle, who was bald and arrogant. In any case, as I said, I'm not free. For a long time, ever since I arrived in the United States more than thirty years ago, I have felt guilty because of my inability to give a satisfactory answer to the questions inevitably put to me by people I meet. Perplexed by my claim to be born both Italian and Jewish, they have questioned me about the circumstances that occasioned this unlikely combination. When did my family come to Italy, they ask, and from where? How many Jewish Italians are there altogether? What is their situation in a wholly Catholic country?

Somehow I have always managed to postpone the effort needed to give a well-considered answer and have put aside the questions. However, being on the point of letting myself go in the selfish pleasure of remembering, I feel duty-bound not to postpone any further. No imaginary and nostalgic childhood memories for me! Or at least, not yet. First of all, I have to ask myself: "What was it like to be a Jewish child in Italy at the beginning of the century?"

What was it like? As a matter of fact, like nothing, nothing at all. There was no observance of rituals or celebration of holidays in my parents' house . . . and that was much more than a failure to preserve the details while maintaining the spirit. Thinking about it now, this attitude was a sort of pride in agnosticism, a pride which my parents shared with many Italians at that time. Italy had come onto the world stage as a nation only a few years before with the motto "Free church in a free state," and the gates of the ghetto had been thrown open to a world where it was not only possible to profess whatever religion one wished, but it was possible, and actually fashionable, to profess none at all. Children, however, seemed to feel the need to be reassured by a religion. Thus, a little after I had learned how to write (and in Europe at that time this was done very early), I composed a graceful prayer which was supposed to serve both me and my younger sister. I still remember the decorated paper that I used, white with red ornaments and a red capital C in a corner. I also remember that my brother made a show of manhood by disdaining to recite the prayer, but that once I heard him refer to me with the words "My older sister is very religious," and that made me proud.

There was nothing particularly Jewish, let me say, about the God with whom I had such an intimate relationship. He was not Catholic, that's certain, because to be Catholic meant to believe in the saints, in martyrdom, and in the Virgin Mary. It also meant dry olive branches on the walls of the maid's room, and churches where my parents looked at the paintings while women dressed in black knelt in prayer; monotonous chants were murmured in the background, and children, seemingly similar to me, approached the altar with a hint of a genuflection and made the sign of the cross. How I would have liked to do the same! Actually, I sometimes knelt and made the sign of the cross in front of the mirror when no one could see me, but I felt sacrilegious and fearful that a lightning bolt might strike me for it. And so I fell back upon familiar prayers in the hope that God would give me credit for them, keep an eye on me and my family, and, naturally, send me good dreams.

Dreams (and their occasional companions, nightmares) were a source of great interest for me at that time, so that my instructions to God to be as helpful to me as possible in this matter were fervid and detailed. He must, if possible, send me good dreams. If he should find it difficult on a particular night, I would be more than happy if he sent me nothing. But please, please, in no case let me have bad dreams, especially those in which one falls, falls, falls, down a bottomless well.

I wondered if adults also prayed for good dreams. It was hard to know, because the only adult of my acquaintance who prayed was my maternal grandmother, and her ways of practicing religion were very mysterious.

I remember Nonna Elisa only as an old woman, although she must not have been so very old when I was a child, especially by current standards. But everyone is old to children, and my memory of my parents is that of a middle-aged couple, not of young and dashing people, who—in the photographs I still have—stand in romantic poses, or hold me, their first born, in their arms. Besides, my grandmother was as frugal with words as she was with smiles, and she intimidated me. It was her reserve, I think, more than the lines in her face, that put her in a world apart for me. I knew, however, that she had been beautiful, and I sometimes stood in admiration before a painting that depicted her as a young bride. Except for the blond of her hair, the whole picture was in blue: the chair in which she sat, the immense skirt falling to the ground, the elaborate embroidery on the sleeves of the little black bodice . . . and, above all, her eyes. Looking at a point beyond and distant from the painter, they confirmed the reserve I intuited in my grandmother, as did her mouth, not completely open in a hint of a smile. But the reserve of the portrait suggested only shyness, a hand not quite extended rather than a hand withheld. Perhaps it was the portrait, then, that encouraged me to ask Nonna Elisa once: "Is it true, Nonna, that you were very beautiful?"

Probably I wanted a complete story of the young woman in blue, but Nonna Elisa only said, with a half smile this time on her thin lips, "They used to say that I was the most beautiful girl in Ancona!"

Ancona, on the Adriatic, was the city where she was born, was married, and where all her thirteen children had been born. Nonna Elisa and Nonno Giuseppe, or Geppino, had been engaged for seven years. Her father did not favor the marriage (I don't think I have ever known why), and so she had waited patiently for his consent, embroidering all that time the letters *E* and *G*, Elisa and Giuseppe, on her trousseau. I don't remember Nonno Geppino, who died when I was very small; I only remember his photograph in the family album and the marble bust on a pedestal that stood in the garden for years until the Germans knocked it down during the Second World War. Nonna Elisa, on the other hand, had an important if discreet role in the early years of my life because we went to her country house every summer, or rather, every autumn. In summer, we preferred to go to the mountains, and only in September to Ancona for the sea air and for family. It was then that Judaism made a brief appearance in my life.

Nonna Elisa would sit in the garden every day, the still and quiet center of an ever-changing group of chattering women. They were daughters, granddaughters, daughters-in-law, some of them houseguests like us; or they lived in the immediate vicinity, or they came from Ancona for an afternoon visit. Once seated, each woman took out her needlework, and this activity, far from interfering with the general conversation, seemed to help it along, making it easier and freer. I have no childhood memory of my grandmother's garden without that circle of women and without me as part of it, trying to learn from one of my aunts how to embroider, or to make macrame, or to knit. But no other undertaking struck me as much as my grandmother's, on whose lap an intricate miracle of crochet work was forever taking form. I was as fascinated by the yards of lace for linens, of ornamental lace of all sizes and shapes, and the elaborate doilies she was capable of making, as I was by the quickness and steadiness of her gestures.

Her hands rested only on Saturday, and on that day, instead of crocheting, they held a worn, leather-covered prayerbook. I can still see its yellowed pages covered with mysterious lettering. Her hands were still; only her lips moved. They were pale lips, with a blue mark on the lower. They moved silently, and every word I tried to catch was incomprehensible. On Saturday the visitors were less numerous and did not stay so long. Again, they were all women because Saturday was a working day, but their hands were idle and the conversation subdued. In whispers the children were told to play less noisily because Nonna was praying.

Sometimes the prayers lasted longer, and Grandmother wore dresses of a special kind: black or gray silk instead of the usual dark cotton prints. Or she fasted for the entire day. Then the mothers said it was "Rosh Hashona" or "Kippur." Thus all the autumn holidays became vaguely familiar, while the others remained in darkness.

2 Thank You, But I *Must* Speak French

The desire to postpone a head-on confrontation with religious instruction in general and the Catholic world in particular must have had some part in my parents' decision to conduct their children's elementary education at home. But only a small part, after all, since this system was followed by most bourgeois Italian families at the time and had to do, more than anything else, with purposes and conditions of an intellectual nature. The caliber of the public schools was low, and their physical facilities nonexistent. There were no private schools, so far as I know. Therefore, the children of well-off families were usually "privatisti"; that is, they studied at home where teachers came to give them lessons. My brother, my sister, and I had two such teachers, sisters, both gentle, cultivated, and unmarried. One of them taught us all the subjects of the official syllabus; the other, a subject requested solely by our ambitious parents: the piano. I began my general education at five years, my musical education at seven. Foreign languages were entrusted to a German governess "in residence," but I, for one, would gladly have dispensed with her ministrations. Three or four such governesses must have passed through our lives during the period before the First World War, at which time speaking German luckily became unpatriotic.

They were all terribly cruel, I thought; doubly cruel, really, because of their tendency to be enchanted to the point of indulgence

with Luciana, the little one with rosy cheeks, and irresistible
Guido, the boy. On the other hand, it was expected, and this was
the trouble, that I must be a good example for both of them, which
caused me to be the object of the strictest discipline. It was with a
wicked pleasure, so I thought, that the current Fräulein used to tie
to my wrist at night the homemade glove without fingers called a
sachetta, or "little bag," that prevented me from sucking my
thumb. With implacable determination, as she hastened to get her
duties over with and leave the room, she forbade me to fold my
clothing properly on the chair near my bed. If at certain times I
managed to frustrate her evil designs, it was only by means of great
cunning and at the cost of considerable sacrifice. I had to stay
awake long enough to see, through the glass door of the bedroom,
the light at the entrance go out, and this could take a great deal of
time, especially when my parents had guests. Only when they (and
the fascinating sounds of their greetings and laughter) had moved
to the dining room, did I slip out of bed and proceed without
breathing to fold my clothes according to a precise and methodical ritual: first the dress, then the blouse, then the petticoat, then
the underwear, and alone on top of all the rest, the stockings.
There was also a robe to put on the back of a chair, and slippers,
naturally, to set underneath it, exactly next to one another. The
whole operation was not a small undertaking for me, considering
that it was conducted in the dark, with my right hand imprisoned
in the "sachetta;" I certainly deserved the deep and uninterrupted
sleep that followed.

When a French children's nurse took the job of governess, I felt
much better. Instead of towering over us, Mlle Robert seemed very
needful of protection herself. Her thin body and white, bloodless
skin gave her a precariously fragile look. Besides, she was a Waldensian, that is, she belonged to a small French-speaking, Protes-
tant group living in Piedmont, and I thought that this fact weighed
in her favor. She, too, was a foreigner, but her beliefs were a little
easier to accept than Catholic ones. Not that I had a very clear idea

of them. Was it the Virgin Mary that Protestants didn't believe in, or perhaps the saints? In any case, there were undoubtedly fewer "people" that they worshipped, so the guilt of not worshipping them weighed less heavily on my shoulders.

I loved Mlle Robert, and it didn't bother me to learn French under her instruction, all the more as the study was carried on in the simplest of circumstances. Except for rainy days (and there aren't any, or I should say there weren't very many in a Roman winter), our French was learned in the parks, sometimes in the little "public gardens" near our house, chiefly at the Villa Borghese, which we reached by a fairly long but not unpleasant walk. The only inconvenience of these walks was the restriction imposed by our mother—to our displeasure and, I suspect, Mlle Robert's— namely, that in no case were we to waste the precious time dedicated to French by playing with other children, who, furthermore, might be suffering from contagious diseases. Thus, whenever another child approached us in the parks, spontaneously pronouncing the magic words "Do you want to play?" we had to answer, "Thank you, but I must speak French." The fatal phrase was always entrusted to me, the oldest, and I tried to put into it the greatest possible dignity. Nevertheless, the look in the eye of a playmate rebuffed, half disdain and half commiseration, was often hard to bear.

Whenever I think of my years in Rome (we lived there until I was seventeen), I see my cousins Mario, Carlo, and Elena. The two boys were slightly older than me, the girl slightly younger, and I loved them very much. I also loved their mother, their house, and whatever they did. I think my mother, too, felt great affection for their mother, who was her sister. They exchanged frequent visits, and we children had the chance to play together as much as our intense course of studies permitted. It was generally acknowledged that my mother was a progressive young woman with intellectual interests; on the other hand, my aunt was a sweet person without imagination. Besides, my mother had been a very romantic girl (as testified by many photograph albums, poems, and manuscripts) and had married "for love," while my aunt had meekly submitted to the common practice of an "arranged marriage." All that placed certain obligations on our shoulders, and my mother would never have dreamed of engaging the same instructors that my aunt had employed before her; she had to find her own. Thus my cousins and we were denied the pleasure of sharing certain experiences and had to limit ourselves to the dubious one of contrasting methods. I always knew that my teachers were supposed to be better, but I couldn't help preferring theirs.

Now that I think of it, my cousins did "Swedish gymnastics" in the same private gymnasium where we did ours; nevertheless, even in this matter they were privileged, because they were not forced by their parents to continue daily exercises at home along with their scholastic work. Every morning before breakfast we had to bend and stretch and lie down on the floor, kicking our legs up and down with great effort, while our mother came and went briskly to and from her bedroom overseeing our activity.

She also checked on our homework, drilling us in arithmetic, as I recall, by means of questions thrown at us in dramatic, rapid succession. "Now, quick," she said, "two plus two, quick!" Or, "Three times three? Quick!" I always knew the answer, being a very conscientious student. I even knew the answer to the sinister "six times seven," but my brother, a year and a half younger than me, got there first. This is the reason why, I suppose, he quickly acquired the reputation of "highly intelligent" if not downright "genius." I don't think that children of that time were very much appreciated for being cooperative or "well adjusted," although they were for being "good." What got the most attention, at least in our environment, was intelligence. The brains of children, like those of adults, were weighed with care and attention, and personalities were judged accordingly. If my brother Guido belonged to the category of "superior," and I thrived for years in the condition of "brilliant but normal," my sister Luciana, younger by only three years, had a hard time living with her inferior label. If she had only known that she was an "underachiever"! But how could she know? All she had been told was that she was slow, and that she took too long to find her way in the labyrinth of "Now, quick, the answer!" that surrounded us.

Sometimes I ask myself what my father was like. Naturally, I have a strong image of him (he died when I was twenty); it's just that nowadays we all have a smattering of psychological knowledge, enough to make us distrust our reactions and memories. Can I say that my father was always gentle, happy, and charming? Or that my mother was stronger and had more precise goals? Or that he, loving her with all his heart, tried at certain times to follow her path rather than his own? When he came home in the evening, he was informed of all our good and bad deeds during the day, and he praised us or scolded us accordingly. I think that my brother had a false idea of him and felt a certain fearful respect toward him. Not I. I always understood that my father would have been happier if he had been free to joke or play. The result was that he played much more with my bigger cousins and with his brother, Giorgio, who was much younger than he and only a few years older than I.

I ask myself if my father, were he alive, would be able to answer those questions about Italian Jews and inform my American friends of the exact moment when our family arrived in Italy. I doubt it, although he was a Coen. Of his father, Adolfo Coen, he spoke little, and I remember nothing. All I knew was that he, too, was a gentle and agreeable man; also, that he had been the chief stenographer of Parliament, and had died in his sleep. It was implied, I think, that having attained such a position was not a small achievement for a Jew, but it was also presumed that one accepts such an achievement nonchalantly, as suits a free citizen of a free state. Of my mother's nine brothers, two were career officers in the navy, one in the army, two others were lawyers, and one was a doctor. Only three worked in the family's dry goods business. The times were prosperous, and hopes were high. Until the First World War.

3 Good Old Alps, Good Old Wars

Scarcely anyone of my acquaintance seems to remember the First World War. I wonder if that means I move among people younger than me, or my friends don't have good memories, or simply that the war, for Americans, was shorter and more distant than for Italians. Not that I remember very much. Nevertheless, I recall the headlines (ITALY DECLARES WAR ON AUSTRIA) that filled everyone with enthusiasm, especially the young. The young, in fact, knew nothing of the treaty Italy had signed years before with Austria and Germany, nor of the debates between those favoring taking part in the conflict and those favoring neutrality. It was only many years later that we read of these debates and learned that this one was an "interventionist," and that one was a "noninterventionist." At that period we were all completely conditioned by a school education that left no room for personal opinions on the subject of the Risorgimento, the dramatic struggle that had led to the unification of Italy a half century earlier. Textbooks, novels, poems, not to speak of songs, described the plight of the divided country, the heroic actions of its martyrs, and the abject role of Austria and the Hapsburg dynasty in suffocating our aspirations and ideals. To this day, in fact, differing interpretations of these events, while attracting my curiosity, make my blood boil. An historian can utter a judicious phrase when speaking of the emperor Franz Joseph as a tragic figure; another can be correct in calling Guglielmo Oberdan, who made an attempt to kill him, a potential assassin. I still feel upset by these definitions because the last words of a patriotic hymn come back to me from my childhood, ". . . and we want freedom! Death to Franz Joseph, *viva* Oberdan!" where the curses are heaped on the wicked emperor and the blessings on the young martyr, whose life was ended on the gallows for love of his country. For children then, in that May of 1915, to go to war again with Austria, this time on the side of England and France and of poor, unfortunate Belgium, was a crusade.

My uncles went to war, even the youngest, my father's brother Giorgio. My father himself was drafted and sent to southern Italy, where he was assigned to drive an army truck. By a strange quirk of fate, after fifty years, after having lived in four countries and changed houses a dozen times, I still have one of his letters in which he asks me to be good during his absence and to set a good example for my brother and sister. My name on the envelope is followed by that of a little town not far from Rome, Soriano al Cimino, where we went every summer during the war, a very modest sort of vacation, in which we enjoyed the fresh air, something still considered a duty in our family and which had a minimal effect on the budget in time of war. We had a large number of playmates, mostly Roman children like us, and, under the direction of our mothers, we all got together at least once a day in a sort of farmhouse up in the woods. We spent the time gathering chestnuts (they were still in their prickly shells and were called "luciane"), looking for the farm animals, cutting sticks and engraving complicated designs in their green bark, and, above all, playing games. The game we liked most was, naturally, hospital, field hospital to be precise. Someone had built a hut for us to shelter our wounded in. It was a pleasant, shaded place, covered with chestnut branches, where we spent much of our time. The girls had sewn as best they could white bonnets with red crosses on the front; the boys were all equipped with pencils, pads for wounds, and little, discarded bottles. Certainly, we had no lack of nurses and doctors. The only thing of which we were in short supply was patients. This problem, however, was resolved unexpectedly by the arrival of a berry syrup provided by one of the mothers to serve as a pretend medicine. The number of patients increased considerably, while the hospital personnel had to bravely limit themselves to tasting the prescriptions.

While the children played, the mothers—at Soriano, just like Ancona—sat in a circle on folding chairs or deck chairs brought from home, each with her own work But in those war years, embroidery, macrame, or lace were banished. All the women worked at crocheting or knitting wool garments to send to the troops at the front.

I remember the wool that was used, colored the same dirty gray, or gray-green of the army uniforms. I'm afraid that all I made were scarves, but my mother and her friends made gloves and balaclavas, a sort of head covering à la Robin Hood, which our soldiers wore in the snows of the Alps. Good old Alps and good old wars! Everyone knew that they were fought only at the frontiers, and if one had just a smattering of geography, one was naturally aware of the fact that the Alps were absolutely the best of frontiers, a natural and formidable protection against any attack. Actually, there had been Hannibal with his elephants, but elephants were a thing of the past which could calmly be set aside. In this way I could enjoy my war, concerning myself almost romantically with my young uncle, the only one of the family's combatants who entered into my evening prayers for the duration of the conflict.

All things considered, I had more pressing things on my mind, because in June of 1916, just one year after Italy's entry into the war, I survived the ordeal of the public examinations and was admitted to the gymnasium.

4 "Pur Non Essendo Cattolica"

I was a little more than nine years old then, tall and slender in the family album, with a pretty, confident smile. That smile, which appears repeatedly in those pages, probably played an important part for me in my youthful years. Above all, it made me appear prettier than I really was. Besides, consciousness of this fact must, I believe, have made me go on smiling. Even now, when I am what is euphemistically called a "senior citizen," it's been said that the smile takes away ten years from me. Except that now the effort involved is somehow greater, and the goal seems hardly worth the effort. In that fall of 1916, when my life as a "privatista" came to an end and I went to school for the first time, everything was a source of joy and, most of all, the school itself.

The Royal Liceo Gymnasium Ennio Quirino Visconti was situated in the Piazza del Collegio Romano, a small, quiet square not very far from the larger and noisier Piazza Venezia. I remember the imposing entry that rose a few meters above the level of the street, before which there were several wide steps, low and circular, where we stopped briefly to greet one another before the beginning of classes, and where we lingered warmly saying good-bye to one another after leaving school. Inside, a gigantic, hospitable courtyard in the form of a cloister was circled by two covered corridors, one above the other, to which the classrooms opened instead of cells. The five classes of the gymnasium were located on the ground floor; the three liceo classes were on the first floor at the end of two long and wide staircases. I attended the Visconti for eight years (the entire period of the First World War and the rise of fascism), but people and events fail to appear in chronological order, and even less can they be evoked one by one in the appropriate context. Rather, they hammer at the door of my memory, all claiming attention and priority, and all seeming equally worthy.

Shall I give first place to Professor Santini, who taught me my first rudiments of Latin, and to Professor Fontebasso, who made arithmetic and geometry seem so simple, so rewarding? Or to their colleagues in the liceo, the unprepossessing and embittered Caccialanza (who seemed to feel the same distaste for Virgil as for his students, and whom we intended to repay with the same coin as soon as we had graduated), and the coarse, insolent Vaccaro (who must have had some idea of algebra since he had been assigned the job of teaching it, but who made it absolutely incomprehensible). It seems incredible that—so many decades later and at an age when I have to make an effort to remember the names of my children—those of my former teachers come instantly to mind. And not only their names. I can see their faces just as well. I can see very clearly the square shoulders and short, white hair of Professor Neviani, who with his brusque manners taught natural history. There are about thirty-five boys and girls seated on the long wooden benches of his classroom with desks and inkwells in front of them. I have been called to the blackboard and Neviani, looking me straight in the eyes, asks me to explain how a fetus can live in the mother's uterus. This is, to be sure, one of the subjects of today's lesson, which the entire class has memorized. Even Sarazani, who is proud of never doing his homework, knows it and laughs convulsively holding his hand over his mouth. Must I explain the subject in front of everyone, thus referring, no matter how indirectly, to the greatest tabu of all, that is, menstruation? I don't want to, and I don't. And at the end of the class, my friends congratulate me warmly for having given the professor a lesson.

My grades naturally fell at the end of the trimester, but that only enhanced my halo.

I can see clearly the gray, bristly face of Professor Pasquini, who taught chemistry and physics. We are going down the narrow spiral staircase that leads from the laboratory into the class, and he is right behind me and is praising me for some experiment that I have carried out satisfactorily. I take pleasure in his compliments, but since I'm paying close attention to the spiral staircase, I don't hear him too well. He is saying something about the Jewish students always being so clever, and also about the responsibility that being Jewish puts on my shoulders. However, he doesn't say "Jewish," but the euphemistic and polite "Israelite." My pride in being Jewish is tempered by awe of the implications suggested by him. I want to be good, but do I really have to be?

Oh, the teachers! I'm afraid of letting them crowd the scene of my memory. But I have to find a little space for the "ricreazoni," the morning break, and recapture for a moment the daily excitement of those fifteen minutes full of noise and chatter and the delicious smell of *maritozzi* just out of the oven, soft and delicious and sprinkled with sugar.

I have to take leave immediately of the *maritozzi* since the school field trips are more important. For example, to the catacombs where the first Christians centuries and centuries ago practiced their religion secretly and where we could barely hear the explanations of the guide, obsessed as we were by stories of the Romans, of lions and the arenas. Or the Sunday hiking trips, which began at five in the morning in a dark and mysterious, almost alien Rome, and ended around midnight with a frenzied ringing of the house bell and a desperate rush for the bathroom.

There! The Sunday outings came back to memory and have vanished. But I can linger for a little while on the daily journeys to and from school; I enjoyed them so much. Strange, I know that I must often have been in the company of my brother Guido. We went to the same school; he was only one class behind me and eventually skipped a year so that we finished in the same class. However, for some reason I seem to remember his presence on those walks only occasionally. He was surely with me one afternoon when we were seen by a neighbor, Signora Martini, gorging ourselves with pastries at a bakery on our street, and our crime was immediately reported to our parents. We must have been very young then, because whenever we met Signora Martini for a certain time after that, we felt a sense of fear. We hadn't foreseen that our mother would consider her behavior that of a frightful gossip and would dismiss the entire episode with a shrug of her shoulders.

Still, where was Guido the other times that I remember so vividly, when I went to school alone?

We lived in the Prati district of Rome, and for many years, until a building was put up across the street, we had a view of the Castel Sant' Angelo. My route took me along the enormous white mass of the Justice Building across the Tiber, through narrow, curving streets as far as the small, elegant Piazza Madama. Here I stopped in hope of seeing my best friend, Maria Pia. She lived not far from there, just behind Piazza Navona, and my hope was often gratified. Then we proceeded together, exchanging comments on our homework and gossip about events at school. A narrow street behind the Pantheon brought us to Piazza della Minerva, which is marked by a curious obelisk at its center and a large church at one side. Sometimes, when we were going to have an oral examination, for example, or a test in class (writing a composition under the teacher's vigilant eye on a subject assigned then and there), Maria Pia would go into church for a short prayer that was supposed to guarantee her divine protection in the trials of the day. If she invited me to go with her, I refused timidly. Instead, I went on alongside the church, taking up enough time so that Maria Pia, leaving from the sacristy toward the rear, could rejoin me. We were used to arriving at school together, arm in arm.

Only once did I go into a church, and it was for a task concerning religion. We had to write a composition on the theme of "my feelings looking at a crèche," and although my family's indignation was great at the choice of so biased a subject, my mother helped me write the composition in a style she considered diplomatic and dignified. I still remember the last line: "Leaving the church, I was profoundly moved. Although not a Catholic, I can well understand how one can be attached to such beautiful rituals." I'm not absolutely certain about the last words. It's the expression "Pur non essendo Cattolica" that still echoes in my mind. I thought my mother was putting the cards on the table right away so that THEY might not think I was trying to pass for something I wasn't. In fact, I was very proud of my mother's style and was quite surprised when our splendid prose only got a "six," barely passing. My mother, on the other hand, smiled like someone who knew a thing or two and said one must expect that sort of thing.

Aside from the incident with the theme, it seems to me that being Jewish at that time was for me more a question of things that I did not do than things that I had to do. I did not take part, for example, in lessons on religion and therefore enjoyed the privilege of going home an hour early once a week. That, however, simply brought an hour sooner the dubious pleasure of playing the piano, while it deprived me of the ineffable joy connected with the sound of the final bell and lingering on the steps outside the school. Afterward, when we were a little older, the entire group of girls and boys used to meet at Sunday mass, or rather, the girls usually went, while the boys waited outside to greet them. On Monday morning I would be informed of what had been said by someone to someone else, but certainly no report could compensate for the fact that I hadn't been there.

Naturally there were Jewish students in the school, but even aside from the fact that they were a small minority, I didn't belong to their circle for two reasons. One of them is clear to me only in retrospect: my parents must have been snobbish in some way of their own, because they classified almost every other Jewish family of the city as *negra,* an adjective not at all racial, notwithstanding its sound, but intended to suggest something unpleasant and inferior in the Italian Jewish jargon of the time. The other reason was very simple: my Jewish schoolmates all seemed furnished with something, no matter how imperfect, to bolster their identity. They knew certain rituals and holidays; they observed some of them; sometimes they might even go to temple. I knew only that I was Jewish, that's all. But I was also different from them. Thus, if Maria Pia could leave me perplexed because one day, putting her arm around me, she said: "I like you, Carla; no one would guess that you're Jewish," Laura (a Jewish girl whose company I had sought out in order to find my identity) irritated me by letting slip now and then some Hebrew words, or observing with a presumptuous air that the fact that I sewed doll clothes on the "Sabbath" was really out of place.

In view of what the rest of my life would be like, this lack of belonging, which I experienced in a certain measure from early childhood, turned out to be no small gift, well worth all the moments of embarrassment and discomfort it cost me. Besides, it didn't bother me much, for during all these years (most of them, in any case) I was in love with a charming young man!

5 Under the Spell of Dante, Wagner, and Fabrizio

I was not aware of being in love, only of being loved, but this limited awareness seemed to be more than enough for my happiness. In fact, it gave such radiance to my daily life during all those school years that it's probably the reason why I've forgotten parts of the general picture. I'm afraid, however, that I was the only person who was ignorant of my own feelings. Professor Salaris, for example, must have known better than I did if he took upon himself the responsibility to call my mother and tell her that I no longer seemed so profoundly interested in my studies as formerly: could it be that I had a boy on my mind? My mother loyally told me about this interview, calmed my indignation by observing that my teacher certainly had at heart nothing but my own good, and tactfully let the subject drop. After having bitterly criticized the guilty party in some heated discussions with Maria Pia, I too forgot about it. Many years later, however, two of my ex-classmates, by then very famous men, whom I met on separate occasions, one in Rome and the other in New York, took to scolding me for having wasted the best years of my life with that little fool, Fabrizio! It was then that I asked myself if they had understood more than I had. In any case, they were mistaken on one point. I hadn't wasted those years; I had lived them fully and joyously, and the modest caliber of Fabrizio's intelligence couldn't in the least mar that joy.

His good looks, I fear, were more important, and so were his warm, easy-going, character and the attentions he heaped upon me. The profusion of these attentions was purely a matter of the heart; naturally, since the practice of going on dates, with their financial implications, was unknown in Italy at that time. By attentions I mean telephone calls, efforts to take part in the same events (a school trip, a ball, a concert); also the attempt, poor boy, to raise his disastrous scholastic average, and, especially, to tell me how much he loved me and how miserable I made him by not returning his love.

"It's only that I can't see us getting married," I used to say, a little regretful that marriage was the only touchstone by which I could measure the intensity of my feelings.

Fabrizio didn't seem to consider my reluctance concerning matrimony as important as I did; nor was he much disturbed by the differences of our religious beliefs. His greatest concern was with the present. Did I return his love or didn't I? Would I send Maria Pia on her way at least once and permit him to accompany me in her place? Would I perhaps allow him, at least once, to kiss me? To answer these questions in the negative was not very difficult, given that the strict moral code of those times left me little room for alternatives with respect to them. It was more difficult not to discourage my friend at the same time from continuing to ask for these things, but apparently I managed to accomplish that feat successfully for some time.

Was I perhaps a coquette? My father, when he teased me about my longing for academic success and my excessively anxious habits of work, used to say: "You could be a frightful pedant, you know? What saves you is that you're a flirt!" I liked the way he said it, his eyes twinkling. And yet that word was the ultimate insult I chose to apply to a schoolmate of mine, Ranzi. So I hope that I wasn't a flirt, but if I was, I'm content not to have known it.

Ranzi was her surname; it is the only one of her names that I remember. The teachers used to address students by their surnames, and the students themselves used to address one another in the same way, at least if they weren't close friends. Ranzi was by no means an intimate friend of mine, but I can still see her clearly: tall, lean, with blond hair decorated with bows, and a condescending "da-ar-ling" on her lips. She knew everything and looked down on everything, an attitude that made a lasting impression on me. Even though I am now calmed by the consciousness that at that time we were thirteen or fourteen years old, I'm still unable to have a balanced idea of her. In my memory she remains an absolute "femme fatale," her charms and wiles far superior to those of any other woman I have met since. Neither the jewels nor the ostentatious furs of those women ever generate the perfect envy in my breast that was aroused by the frill of white lace that Ranzi managed to slip around the neckline of the black smock that all the girls had to wear, or the silk stockings, or the high-heeled shoes that she flaunted. If Ranzi wasted any of her "da-ar-lings" on me, it must have been because of Fabrizio. His devoted attentions during the three years of liceo contributed decisively to my social position, making up for the fact that I was a model student and a grind.

I can also credit Fabrizio more than my piano teacher for my love of music, since I was only moderately fond of music lessons and a good deal bored by the continual practice required of me by my mother. Unfortunately, she had decided at an early stage that I was highly gifted, and she expected me to practice every day as soon as I returned from school and before I became absorbed in my homework. She also wanted me to practice even more intensively during vacations, and I can still remember certain sweltering afternoons in rented apartments at vacation resorts or elsewhere when I had to sit at the piano while Guido and Luciana took a nap. I couldn't bear a grudge against my sister, poor thing, since she was, to use my mother's words, "without a gift for music." I could, however, and I did, feel resentment toward my brother, who had somehow preserved his reputation as "gifted," despite having managed to abandon lessons after the first year. Anyway, my unhappy fate had some reward, because I and only I had the privilege of accompanying my parents to the Augusteo on Sunday afternoons.

The Augusteo was an enchanting auditorium that owed its name to the fact that it had been built upon the ruins of the Mausoleum of Augustus, the first Roman emperor. Mussolini later decided to demolish it so that the public could enjoy the sight of the glorious ruins. They, however, turned out to be so ugly and shabby that they had to be covered up with all sorts of trees and bushes. But right after the First World War, when I was thirteen and fourteen and began to attend the concerts, it was still standing. Similar in plan to our symphony halls, it was more intimate and appeared extremely attractive to my adolescent eyes. Just hearing the instruments tune up made my heart leap with excitement. We always sat high up in the amphitheater; we had a subscription, I think, and were vaguely proud of the location of our seats. It was always understood, even if not openly said, that the people provided with enough money to permit themselves seats close to the orchestra, were not sophisticated enough to understand the music. Fabrizio sat lower down, I'm sorry to say, with a very dear and rich friend. Did his friend pay for him, I asked myself, since his father was only a member of the fire department, perhaps chief of a brigade? Fabrizio looked at me from the orchestra, constantly raising his binoculars in my direction. I hardly looked back, but was conscious of his gaze and basked in it. That was how I encountered my first symphonies and concerts, how I was fascinated for the first time by Mozart and Beethoven, the "Unfinished" of Schubert (which I was advised to admire only warily, but instead I adored), and Strauss's "Don Juan," the motif of which was "my passion," as I was in the habit of saying then about a multitude of things. Half a century later, there come back to me from nowhere the comments in the program notes for "Don Juan": ". . . the fire is out, and nothing remains in the fireplace but cold, gray ashes."

No doubt Fabrizio's presence greatly intensified the excitement of my first encounters with symphonic music. Had he also chosen to attend the opera, my whole relationship with that art form would have taken a different course. He did not, however, and I was left entirely to the company of my parents and their rather austere taste in that sphere.

Strange! I have memories of my mother at the piano playing passages from *La Bohème* or from *Otello,* while Papà and their friends happily sang in loud voices this or that aria. Nevertheless, when it was a matter of really getting tickets for the opera, Puccini or Verdi were not good enough—only Wagner would do. So it was by way of the *Ring of the Niebelungen* that I got to know opera, and, alas, it was hard going. Nor were matters made easier by the circumstances that accompanied our visits to the old and ornate Costanzi Theater. Our seats, located high up in the last balcony, were narrow wooden benches, easily turned over by the least movement of their occupants. Besides, the idea of "only listening" to Wagner would have seemed sacrilegious to devout music-lovers like us. Our backs bent, our eyes squinting, our hands furtively manipulating a pocket flashlight forbidden by the rules of the house, we never lost sight of the libretto, which alone could open the doors to the fantastic world of our hero. Yes, all things considered, Fabrizio was probably wise to avoid all personal involvement with Wagner . . . although I'm happy in retrospect that he let himself enter into a sort of relationship with Dante. Our first encounter with *The Divine Comedy* took place in class and produced confusion more than anything else. According to the official program in force in all the Italian schools, the study of the "national Bible" was very conscientious and extended over all three years of the liceo. Unfortunately it was limited to paraphrasing the magical poetry in explanatory and very pedestrian prose. What remained for the students was a superficial story, the historical implications of which seemed to constitute the principal object of attention of most of the instructors, and of innumerable, terrible quizzes. Occasionally some vague reference was made to philosophy and to allegory. Drama, poetic images, lyricism, beauty . . . never. Conscious of the fact that before us was one of the greatest masterpieces of all time, we diligently did our assignments day after day, week after week, asking ourselves if boredom wasn't by chance the constant companion of greatness. Then, one fatal spring, something extraordinary happened to us in the person of an unprepossessing Catholic priest with big eyeglasses.

Father Luigi Pietrobono, a famous Dante scholar, came to give a series of lectures on *The Divine Comedy* in our school. The series, in no way connected with our curriculum, was free and open to the public on Wednesday evenings. Because of this unusual time, I thought my parents would oppose my desire to attend the lectures. I should rather have known that their worship of learning, or "culture," had no limits. As a girl my mother had tasted some of the pleasures of learning, in spite of the fact that her father, Nonno Geppino, had never seen the need for female instruction. But chance had it that he was a good-hearted man, deeply conscious of his responsibility toward the less fortunate. And so he consented to piano lessons as well as tutoring in literature for his daughter because of two "pitiful cases," one a blind music teacher, and the other an unmarried, middle-aged woman who had a diploma but was penniless as a result of family circumstances. Thus my mother had enjoyed the benefit of a certain instruction; on his side, my father had begun work at the age of twelve and never had time for intellectual pursuits. However, their different experiences had made them both anxious to give their children the gift of education, Papà because this privilege had been denied him, Mamma because she had tasted it. Thus I received permission to attend the course on only one condition: that Guido come with me. The late hour required a certain consideration for public opinion, or as we used to say, "gli occhi del mondo."

Guido agreed reluctantly. Maria Pia and Fabrizio were part of the project from its beginning. And so that spring we four went back to school every Wednesday evening, and the chief reason, I believe, was the incredible enjoyment of meeting again in the evening, instead of doing homework at home as usual. But even if this is true, what miracle took place on those Wednesdays that kindled the flame of my love for Dante?

I can still see the hall where the lectures were given: bare, ill lighted, the benches only partly filled, and the stupefied faces of King Victor Emanuele III and Queen Elena on the walls adding to the general gloom. Truth to tell, Fabrizio sat next to me whispering affectionate words from time to time, but it wasn't his presence alone that caused the growing happiness that I began to feel. What sort of wonderful message did Pietrobono have for us? Did Catholic dogma play a part in it in some way? I don't know anymore; perhaps I never did know. All that I remember is the priest's soft voice, his unanticipated reading, free of bombast, and the slow revelation of the poetry under its spell. I found myself whispering "quiet" to Fabrizio. And this makes me wonder: could it be that just as his presence enriched my first encounters with music and poetry, did these encounters enrich our own limited relationship? I imagine so. In any case, I was lucky—I can see that now—to be able to enjoy to the full both these pleasures, protected, even if sometimes irritated, by the supervision of adults, not overwhelmed by the tormenting problems that fate has reserved for today's youth.

6 My Version of the Facts

Although believing firmly in the right of every individual to his own personal version of the facts, I have always been inclined to place particular trust in my own. Thus I could listen in respectful silence to the absurd recollections of my children concerning their early years and my role in them; nevertheless, while restraining myself from interfering in the discussion, I can do no less than maintain a firm vision of the circumstances as they really took place. How does it happen, then, that when it comes to questions of politics, I seem to lose my confidence and grow afraid of the experts? "It's true, I was an Italian in Italy during the rise of fascism," I say to myself, "but wasn't I perhaps too young to understand, too deeply immersed in all of it to see it?" And, above all, haven't the historians of the years that followed influenced my recollections? Certainly, they are affecting me now as I try to reorder my memories, since—left to my own devices—I might very well have failed to see the connection between the rise of fascism and an incident of which my uncle Aldo was the protagonist.

Uncle Aldo was one of my mother's nine brothers, one of the youngest and most dashing, the pride of the family. A naval officer, he believed firmly in honor, country, and king, and had always been ready to give his life in their defense. The First World War offered him the chance, and he distinguished himself on board the pontoons that protected Venice to the point that he received three silver medals, one of bronze, and innumerable citations. Immediately after the war (he was then assigned to the Ministry of the Navy in Rome, I think) he was leaving our house one day, the embodiment of glamour in his uniform resplendent with decorations, when Mamma called him back inside. "Aldo," she asked, "do you think it's prudent to go out in the street with that display on your chest? What will happen if you're beaten up?" I couldn't believe my ears and was relieved when I heard my uncle respond, "Let them try it!" I did not understand that I was indirectly taking part in a prelude to fascism, since fascism—we have now been told—spread as a sort of law and order reaction to the unrest that followed the war.

The war had been won; the wicked Hapsburgs had fallen; Trento and Trieste had been liberated, and even we children had duly marched in the streets of Soriano al Cimino waving flags and singing patriotic songs to celebrate the event. And yet some Italian-speaking territories were still in foreign hands and, above all, the economic prosperity that everyone had expected as recompense for four long years of war had not been realized. The peasants were no nearer to satisfying their dream of a greater share in the benefits derived from the land they cultivated; the workers, awakened only recently to their rights by a few imaginative leaders, were divided between calling for gradual change and a vague consciousness of more substantial and more immediate gains obtained in other countries. As for the lower middle class, hit by new taxes and deprived of sure profits because of rent controls, it had still to face an overall rise in the cost of living, the lack of jobs for returning sons, and occasional outbursts of violence. The fear for her heroic brother that I had noticed in my mother's voice reflected the resentment felt by many hotheads toward the supporters of a war that had been won, they thought, only on paper. There were other fears that we, as preadolescents, could discern only vaguely yet nevertheless seemed to be all around us.

I still remember the threatening "Land to the peasants" that I didn't know how to connect to the family property near Ancona, nor to the peasants with whom we had such friendly relations; and the mysterious references to occupations of factories in the north; or the terrible "red week," which brought to mind the idea of bloodshed rather than of communism. I don't know what my parents' opinions were about all this. Certainly, they were concerned with shielding us from certain information, and probably they were helped in their efforts by the wish, common to all children, to hide unpleasant thoughts under several layers of rugs. In any case, my brother, my sister, and I passed through the times with a notable lack of interest. In fact, the years between 1918, when the war ended, and 1924, when our family left Rome for Florence (fascism was already entrenched in power), might well have been the happiest of my life.

They were the years of *thés dansants,* which I attended escorted by my mother, carrying a card where my schoolmates wrote their names; the years of Thursday matinées at the theater, since Thursday was the day when there were no afternoon classes; the years of Fabrizio and Dante, of trips to the mountains, and of Anatole France, of Tolstoi, of Dostoyevsky. When, returning home from school one day, my brother and I found ourselves face-to-face with Friesland horses and heard sounds of firing, we had a short discussion on what line of action to take (Guido wanted to go and see what had happened), but in the end my more prudent idea to turn around and take another street prevailed. When one afternoon at home, we heard rapid shots from the street below, mamma explained to us that the "royal guards" were dispersing some hotheads; reassured, we limited ourselves to following her advice to keep away from the windows. When, finally, we heard that the king had refused to sign the state of emergency, which would have placed the military in opposition to the Fascists, and following that had called upon Mussolini to form a new government, we didn't pay much attention to the worry we observed on some faces, but shared anxiously the relief that clearly showed itself on others.

Good little king! Who would have expected him to do something worthy of attention, much less save us all from civil war? His tiny size had always deprived him of credibilty in our eyes. Emphasized as it was by the Junoesque proportions of Queen Elena, it came close to rendering him an object of derision or at least of great embarrassment. We knew he had gone to Montenegro to marry her just because of her build, as a way of infusing new blood into the House of Savoy, and the results had been noteworthy: five children, four girls and a boy, all tall, slender, and handsome. The Italians followed their births, anniversaries, marriages, etc. with great interest, fascinated by them, as they would be years later by the goings-on of movie stars. I was no exception to the rule; my interest shifted at one point from Prince Umberto (too handsome, I'm afraid, to be nothing but a fool) to Queen Elena herself and the difficulties she had encountered living with the Queen Mother, who had been celebrated in the work of our national poet, Carducci. And now the king had called Mussolini to form the new government! All of us, grown-ups and children, people who were interested in politics, and people who said, "Sorry, I don't bother with politics," sceptics and those full of hope, crowded windows and balconies to see the victory parade in honor of what came to be remembered as the "March on Rome," but which in reality was a march *in* Rome.

The year was 1922. I don't know when it happened that the Italians as a whole became conscious of the dangers and implications of fascism. Quite early, I would say, if I can draw any conclusions from two of my vivid memories. One is connected to a summer we spent with one of our uncles at his property near Ancona and the fear we experienced every time a truck full of Fascists roared by in the vicinity on one of their "punitive expeditions." It was known that they carried two weapons with them: clubs and castor oil, which they forced down the throats of dissidents. I had never been able to swallow a drop of castor oil, and my revulsion at the thought of it magnified the feeling of humiliation inspired by that practice.

My other memory was that of a large, dry bloodstain on one of the sidewalks along the Tiber. It was Matteotti's blood, a Socialist who had dared defy Mussolini in the Chamber of Deputies and was killed for it. People passed by in silence, afterward exchanging comments on Mussolini's declaration carried in the press that "only his enemies thought they could serve him by such means." *

That was in May of 1924, and in June of that year my brother and I, having passed the state examinations for our liceo diplomas, rejoined our parents and Luciana, who had already left the city and moved the household to Florence.

* Matteotti, I now learn from history books, was actually abducted in the city but killed in the suburbs. So what I remember so vividly must have only been the spot where a memorial was placed and where people brought flowers in his honor. But I am reluctant to change what I recall. My memories seem to have a life of their own that challenges historical truth.

7 Small Shops, Small Talk

Our move to Florence was the result of an attractive business opportunity that drew my father out of his lifelong routine. It involved the sale of the Roman store (of which he alone had the management since the death of his uncle) and the purchase, in partnership with a friend, of a prestigious jewelry shop on the Ponte Vecchio. The transaction itself and its impact on the life of the family had been subjects of careful consideration for several months. However, since in that period the opinions of the young were not usually consulted, my brother, my sister and I had not had any say in the matter. I remember having spontaneously offered my opinion on one occasion, saying with a certain hesitation that, for my part, I would prefer to live in Rome and "be poor" than in Florence and "be rich." My statement was received with benevolent smiles, and my mother afterward explained to me that it was not only a question of money, but that my father would have the possibility of entering into a more exciting world of business, in which his abilities would be more greatly challenged. Was she right, and did that excitement really interest him? He seemed to me perfectly happy; he laughed, joked, and teased continually, played bridge with his and my mother's friends, and rowed on the Tiber with companions from his club. But naturally I knew that he had gone to work very young, stifling his desire to study, and I wanted him to be happy with all my heart. In fact, I asked for nothing better than to continue being happy myself. But I couldn't. I cried my heart out for months.

Oh, Florence, cradle of the arts, polished jewel on the banks of the Arno, monument of the glories of the past . . . how can I do you justice and at the same time speak of the somnolence, the melancholy, the dullness that you had in store for me when I was seventeen years old and you became my home? Narrow streets, small shops, small talk, fog, rain . . . they seemed the echo of my nostalgia, my frustration. Would it have been different, I ask myself, if I had continued my studies and graduated from the university there? Perhaps not, since Guido, who was then attending the Faculty of Law, seemed as depressed as I; but at that time the study of law in Italy fostered the most peculiar pattern of life: after having spent the whole year a prey to inertia, one suddenly switched to frenzied bursts of activity in the weeks immediately preceding the exams. I would have wanted, at least, to study literature and attend the Faculty of Letters of the University of Florence. But my academic career was thwarted very early by my presumed musical gifts when the pianist who examined me faced me unexpectedly with a sort of ulitimatum. I had talent, he said almost aggressively, and he would train me, but on one condition: that I would agree to commit myself entirely to the work and put everything else aside. I don't think I really believed him. Even if I was talented, I lacked one important element in the formation of an artist, faith in myself. Only with difficulty could I imagine myself sending the public into raptures. But I was flattered. Agreeing to the maestro's conditions, I set to work under his guidance. This made me a private student once again, since I studied at home with a teacher chosen by me, and I presented annual examinations at the Luigi Cherubini Conservatory for a diploma in music.

When I look back at those years, this is how I see myself: at the piano for hour after hour every day, or going shopping with mamma and Luciana, or going to a tea, or taking an English lesson from a blond English gentleman with thick eyeglasses whose portfolio was full of mimeographed sheets with irregular verbs in purple ink. Compared to the exuberantly irregular behavior of Italian verbs, the English ones seemed very simple to me, and I couldn't understand why such a fuss was made over them, but proceeded willingly to memorize all the "break, broke, brokens" so dear to my teacher's heart and that made him so happy.

When we lived in Rome, we were surrounded by relatives; in Florence we had no one, or almost no one, the only exceptions being a second cousin of my mother's and her two daughters. Lucia and Lina were a little older than me, not more than five or six years, and I attached myself to them with hopeful affection. But they too, like the Florence in which they were born and grew up, seemed to emanate sadness. Was it because of their father, a small accountant with a difficult character (so it was said in the family) who had died years before and left them without means? Or because of their mother, a gentle and warm woman whose modest charm seemed to have been suffocated by the demands of marriage, motherhood, and practical necessity? Or because of their Victorian house (heavy buffets, heavily decorated; dark velvet divans with wooden trim; leatherbound books that looked out from behind glass, prints and paintings that vied with one another on the walls)? Unless the melancholy aura of our cousins was, after all, in the eyes of the observer, little snob that I was, with a condescending view of any unattractive woman over twenty who worked for a living. Be that as it may, I can't recall Lina's and Lucia's teas, the first socials in which we took part in Florence, without a pang at my heart.

All the women who attended these gatherings were friends from childhood; all were married and busy raising children, with one exception: a person of sharp and authoritarian features, who shared the unmarried condition with my cousins, but nevertheless had several aces up her sleeve. One was money; another was a "pure" relationship with a bachelor, whose regular visits added luster to her status.

We would gather at five in the afternoon, filling up the little drawing room and engaging in small talk until a decrepit maid, who had been in the family for years, came in, dressed impeccably, with the tea and everything that went with it in those days. How we could have eaten a myriad of little sandwiches, canapés, and sweets in the middle of the afternoon and then begun again at dinner time baffles me, but we did it at my cousin's gatherings as well as all the others, which every guest organized in her turn. The surroundings changed; the ritual remained the same. If our apartment, sunny and spacious as it was, lent itself to these entertainments better, generally speaking, than my cousins' house, in practice it gave only a little luster to our meetings, since the guests, the sleepy proceedings, and the aimless conversations were all the same.

I remember that apartment very well and, to my great surprise, I still find it occasionally as part of my dreams. Or rather, I dream of entering the door of the little building that stood opposite the beautiful and well-kept public park in Piazza d'Azeglio and climbing the few, easy steps to the second floor where we lived. This climb, however, is without event or conclusion. I never meet our landlord, Count Colloredo, who occupied the third and uppermost floor, or any of his seven daughters (no male heir, alas!). Nor do I ever succeed in entering the apartment, a goal so impatiently anticipated during the climb. Right on the landing, before I can ring the bell, I wake up. What am I looking for in my dreams, and why does waking leave me with a vague sense of disappointment? I didn't like the apartment very much when we lived there; in fact, I was almost repelled by several pieces of antique furniture we were now able to permit ourselves. I can still see the stiff furniture of the living room, in the style of some Louis or other—gold and pale green against the yellow silk that covered the walls. Even my piano seemed uneasy in the midst of all this. Duly camouflaged by means of a valuable but worn tapestry, it looked like a thoroughbred out of a Renaissance painting, its grace weighed down by an elaborate harness.

It rained a lot in Florence in winter. In the late afternoon and after dinner I usually read a great deal, books of every kind. I read all of Anatole France, I remember, although I can't understand very well why. I also wept over Baudelaire and copied passages from the works of Nietzsche. Blissfully unconscious that one day he would be considered responsible for the birth of Nazism, I used to write in my notebook, the pen trembling with enthusiasm, that "it's a poor way to reward a teacher, by remaining faithful to him forever." I promised myself fervidly to betray all the mentors who would ever cross my path.

My father, who was never particularly impressed by my musical successes, was very proud of my love of reading. He even used to go to the trouble of reading certain books himself in order to be able to discuss them with me. He was particularly proud of my interest in history. For my twentieth birthday he gave me a beautiful leather-bound edition of a *History of the Popes* in seven volumes, hiding his pleasure under his usual jokes. "Here," he said, "years from now you'll be able to look at these books and say: 'These were given to me by my late father when I was twenty years old.'" Four months later he was dead.

8 The Afternoon Clouds Over

Periodically I try (I imagine everybody does) to put a little order in my papers, each time assigning myself the task of a quick inspection, a final good-bye, and a pitiless discarding that should leave both my drawers and my mind happily cleaned out. Needless to say, I'm brought to a standstill at the first stage, pondering over old letters, faded photographs, and newspaper headlines. Then, suddenly reawakening, I mechanically tear up a piece or two and slam the drawer shut.

In one of these searches, quite recently, I came upon several forgotten pages I had written for myself, when I was young, on the death of my father. They faithfully record events lost in the distant past: a minor indisposition of my father, a doctor's advice that the whole family should spend the month of July on the beach at Forte dei Marmi, Papà's imperceptible worsening between beach and bed, the summoning of more doctors for consultation, the disconcerting arrival of a few close relatives, and almost on their heels, against the absurd background of a family *pensione,* the implacable appearance of Death itself. Written carefully by hand, these pages express, with a pathos at once genuine and conventional, my personal sadness and the suffering that enfolded everyone. And yet, whenever I think of those days and my first face-to-face encounter with death, it's not suffering that haunts me, but the absence of suffering.

My mother, I still remember, is telling me that my father's illness seems to be lasting longer than was foreseen. Has the doctor, perhaps, shown some concern? I don't know any longer. I only know that she suggests that my brother and I not go dancing that evening, as had been decided, and I agree. But do I really agree, that's the point, or do I submit? Because this is to be the first time I would have gone dancing since Rome, the first chance to escape from the monotony of the afternoon teas of Florence. Thus, it's only my reasoning that is in agreement, while a short but sharp flush of resentment strikes at my heart.

Then another moment. This time the doctors must have expressed concern, because my father calls us children to his bedside and directs a few words to each of us. To my brother he says: "I entrust her to you," meaning that he confided my mother to his care. He says nothing to me, although I am the oldest. He only kisses me painfully, and his kiss is moist. Instinctively I dry my cheek with the back of my hand.

The pain of his loss went away in time, though occasionally revived by other losses, other pains. Those two moments (the flush of resentment, the instinctive gesture) have retained their intensity undiminished. So, too, the moment when I found myself laughing again, only a few weeks after the funeral. Look, I'm laughing, I thought with surprise but not with regret. I knew then that not only would I live, but I would enjoy life, and I felt immensely relieved.

We went to Ancona, or rather to the family country house at Le Grazie, a nearby village, earlier than usual that summer of my father's death, in the middle of August. Nonna Elisa, my mother's mother, still presided over the family at that time, which included a daughter and two sons, all unmarried, as well as a maid, a cook, and various part-time helpers. My aunt and uncles loved us very much, and we adored them, so that their welcoming us in that particular circumstance was a great blessing. The very monotony of the family routine and their daily rituals calmed our anguish. Established so long before our birth, familiar companions of our childhood, these rituals would continue unchanged for years until fascism and its war put an end to them.

The arrival of the barber, for example, early in the morning. He was admitted directly to the bedroom of Uncle Vittorio, the head of the family's business affairs and our favorite. Fifteen minutes later, he went into the bedroom of Uncle Roberto, the state's attorney, whom we regarded with a mixture of pride and awe. Then the barber went down to the kitchen for a cup of coffee and a little gossip with the chauffeur while waiting for a lift back to the city. We children had few contacts with him except for a casual greeting. However, through the half-open door we could sometimes observe his way of conducting himself: casual and facetious with the first client, formal and deferential with the second.

The uncles left for the city twice a day and returned twice a day, the first time for lunch, the second for dinner, announced each time by the sound of the automobile on the gravel of the garden and by the following communication intoned in a singsong by my aunt: "Wash your hands, and everyone to the table!"

Another ritual (although it seems unlikely that it took place every morning, as I remember it) was the counting of things that needed to be laundered in the hall of the upper floor outside my grandmother's bedroom: personal linen, towels, pillow cases, kitchen cloths, all divided into piles on the tile floor and then picked up by the strong arms of the laundress and gathered into a single large sheet, the four corners of which were tied together in two big knots. The laundry was done in the best possible way, by putting the wash under ashes, a method that remained forever mysterious to me because images of gray dust obstinately came to mind to contradict the assurances of immaculate results.

Later in the day came the hour of the siesta, when everyone except the children slept, even the servants in their room on the ground floor, and one could only talk in a whisper.

And at sunset the gardener watering the flower beds, water dripping peacefully over plants, gravel, walls (Should we move our chairs? Yes, it would be best to move them).

And later still, the maid clearing the dinner table, sweeping away the last crumbs before taking off the tablecloth and bringing some ashtrays, cigars, and playing cards for the games that Nonna Elisa played in turn with her two sons. We exchanged visits with the cousins who lived nearby, or sat around reading or knitting. A little after ten, cooling drinks were brought round: *granatina* made with pomegranate syrup, red and very sweet, or *orzata*, white with the taste of almonds. After the drinks we all went to bed, lulled to sleep by the slow freight trains that went puffing by in the valley below.

That summer of my father's death we must have done little more than let ourselves be, taking the days as they came and letting our loved ones take care of us. Except for tennis, naturally, because there had always been tennis at Le Grazie since long before we were old enough to play it. Actually, there were two private tennis courts available to us. One belonged to a doctor, a lively and perennially sunburned man of our parents' age, who kept his court in good condition, partly because of his love for the game, and partly because it allowed his beautiful daughter Sissi to carry on her social relations directly under his vigilant eyes. All of us, although criticizing his strictness (we cheerfully made the prediction that Sissi would elope someday), had to admit that we were indebted to Dr. Sorrentino for many good times. His house was located in an ideal spot, a few steps not only from my aunt's house but also from those of various young friends. It was also a stone's throw from the stop for the tram to Ancona, and so was accessible to our cousins who lived there and to their friends. One summer we even persuaded the "goodhearted grouch" to let us use the tennis court for a masked ball, an event that would remain unique in most of our lives.

The other tennis court was very different. Considerably run down and less enjoyable because accessible only to a few of us, it nevertheless made part of a most romantic setting, the ample and shady property of a family friend. An impressive gate and a wall of heavy stones protected this place from the eyes of the curious, so that, even though we were familiar with the old lady, and her brusque manners, who squinted through the window of the gate-house, we couldn't help but pull the long metal handle of the bell with a certain trepidation. Once the lock was open, we gained courage and began to climb slowly up the long, winding road, dark under enormous trees, that led to the main house.

We rarely met the owner, a sad, gray man, who had been wid-owed years before with a horde of children. The oldest of them, who had helped raise the family, was now married. Four others, grown men and women, appeared and disappeared at the house and tennis court following events and travels that were always wrapped in mystery. Only the younger children were our age, and it was they we came to see from time to time.

The tennis court was located in a corner of the property, below the hill with the greenhouse, and completely hidden by the growth of trees and shrubs. Most times we went directly there without stopping at the main house, but sometimes we were invited in, be-fore or after the game, for cold drinks and sweets. It was an enor-mous house with a vast, dark kitchen, many stairways and corri-dors, bedroom after bedroom on the upper floor, and a large drawing-room on the ground floor worthy of the pen of Chekhov, full of plants in pots and languid, elegant figures. Or perhaps they appeared languid to me, influenced as I was by the stories whis-pered at home of young orphans, nervous breakdowns, and faded beauties. I even imagined them playing tennis languidly, because I never saw them except when they left the court, since the younger group had to wait when the adults were playing.

Was it all, I now ask myself, like the film *The Garden of the Finzi-Continis?* I imagine it was, although many other things were different. No library adorned the villa; no old carriage lent itself to amorous encounters in the garden; no meticulous elegance

regulated our simple refreshments. Nor was the sadness that em-
anated from the house in the late twenties yet the end of an era.
That sadness didn't depend on the fact that its occupants happened
to be Jews any more than the carefree time spent at Dr. Sorrentino's
depended on the fact that he happened to be Catholic.

And yet, all of a sudden, I'm not so sure.

9 The Mysterious Power of American Girls

Whether the slower rhythm of our Florentine life was caused by the city, or was a consequence of the fact that we were new arrivals pining for the world we had left behind, its disadvantages were emphasized by my father's absence. The family no longer provided an antidote to them because Mother, while she became more dependent on us, also became bossier.

Of her three children, I was probably the one least affected by her increased display of authority, either because I was the oldest, or because I was the closest to her in tastes and temperament. Besides, I was sent to England that winter. My brother had gone there the year before and had acquired an excellent mastery of the language. It was supposed that my visit would bring the same result and, at the same time, provide a diversion from my grief. In the end, both of these goals eluded me, since the girls' school I attended in London was as academically incompetent as it was gloomy. As a result of my trip, however, I was spared the full impact of Mother's tenacious energy that had been set into motion by the loss of her husband and a renewed sense of mission. Her first target was Alice, a young American girl who had become an intimate friend of Guido.

It doesn't seem possible that I never met Alice. I feel as though I know her well, so important is the place she has held in family discussions since those days. She was sixteen years old at that time, very pretty, very sweet, and very much in love with Guido. If Guido, tall, dark, and good-looking, must have embodied the ideal man in her eyes, Alice (blond, with blue eyes and white skin) answered to all the expectations that young men then had when they met an American girl. However absurd it may seem now, these expectations did not go much beyond the abovementioned physical attributes, and for the rest, were often confined to the pleasure of a kiss and the supreme happiness of an unchaperoned meeting. If that was enough to make American girls objects of desire for young Italians, it was more than enough to endow them with mysterious and malignant powers in the eyes of Italian mothers. Ours did not lose any time in setting out on a crusade against the treacherous enemy.

My father's brother, Uncle Giorgio, was summoned from Rome to take the place of head of the family in the emergency. Armed with a letter that no one ever read but which, it was said, spoke very bluntly, he was dispatched to visit Alice's mother. None of the details of that visit were ever divulged; nevertheless, enough came out to make Guido recoil in shame, horrorstruck. The reaction of Alice's mother was swift and drastic. She told my uncle to go to hell, took her daughter, and left Florence. When I came back from England soon after, it was all over. I found Mamma inflexibly convinced of having done her duty in protecting a fatherless boy, who was inexpert in the wiles of an intriguer; and Guido, heartbroken and bitter in a resentment that would never weaken.

Did Mother meddle in her daughters' love lives as well, I wonder. Certainly she did. Except that Luciana's had not yet taken form, and mine, I can see now, was so innocuous as to run absolutely no risk, given the consultations that Mother and I held so frequently and which we enjoyed so much.

As, for example, the first time that a man followed me in the street, in Rome, when I was returning home from school. I was frightened to death and ran to an aunt's apartment, which was providentially nearby. Aunt Lilla gave me a cup of strong coffee, my first, and had her serving woman accompany me the rest of the way. It was my mother, however, who explained to me that, since I was taller than my fourteen years, I would get involved more and more often in similar happenings. She taught me how to walk, erect, indifferent, looking straight ahead so as to discourage beforehand anyone who wanted to follow me. I liked the lesson and made good use of it, so much so in fact, that it took some time after my coming to the United States years later, to discover that I could relax and let my eyes wander.

Or the time when a cousin younger than me gave me a very sketchy account of the facts of life. It would have been very dangerous for me to be left to my personal reflections, or worse, to my feelings of guilt. If sharing the information with Mother didn't throw any light on such a confused subject, our conversation served to transfer the guilt from my shoulders to my cousin's, which was no small accomplishment in the circumstances.

Or the time when my piano teacher, the one who had so highly valued my talent and was so strongly conscious of my obligations toward it, began to move his chair closer and closer to mine, first brushing my back, then my shoulders, and at last my breast, while all the time making authoritative comments on my artistic successes. It was Mother who told me how to deal with him, with a firm voice and words not directly referring to what had happened. After I had curtly said that I could not bear any impediment to my movements as I played, the poor maestro must have asked himself if I rightly understood what he had been doing, but he backed away courteously.

As for the young men I encountered in Florence, or Ancona, or in hotels in the Alps where we went every summer, they all seemed very much alike and behaved in similar ways; strangely and obstinately, they were intent on marriage and lost little time in courtship. I can still remember two of them, whose parents spoke to mine before their sons had taken the trouble to speak to me, and who, like Barkis in Dickens, were "willing." It was great fun discussing them with Mother and getting her proud nod of assent to

my impassioned affirmations concerning love, and waiting, and—
why not?—remaining single forever.

Once a man, much older than I, of about thirty-five years, I
think, was really in love with me. He didn't speak to my mother
first; he spoke directly to me. But I didn't know what to do about
his feelings; I was not ready, and he frightened me. I don't know
anymore if it was he who spoke of suicide, or if it was us, Mamma
and I, who thought of such a possibility because of the intensity of
his feelings. I remember the room in the Milan hotel in which we
stopped on our return trip to Florence from a vacation spot in the
mountains, where Mother left us alone for a meeting he had requested. This time, too, she instructed me to be firm, but she
taught me a compassion that I was still too young to feel. The man
did not kill himself, but he never did marry.

No, I'm wrong, Mamma did not meddle. She only looked on,
and I did better for it. I don't know if she ever was tempted to intrude when Alex came on the scene. I think that he must have confused her at first, and when she had figured him out, it was too late
to intervene.

10 Enter Alex

When I first met him, toward the end of spring in 1930, Alex was Alessandro or Sandro to his Italian friends, Shura to his family. Ten years before, his parents had sent him away by ship from his native Russia, terrified at the idea that on his next birthday, his eighteenth, he would be eligible for military service. Which army would have enlisted him was far from clear in those confused times, and in the end it was the Bolsheviks who, in the wake of the departing Allies, took the upper hand only a few hours after the young Alex's escape.

He and I met accidentally thanks to Guido's having second thoughts when he left the house one evening for "the theater with a friend." "Would you like to come with me?" he asked, I don't know why, since he had never asked before. I don't even know why I went, given that by temperament I am usually inclined to stay at home. The play was Ibsen's *Peer Gynt;* the friend, a dark-haired young man with bright eyes, a bit thick-set, analyzed it brilliantly from beginning to end, and a few weeks later we were engaged. The talent for analysis that Alex revealed at our first meeting would sustain his fascination for me during our entire married life. So would the way he talked about his adventurous past, half dramatic, half ironic. Beginning with his flight at the last minute on board a crowded ship (the last one to leave the port of Odessa), his stories included a precarious life in a Constantinople teeming with refugees and steeped in xenophobia; a miraculous crossing of the Balkans not long before the Greek-Turkish war; a stay in Vienna selling typewriters; another in Leipzig studying philosophy at the university and being initiated into the fur trade . . . finally, settling down in Florence, where his parents had joined him.

Alex's younger brothers, Emanuele and Raimondo, although acknowledging his successes, were in a way critical of his choice of Florence instead of the city that had long been a beacon of culture and taste to Russian eyes: Paris! Needless to say, I had no quarrel with his choice. For me, Florence was the perfect ending to a very romantic story. When my girlfriends asked me who was this man I was engaged to, I used to answer casually, "a Russian," as I might have said, "a count" or "a duke."

The exotic past of my beloved didn't have quite the same fascination for my mother, who was much more interested in his present circumstances. These too, however, seemed quite promising. In the days when Alex's and my paths crossed, an imposing brass sign next to a wide entrance on the Via Tornabuoni in Florence advised passersby of the presence in the building of the wholesale fur company "H. Pekelis & Sons" which Alex had helped to create. Nevertheless, Alex himself dedicated only a part of his time to the firm. Having succeeded in finishing his law studies in his free time, and passed the bar, and published a book, he was now beginning a professional and academic career.

I never met the H. Pekelis of the sign, Alex's father Haim. He had died suddenly a few months before, after an operation. If Alex, the oldest of his three sons, was now the head of the family, its soul was Mamulia, little Mother, adored by all her sons identically. Mamulia was a small, plump, energetic woman whose warmth and devotion I would come to appreciate in due time. Our first meeting, however, was far from being a success and put my romantic mood to a hard test. Alex had prepared me for the little apartment, barely furnished and sad, located at the back of the business premise, the window of which opened on a dark courtyard. "You will see," he told me jokingly, "you won't find any of your mother's bourgeois knickknacks in our house!" What I wasn't prepared for was that his mother, still in mourning, received me in tears and refrained from weeping only long enough to feed us, and then began again with the greatest gusto. Her tears, presumably, were owing to the fact that Alex's father was not with us to share the happiness of the occasion; however, they didn't exactly help to make the occasion festive. Meanwhile, some of Mamulia's comments on Italy aroused in me a vague suspicion that she might consider the prospect of having an Italian as daughter-in-law a dubious blessing. Not one Italian thing that we happened to mention at that first meeting or most of the following ones could bear comparison, according to her, with its Russian counterpart. Not the food, not the shops, not the people. Even the brass plate at the door was a falling off from that (black letters on a bright metal plate) which had adorned the four bay windows of the Pekelis store on Richelievskaia Ulitsa in Odessa! Nor did the fact that I was Jewish compensate, I fear, for my being Italian. In fact, that could have been another source of concern in Mamulia's eyes, since—as I discovered later—she had a very low opinion of Italian Jews. If the totally ignorant ones like me deserved at least a condescending pity, the others (who worshipped, ate, and behaved in the most strange and unorthodox ways) were the objects of a most disdainful criticism. And as a matter of fact, of the many elements that made Alex's youth completely different from mine, the most important may well have been the approach to Judaism.

While I had grown up in an atmosphere of vague identity and comfortable ignorance, he had been raised in fear of pogroms, which had pursued his forebears for generations. As a boy he had had to repeat the admission exams to the gymnasium many times in order to reach the highest grade, since only thus was he in a position to surpass the *numerus clausus* that limited the admission of Jews to public schools. The Jewish identity, therefore, was above all an indisputable fact to him and, at the same time, an act of dignity, a weapon and comfort in the eternal struggle. The observance of rituals helped to preserve this identity, and he practiced them with complete faith in the symbol, if not in the letter. I learned all this quickly and was very willing to share it with him. However, the going was not always easy.

I remember our first Yom Kippur. We were just engaged, and at that time Alex was our guest at dinner every evening. He said that he would not come on Yom Kippur eve because he would have begun to fast at sundown. I accepted the fact indifferently, and indifferently spent the following day in ordinary activities; only when I greeted him in the evening did I realize that I had profoundly disappointed him by not even making an appearance at the synagogue on the holiest of days.

I was staggered. "But I've never gone into a synagogue in my life," I protested, nevertheless determined to conduct myself better from then on. My first visit to a synagogue finally took place on a Friday evening in Genoa during our honeymoon, and I was filled with dismay.

I knew beforehand, of course, that I would not be seated next to Alex, but on the floor above with all the women. For some reason, however, I had not expected that the gallery would be so small and confined, the separation from the men and services below made complete by an elaborate marble grating. Nor did the Hebrew-Italian prayerbook I had brought with me provide any help, since the ceaseless chattering that filled the place left no room for anything else. Lower middle-class housewives, tradeswomen, and shopkeepers, the women around me were not as I expected the celebrants of a High Holiday to be. Knowing the order of services well, from time to time they proudly threw out a hurried response in Hebrew to the mournful chant of the cantor below. But their principal interest seemed to be an intense and undisciplined exchange of news concerning the widest variety of subjects. In the meantime, children ran noisily along the rows of benches, occasionally provoking an absentminded slap. A frowning attendant, strangely like a eunuch in a harem, surveyed the goings-on and at certain moments ordered silence with an authority ignored by all.

I don't think any of the services I attended afterward equaled the hopelessness of this one in any way. None of them, however, was to give me consolation, or strength, or even the possibility of meditation. Perhaps one cannot hope to find these blessings by asking for them; they must enter the temple with us. Perhaps this is the reason why the women one sees lost in prayer in the half darkness of Italian churches seem reluctant to leave. I, too, have once or twice tried in those churches, if not to pray, at least to think. But it did not happen during the religious services.

The only ceremonies that brought me close to a religious experience were those that Alex celebrated at home: blessing the wine over the table on Friday evening, rejoicing at the promises of the new year, presiding at the Seder of the first two evenings of Passover. Since we didn't have a child big enough to ask "Why is this night different from all others?" I was the one who put the question out loud in faltering Hebrew. To make his answer understood, Alex used to say it first in Italian: "Slaves we were in the kingdom of Egypt!" His voice sounded strong and clear speaking of slavery and redemption; then it became softer in a gentle parody imitating the Talmudic subtleties of Rabbi Eliezer, Rabbi Joshua, Rabbi Elazar (the son of Azariah); then he allowed it freely to sing the ballads and rhymes. He never skipped a line or a chorus or pronounced them in haste, since haste is not worthy of a wise man and is disrespectful to God; in any case, his public (his mother, brothers, and an occasional member of my family) stayed with him from beginning to end.

Looking back at our years spent together in Florence (there would only be seven) I rarely am able to see again our first little apartment where, comfortably provided with a serving woman, I continued to lead almost the same life I had led as a girl. "What did you do this morning?" Alex asked when he came home for lunch, and again "What did you do this afternoon?" when he came home for dinner. He was not exactly struck by my progress, including, I'm afraid, that in the field of music. The whole world was before us, he thought, ready to be conquered. The sooner we were engaged in this task, the better. I should study Law; I should work with him in an office of our own, and incidentally, not have children for at least ten years.

However, as the Italians say: what woman wants, God wills. By simple passive resistance, I avoided the Faculty of Law for a bit longer and became pregnant the following year. We left the little apartment to have room for the child, and this time Mother was able to persuade us to take an ugly but large apartment two blocks from hers, which would allow her to help me out at the moment of birth and to help me care for the baby. I think I agreed with her, especially in connection with the birth, for which I thought I needed all the help possible. Still, I absolutely hadn't yet foreseen the event as the complex public affair it turned out to be.

It took place at home, as was the common practice at that time, under the direction of the midwife, a dark woman with mustaches, muscular, of great reputation, who rained blows upon my stomach with her fists when she thought the pains were too weak and too far apart. Also in attendance were my mother, who was second-in-command, her serving woman, my serving woman, Alex's mother and the doctor, who finally arrived to examine the situation.

As for Alex, left to himself in the living room under a burden of orders and comments spoken by excited women, he didn't even have the traditional comfort available to a man, since he didn't smoke. Nor did things change appreciably after the birth of our daughter, because Mother installed herself determinedly in our bedroom to care for the child and me, while the serving woman traveled continually between her apartment and ours with all sorts of refined dishes, which Alex accepted reluctantly but devotedly gulped down.

It took us ten days to recover possession of the apartment and ten months until we left it altogether for the one that would become our true home, alas, for too short a time.

11 The Noose Tightens

We answered an advertisement for a three-story apartment building on one of the busiest streets of Florence, Via Cavour, because the location seemed perfectly suited for a law office that Alex intended to have in the apartment. The garden that we found behind the entry came as a surprise to us and made my heart beat hopefully. It was enough to enter the apartment itself, on the third floor, and give one look at the well-lighted hall with its two french doors opening on a long terrace overlooking the garden, for me to squeeze Alex's arm and whisper to him, "I love it!" Notwithstanding the fact that, as Alex remarked afterward, any chance of negotiation is precluded to a man if his wife spontaneously shows her feelings so openly, we rented the apartment. Alex had his office of two rooms with a separate entrance, and I my terrace. The part I had seen first, equal in size to the comfortable, square entrance hall, was the largest; a narrower strip ran along the entire rear of the apartment past a second, smaller hall that led to the kitchen, the bath, and the bedroom. The garden below belonged to an old lady, who never left the little villa she occupied. I liked to watch her sight unseen, and wished her many years of serenity and good health.

We must have used the terrace less frequently than I remember, since even in Italy winter makes its appearance from time to time, and in Florence in particular it's often accompanied by rain. And yet, looking back, I see only sunshine, lounge chairs, plants in bloom. Geraniums especially, of every kind and color, sometimes an azalea or a daisy, and every April for my birthday a gardenia that Alex and I bought together at the flower market around the corner. It was on the terrace that I sat with Daniela and her toys, walked impatiently back and forth in the pains of other child-births, read, knitted, and received my friends' visits. In the evening, when the children were in bed and late meetings kept Alex in his office, I waited for him as the sun went down, not daring to turn on a light for fear of breaking the spell. It was always Jole, our young maid, concerned as she was for the fate of the dinner she had prepared, who heard Alex first. We hurried inside for the meal to please her, and then went back outside with cups of coffee in hand and, in the darkness, exchanged the news of the day.

If it's true that, as the Italians say, "happy people have no sto-ries," we were unhappy even then when we were hardly conscious of it, because our evening conversations were always full of stories. Some surely had to do with the family. Guido had married, had had two children, and then, tired of all that, had retired to a bachelor's apartment complete with a butler in white gloves. Luciana tried to escape from life with Mother by getting engaged to a certain young man only to discover that he was too high a price to pay for that purpose, and she rid herself of him decisively; her wisdom was re-warded not long after with a good husband and children. Alex's mother became sick and stayed with us for a year. His brothers went through an exorbitant number of ups and downs, profes-sionally and otherwise. In the meantime, the world around us was breaking up, and although we kept putting off doing something about it, we were obsessed by this fact.

Fascism had grown much stronger in power. The head of the government and the party, presumably for life, Mussolini—who had corrupted the parliamentary institutions, suffocated the press, and imprisoned or exiled the opposition—relied on a few positive achievements to impress the respectable folk at home and public opinion abroad. The rest of us, highly conscious of the state of things, took futile refuge in passionate discussions and the endless exchange of jokes.

"Did you hear the one about the Duce talking to a peasant? Or the afterwork group that was taken to hear *La Bohème*? The one about the pedestrian crossing the street? Let me tell you the latest rhyme, limerick, song. . . ." Occasionally someone would lower his voice and indicate the maid who might overhear. It was taken for granted, however, that the maids either didn't understand or weren't interested, and unguarded comments were a common outlet. It was as if being satirical about the evils of the times was all the catharsis we needed. Many determined opponents of the regime, in fact, had the party card in order to avoid possible problems in looking for or finding work. This double game was amply justified in their eyes precisely because of the arbitrariness of the demands and regulations imposed on them. On this point, I also felt ambivalent. I remember challenging Alex with my questions in relation to his career, since he was offering a "free" or optional course in the Philosophy of Law at the University of Rome, one that had little prestige and no academic future. To become a full-fledged professor in any university, he would have had to take part in one of the competitions held in Italy when there is an available chair . . . and for this, at the time, a card was necessary.

"Why not get one?" I pressed him. "Why play *their* game, limiting your teaching to those few students who may wander in and out of an optional course? Wouldn't you be better off among the others, teaching the young to think and protecting them from indoctrination?"

He listened to me nodding as if in agreement, but in the end shook his head with a sad smile. "I know, I know," he said, "it seems sensible. But it's too easy! I simply can't allow myself to believe in it!" And that was that. Soon enough, in any case, the humiliation of getting a card was no longer enough. All university teachers were asked to take an oath of loyalty to the regime, and nine professors who refused lost their positions.

Historians always bring our attention back to the fact that totalitarian regimes, when they need to divert their people from internal difficulties, turn to the international sphere. Mussolini's involvement, first in Ethiopia and then in Spain, may probably be seen in this light. But I don't think we were conscious of it at the time. When Italian troops entered Ethiopia in 1935, we only thought that Mussolini's speech about "living space" and "a place in the sun" was a lot of nonsense, and that looking for them in the barren soil of such a distant region was an act of folly. For a while we even hoped that the rest of the world would protest the undertaking. Unfortunately, the economic sanctions voted by the League of Nations and applied almost reluctantly could not achieve the purpose of weakening the Fascist war effort and only succeeded in spreading among the common people a slight surge of patriotic feeling. Some months afterward, Mussolini, by now completely alienated from England and France, joined Hitler in his support of Franco in Spain.

Far from taking our minds off domestic troubles, this action came as a new burden. It was small comfort to know that a group of Italians (for the most part exiles) were fighting in Spain on the opposite side of the barricades. Their motto was: "Today in Spain, tomorrow in Italy," and one of their leaders was Carlo Rosselli, a longtime anti-Fascist, who had undergone prison and deportation, and was then the editor of a militant opposition paper in Paris. His brother Nello, whose ideology was also well known, was one of our friends and lived in Florence with his wife and small children. Although his activity was limited to the publication of scholarly books on the nineteenth-century Risorgimento, he was under strict surveillance by the Fascist police.

I remember the morning, at the beginning of June 1937, when Alex called me from the bathroom. His face half covered with lather, his eyes full of tears, he pointed to the morning paper that lay open on the dresser next to the sink. Carlo and Nello, who had gone to meet him, had both been killed in France, officially by French *cagoulards,* members of a right-wing terrorist organization. There was never any doubt in anyone's mind about who had secured their services.

12 Jews Are Not of the Italian Race

The death of the Rosselli brothers was not, of course, the first example of Fascist violence to claim our attention. Just at the beginning of our stay in Florence, for example, when the regime was still trying to consolidate its power, there had been insistent rumors of a night of "purification," when several eminent anti-Fascists had been picked up at their homes, arrested, and later executed. In the absence of a free press, however, the rumors remained rumors and were easily stifled. When the Rossellis were assassinated, we were forced to look the tragic event in the face, not only because we felt the blow personally out of love for our friends, but because there was absolutely no possibility for us to take refuge in the labyrinth of: "Are you really sure? Isn't it perhaps just talk? Aren't you making too much of it?" which had protected us on other occasions. It was as if this event signaled the beginning of a period of more acute awareness; as if until this moment we had been expecting the fall of fascism because of the economic situation, and only now did we come to realize that people would first have to suffer a great deal. We only partially guessed that we would be high on the list because we were Jews.

There had already been sporadic attacks against the Jews for years in the sectors of the Fascist press closest to Nazi Germany. Most of them, however, came from the pens of particular journalists, some of whom had even been criticized by other journalists. As for the Duce himself, he seemed to avoid going on record on the subject, while at the same time encouraging optimism on the part of the potential victims. Of the many statements attributed to him (to Chaim Weizman in an interview of 1934, to Nahum Goldman later that same year), the one that circulated most widely referred to the remark he had made in a speech given, I think, in Bari. Dismissing the rumors of a possible alignment on his part with Hitler's antisemitic measures, Mussolini had affirmed: "The Jews have wept over Caesar's tomb; they won't be touched!"

However, when his paper, *Il Popolo d'Italia,* began to publish antisemitic articles, or reprint sympathetically the criticisms, insinuations, and slanders published by other papers, the direction being taken became tragically clear.

Looking back, I can't understand how, in the fall of 1937, I could have had so much faith in life as to enroll in the Faculty of Law and plan for another child. Our second daughter, Simona, had been born the year before, and Alex thought that two children were more than enough. And he took up the subject of law school again, in a way truly typical of his character. He maintained that actions must be prompted by impulses and convictions, without an excessive concern for circumstances. "If I had waited for a green light," he used to say, "I would still be in Odessa!" But I, I had always had the highest respect for green lights. How could I want to bring another child into the world we were living in? How could I think that my law studies had any sort of future, that I would practice law together with Alex one day? And yet, all I did was tease him jokingly. "I'll go to the university," I challenged him, "if I can have another baby!" And that's the way things turned out.

During that winter I worked very hard and, so far as I can remember, very happily. I didn't in the least miss my friends and games of bridge. The university was only a few blocks from our apartment, and I could stay in class until a certain hour and be with my children immediately afterward. The children didn't even feel my absence very much. Not only was there a faithful nanny at their disposition, but there were grandmothers, aunts, and cousins only too eager to help. The transformation from young mistress of a house to a student was in itself exhilarating. To discuss the material with Alex, to work with him on some unimportant matters, to find that at the ripe age of thirty my mind had not become rusty were new sources of satisfaction. As for what awaited us, I must conclude that—conscious as we were of the circle around us steadily growing tighter, and influenced as we were by an impending doom—we must simply have lacked imagination.

Our third daughter, Rossella, was born July 10, 1938, and we welcomed the event with a joy that was not obscured by circumstances. In those days it was assumed that a woman would remain in bed for a week after giving birth, and I enjoyed the rest. My bed was only a few steps from the french windows that opened on the terrace, and beyond that my eyes lingered on the trees in the garden of the neighboring house. One of them, a magnolia, gave out a pungent, irresistible fragrance. The week was not yet finished when I picked up the morning paper that Alex had forgotten when he had gone to have breakfast. It carried an enormous headline on the front page: THE JEWS ARE NOT OF THE ITALIAN RACE. Underneath came what was called "The Manifesto of Race" that listed ten points to make clear the concept of race and the relative position of the Jews. The ax had fallen, although people, including the Italian Jews, still needed a long time to absorb the implications of it all.

That summer we rented a house in Gavinana, a little vacation spot in the Apennines not far from Florence. We carried on with our plans, waiting more or less for what would happen. My sister and her family joined us there. Also Uncle Giorgio and his wife from Rome. All of us felt the need to get together and consult about the next step. It was evident that the publication of the "Manifesto" (the signatures of various "scientists" had been affixed to it a few days later) was only the beginning. Beginning of what? It was plain that the best thing we could do would be to emigrate. But when? And where? Mario, Luciana's husband, was a fervent Zionist and intended to move to Palestine, then under the British Mandate. Giorgio had a brother-in-law in Argentina, and they were thinking of South America. Only we were uncertain. Meanwhile the days were passing; I was nursing little Rossella, playing with the older girls and Luciana's children in the yard behind our house and preparing stubbornly for my law exams in the fall session. Photographs, which strangely have followed me until today, show a five-year-old Daniela holding her little sister with both fear and awe; Luciana and I who are looking elsewhere, arm in arm; and Giorgio and his wife smiling and looking at the camera. Gestures and expressions no different from those common to all family albums. Behind them was the feeble awareness that our world was coming to an end.

The first racial laws made their appearance at the beginning of September 1938. All Italian Jews were forbidden to attend public schools and universities (and these last are all public in Italy) as well as to teach there. The Jews who were naturalized Italians, Alex among them, *ipso facto* lost their citizenship and were invited to leave the country within six months. "Why?" said Mamulia in dismay and confusion. "The king himself signed my citizenship papers!" Poor Mamulia! She, an immigrant from the land of pogroms, had faith in the integrity of Vittorio Emanuele III, King of Italy.

The fact that Alex had lost his Italian citizenship attracted a great deal of sympathy and affection from relatives and friends. However, it was really a blessing, since it prevented any further beating about the bush on our part. True, a special proviso allowed foreign Jews married to Italians to remain in our territory, but it would have required incredible ingenuousness to rely on this pretext. Thus we decided that Alex must leave immediately, while the children and I should remain, ready to leave as soon as he had given us a sign that the way was clear.

The months that followed, the last in my native land, were so hectic with respect to every kind of practical detail that little room was left for sadness. Not only did Alex's absence increase my daily responsibilities, but it was necessary to proceed with closing the house as well as the law office, and this had to be done discreetly, because our departure, though it was forced, might yet encounter resistance. To all this had to be added the continual and very wearisome talking with hundreds of friends and relatives who wanted to say good-bye to us and show us their sympathy, or were merely curious. Some lived there in Florence; others came to look me up from out of the city. Strangely enough, the Jews among them did not seem to feel personally threatened by the way things were going. For most of them, I was a special case because I had married a foreigner, and their profound involvement in my plight did not appear to be troubled by personal fears. If the rights of all Italian Jews were being stripped one by one (to attend schools or to teach, to employ "Aryan" servants, to marry non-Jews, to hold public office), these deprivations seemed of little account in the light of a general and passionate desire for reassurance. Far from being seen as the prelude to worse evils, they were considered as mere concessions by Mussolini to Hitler "to keep him happy."

As for our friends who were not Jews, their attitudes ranged from bewilderment to perplexity to indignation according to their degree of political awareness. Our greengrocer shook her head sadly. "Poor lady," she commiserated, adding hesitantly with her typical Florentine cadence, "But what does it mean, Jewish?" My friend Bianca, whose parents came from landowning stock of the upper bourgeoisie, whose younger sister was a nun, embraced me with her usual warmth. "Poor, poor Carla," she sighed, "I can find only one explanation for this drastic measure. Some Jew must have done something terrible, something that can't be revealed. And you're all paying, atoning for this fact!"

Strength and support came from those who had always been intellectual opponents of the Fascist regime. Among them I did not find myself an object of pity, but rather a symbol of the evils that beset us all, and I could feel like a combatant rather than a victim. By the time Alex decided that he ought to settle in Paris, it was the end of autumn. It seemed crazy to face an expensive and cold winter in Paris with three little children, but it seemed equally crazy to lose more time in Florence. The caprice of a new rule could, at any moment, separate us forever. Thus it was decided that the children and I would cross the border, but spend the winter in Nice. The trip (so short, but so fraught in my mind with a thousand dangers) was easily accomplished. At the first stop after the French border I pressed my face to the window, trying to see from the lighted compartment into the darkness of the platform. I saw Alex and waved to him. He did not answer my greeting; nor did he board the train immediately. He remained motionless, touching his right hand first to his lips, then to his forehead. I knew that he must be murmuring in Hebrew his thanks to God.

13 "Safe" at Last

The period that the children and I spent in Nice remains in my memory as completely desolate. I feel guilty admitting it because after all we were safe, in good health, and comfortably situated in a family *pensione*. But as soon as Alex had gone back to Paris and I was alone, separated irreparably from my friends and my country, the understanding of all that had happened struck me with sudden violence. I could manage in one way or another to live by day when the brilliant sunshine of the Riviera seemed to deny both winter and sadness, but I couldn't bear the nights that descended abruptly and filled me with anguish. The chores that marked the end of the day (bathe the littlest child, nurse her, dress the others for dinner) instead of helping me take pleasure in the beautiful things that were still mine, only made my longing for my lost home more acute. "What is it, Mamma?" Simona asked, more curious than frightened, exploring my wet cheeks with her fingers, and her innocence made fresh tears come to my eyes. I must have communicated my suffering to Alex in the letters I wrote him, because when he came to see us on New Year's Eve, he told me he had rented a small furnished apartment in Paris and we would again be together.

Thus at the beginning of January 1939, we left Nice behind us, the first stage of what would become a long voyage, and we took possession of our new dwelling at No. 9 Rue de Bassano, an anonymous street, narrow and crowded, beyond the Champs Elysées. By now I remember that house only vaguely, just a room or two, and the suffocating sense of too much furniture and too many people among faded wallpaper and low, gray ceilings with stucco decorations. Not only had my mother and mother-in-law joined us from Italy, but it seemed that every sort of visitor came and went at the house at all hours. Mostly they were fellow refugees in search of company and advice. Some were clients, since Alex, with an ability equaled only by his courage, was already immersed in the French legal system. Some, alas, were doctors, for all of us were sick that winter with a variety of illnesses. In the middle of all this there was a constant stream of cleaning women, maids, and cooks, who kept our doorbell ringing, a note from the agency in their hands, only to leave promptly, frightened by the size of the family and the feverish atmosphere. Some stayed for a few days, long enough for us to catch a glimpse of pretty faces and taste an extraordinary leek or potato soup. Then they disappeared, with a look of contemptuous disapproval in their eyes.

It seemed to me that my days were almost completely given over to regulating the traffic, a responsibility that included taking the children out of the house when some important person was with Alex in the living room, or simply keeping them quiet when that someone was just a friend but who had no less right to tell the story of his misfortunes without interruption.

The goal of my walks was invariably the immense, sprawling Place de l'Étoile and the precarious haven offered by its intricately arranged flower beds between gravel paths. The arrangement is completely dimmed in my memory, but the sharp cold of my first winter in Paris still makes me shiver when I remember it. How many times did I actually push the carriage (Rossella asleep inside, Simona perched on a seat between the handles) as far as Place de l'Étoile? How many times did I retrieve balls, untangle jump ropes, or read from picture books? Probably not many. In memory they make part of a single interminable morning during which I am continually looking at my watch, longing anxiously for mealtime which would put an end to my ordeal.

In sharp contrast to the long demanding days, my evenings with Alex away from the house, in the city, were fascinating, unreal. We met friends for dinner, or more often, after dinner at one of the many *boîtes* that flourished unobtrusively under dark entrances, down in basements, in winding alleys. Those evenings were most disconcerting, for in some way they made the whole business of ex-ile appear like an adventure, and what is more, a social adventure. But back in the little bedroom that Simona and Rossella shared with us, it was hard to fall asleep. From the apartment above, a continual creaking preyed on my already restless mind. I had been told that it was caused by a sick old lady, close to death, who rocked all night in her pain. It was almost dawn when the sound stopped, and a few minutes later little Rossella rolled out of her bed into mine with gurgles of laughter. Together we got up be-tween shushes and kisses to begin the new day.

I don't remember when we understood that the forwarding of our furniture from Florence, however much it might cost, would really be a good idea. By allowing us to move to an unfurnished apartment, it would give us more breathing space and would result in an economic advantage. I think we moved to No.186 Avenue Victor Hugo in the spring, because the first tender leaves on the trees and the first buds in the flower beds found the children and me at the Bois de Boulogne, just a stone's throw from our new apartment. This apartment occupied the fifth floor of a rather im-posing building that had a majestic front stairway (an elevator rose smoothly in the central space) and a rear stairway without an ele-vator for deliveries and the servants. Of these last we now had three: one half-time for cleaning the house, one in the kitchen, and one who served meals and took care of the children. To this day I really don't know if the ease of our domestic life on Avenue Victor Hugo depended on the fact that the new house gave us a certain

degree of respectability in the eyes of the help, or if it was the presence among us of Anne Le Bouédec.

Initially hired as a cook, Anne quickly became our principal
support and best friend. Saying that our inexperience put us at the
mercy of those she called "the first to show up," she assumed the
task of deciding who the rogues were (cheating suppliers or un-
scrupulous domestics) and of foiling their plots. Sturdy, dignified,
with gray hair, she had been born in Brittany about fifty years before. This origin constituted a sort of elevated lineage, and she referred to it with a certain pride. If her social standing was a bit inferior to ours, being a Bretonne compensated amply for it. The fact
of being able to teach us the French word for leek permitted her to
look down on us and love us all the more. Apart from Brittany (and
a niece who still lived there), Anne had two other reasons for pride:
her hair and her "room on the seventh floor." French apartment
buildings then had (I don't know if they still do) a floor, the top,
reserved for the maids of the tenants. The one that Anne loved so
much was not, however, that to which we were entitled on the top
floor of our building. She was the owner of her own room, situated
in another building on the Boulevard Flandrin a few blocks away.
She had been given it by an ex-employer in his will, a will that figured prominently in the stories she told to us and to the children.
Although she had to climb up to her nest every evening, Anne was
back in our apartment every morning in time for our breakfast
with a long twist of fresh bread under her arm. The maid and cleaning woman conceded the right of precedence to her, and so did we.
Even my mother and mother-in-law, potential rebels, had to restrain themselves from open opposition on the ground of language. As for the children, they became attached to her from the
first moment, perhaps for the many songs she knew, songs they
were able to sing and understand long before their French was good
enough for her stories. Their ecstatic appreciation of "Toulouse,
Tou-lou-se, *jolie fleur d'été*" delighted Anne, who was inclined to

believe that they could do no wrong. Their tramping on our floors could provoke cries of "Slippers, slippers!" from the floor below. She maliciously said that intolerant people like the "gentleman on the fourth floor" shouldn't live in apartment buildings, but ought to remove themselves and their idiosyncrasies to the country.

Yes, all things considered, the spring of 1939 was good to us. Very much so, in fact, if I could think of following the doctors' advice and take Daniela to the mountains for the summer. For some time, during that period, she had been subject to sudden, violent high temperatures, and X-rays had revealed that it was a case of tuberculosis. The doctor had explained that such cases were frequent among children, although they often went undiscovered. A few weeks in the mountains would be beneficial for the healing process and would prevent the recurrence of similar episodes.

Just then my Roman cousins and childhood friends were in Switzerland, at Champex, ostensibly on vacation but in reality trying out the first stage of emigration. So Daniela and I went to Champex, installing ourselves in the same hotel and indulging for a bit in the pleasures of a lovely, unreal interlude. If the adults' conversations, far from the ears of the children, reflected the menacing quality of the times, family life followed the quiet, unconcerned rhythm of a vacation resort. Every morning, their knapsacks proudly flaunted on their shoulders, the children set out on shady mountain paths, while their parents followed after. Picnics took place among wild flowers and grazing cows. Daniela's cheeks were taking on a rosy color and her eyes an excited brightness.

All this lasted but a short time. The announcement, charged with foreboding, of the Russo-German pact, sent Daniela and me back to Paris and my cousins—unpredictably—to Rome.

Our fears were justified. On the first of September 1939, Germany, its hands now free, invaded Poland.

14 Pierre

The Poles were overrun, first by the Germans and then by the Russians, in the course of a few weeks. In protest, France and England entered the war, and we, once more, began to wait. Not in fear as two years ago, when we had waited for the ax to fall, but rather with impatience, almost with longing. The definitive engagement with the forces of evil was finally at hand, and we had no doubts about its outcome!

As an immediate measure of precaution, we moved the children, our mothers, and Anne to Pau in the Pyrenees, far from the "front." Alex remained in Paris, and I began to travel back and forth according to the needs of the family and the office. January found me again in the mountains with Daniela to complete the cure that had been cut short in Switzerland, this time at Font Romeu, another village in the Pyrenees but east of Pau and higher up. In February I was back in Paris with Alex. As far as the war was concerned, nothing was happening. A few skirmishes, some bulletins, strict application of the blackout rules, and a great many rumors. The French had already found a name for this situation: they called it *cette drôle de guerre,* "the phony war." And they laughed at Hitler, letting themselves relax at his delay in making a move. Let him take all the time he wants! France can wait. The Maginot Line will be there, an impregnable bulwark, when he makes his decision.

In darkened Paris night life went on as usual. Occasionally Alex and I took part also, under the expert guidance of friends who initiated us with a certain pride into a world they considered highly sophisticated. They were Russian émigrés of the twenties (tied in some way to Alex's past) or French by birth, all of them intellectuals who somewhat intimidated me. I tried hard to live at their level and enjoy myself, but most of the time our explorations seemed to yield slight results. The evenings began in some unusual restaurant (I remember one called "La Moschea," where the darkness and an oppressive smell of incense made eating a difficult chore), and they ended in one night club or another, with whispered songs, mournfully uttered from the most minuscule stages. Edith Piaf, Agnès Capri, Suzy Solidor. . . . There were moments when, as they sang their attractive melodies, I could almost imagine myself one of their ardent admirers. Then a strange, eccentric display would suddenly interrupt my initiation, leaving me embarrassed and bored. Not Alex.

I remember one evening when two enormous, bearded men, standing upright and motionless on the stage, their arms hanging at their sides, sang like robots: "*La sainte Catherine, lazi-bumbum, la sainte Catherine était fille du roi, voilà, voilà, la sainte Catherine était fille du roi.* . . ." I knew the song well; it was one of those Anne sang to the children in the evenings when she put them to bed. When we were coming home, I gave vent to my irritation to Alex. "All right," I said bitterly, "let's say it's absurd on the lips of those men in that place, therefore sophisticated; it's so impossibly out of fashion, it becomes the fashion. All right, I get the point. I still say it's not at all amusing, and I was bored to death!" Alex, waving away my irritation, pronounced himself more worried than bored. "I'm afraid," he explained, "that all this shows that European civilization has reached its highest stage of superficiality. The next step can only be decadence!"

By then it must have been February. Finland had been swallowed up by Russia to the great indignation of France and England. And yet France and England were still waiting for Hitler to make the first move, and the wait began to make itself felt among the refugees and their French hosts. The land that had seemed an ideal haven from totalitarian persecution, that had embodied for so many of us the essence of human dignity, gave signs of uneasiness, hostility, even resentment. Work permits, residence permits, all was still possible for those among the refugees who were strong, had means, and knew how to find their way around and how to get hold of the right person. The others, exposed to the expiration of this or that permit, to lack of funds, to the impossibility of working or the risk of deportation, were falling prey to panic. The threatening specter of anti-Semitism was raising its head. Carved on a seat in a lecture room, scrawled on the walls of a toilet, we could read the words DEATH TO THE JEWS!

"Nonsense," said Pierre when I told him about it. "You can't take such expressions seriously. They have absolutely no relation to the real France. They're the products of sick minds. Forget about them!"

He spoke with the energy and authority appropriate to a French diplomat, albeit a young one assigned to a minor embassy. He didn't know that as an Italian (and an ordinary Italian, for that matter) I had been taught to look down at his profession as the traditional refuge for untalented children of the aristocracy. Although I was anxious to be reassured, I was also inclined to discount his opinion as simply wishful thinking.

Pierre was not himself Jewish, although his wife Jeannette was. I don't remember anymore how Alex and I made his acquaintance; I think Pierre had helped Alex to solve some problem. In any case, both of them were already part of Alex's world when I joined him in Paris, and we four began to meet from time to time for an aperitif, a meal, a visit to the theater. Alex, I recall, thought that Jeannette was "an interesting ugly woman" whose vivacious personality gave the couple flavor. "You'll see," he said before I met them, "without her Pierre would be an absolutely banal individual." For my part, I found Jeannette pretty, gay, animated, but not original, while I was completely fascinated by Pierre. Maybe he was a banal individual, but how was I to find that out? Tall and slim, with eyes and hair black as a raven's wing, he was at the same time reserved and intimate, ironic and warm, snobbish and sympathetic. I enjoyed our meetings as a foursome, and it was with a certain surprise that I noticed that they were gradually becoming a burden in Alex's eyes. More and more often it seemed that there were things that he had already done, people he had already seen.

"You used to like them," I reminded him reasonably. "Not very much!" he replied, referring to Pierre's frequent telephone calls. Soon it was left to me to answer them as seemed to me most suitable . . . postponing, that is, or accepting invitations on my own. "Why don't you go?" Alex suggested, if he foresaw being out of the city or busy with a client. "It will be a change from all your chores at home and . . . I will avoid the boredom this time."

All of this doesn't quite explain, I fear, how it happened that I always saw Pierre without Jeannette. Not that it happened often; not more than three, perhaps four times altogether.

The first time must have been before the war; I mean before the "phony war." It was summer or perhaps early fall, and I had been sick with the flu. I recall that Pierre dropped in one afternoon without Jeannette, looking for Alex who was out. He asked me then to go for a ride in his car with him, saying that breathing a little fresh air would make me feel better. The grandmothers and children accompanied me to the door, the first hoping that I enjoy myself, the others complaining: "Why can't we go with you?" We had tea in some part of the Bois de Boulogne. I can still see the spacious, open terrace of the restaurant, our table in a corner between the wall and the balustrade, and the flowering shrubs beyond. Pierre showed me how to drink from the wrong side of the teacup; he insisted that the right side was always stained by traces of lipstick, whether or not it had been washed. I had some fun teasing him about his squeamishness and felt young, elegant, free . . . while family and household faded into the distance.

The second time was in the morning. I met him at the bar of the Hotel Crillon, and we drank a Dubonnet together. I liked the Crillon even more than the Bois since the mysterious obscurity of the bar went to my head as much as the wine. We spoke and held hands. Pressing his leg against mine, Pierre told me that I was beautiful and he loved me. As I was obliged to do, I answered that he must not, because nothing could come of it . . . but how pleasant it was to hear his tender pleading, so incredibly remote from the reality of those times. He brought me home in his car, but I asked him to let me out well before the building where I lived. I wanted to walk a little, think about "it," digest it. As I left, he kissed me.

Some days later (or perhaps weeks, because I remember that Pierre was already in uniform; he was on leave, in fact) we took a short drive to the outskirts. In the lingering afternoon sun, the French countryside was more beautiful than ever. He hardly spoke, holding back from saying good-bye, but we were both sadly conscious of one another and of his precarious situation. Looking at the young leaves and the houses wrapped in silence behind their closed shutters, I thought that some day I would be able to forget the brilliant Paris of peacetime, its shops, cafés, night clubs . . . but never this Paris of wartime and the dramatic beauty of its fateful days.

Soon afterward Pierre returned to his unit and I did not see him again until Perpignan; but this was much later, when France's war was over. Later still, in the United States, I tried to tell Alex what my feelings were toward Pierre. "My dear," he said drily, "you don't understand. Every man wants to be the lover of an honest woman." I felt disconcerted and disappointed because his remark deprived me involuntarily both of my romance and my confession. However, I deserved the disappointment . . . for having abandoned myself to the selfish need to tell all. Only later in my life did I come to understand how little that need has to do with honesty or the quest for truth.

15 Passover in Exile

The history books place the end of the "phony war" at the beginning of April 1940, when the Germans landed in Norway, and in a
diary I had begun to keep a couple of months earlier, the German
aggression is touched upon with renewed indignation. However,
our personal lives still seemed unaffected by it. We were preparing
to celebrate Passover and, lo and behold! for the first time in my
life I had the job of making the necessary purchases.

It was Mamulia, Alex's mother, who had always overseen the
domestic preparations associated with every Jewish holiday. She
devoted herself to this task with the skill of a professional and a
professional's reluctance to share the secrets of her craft with out-
siders. Alex saw his mother as a gentle person, and the Russian
words of endearment he used for her reflected this image (*maia mi-
laia,* he called her, *maia krotkaia*). Needless to say, she collided
with me quite forcefully; still, just for that reason, I was aware of
her plight. In Russia she had been the pivot of her family's life, at
the center of all vital decisions, and had taken great pride in her
role. Emigration to Italy, depriving her of the habits of a lifetime
and of her mother tongue, had drastically limited her capacity for
expression and in some way had stripped her of her identity. The
Jewish holidays periodically restored her status and her spirits. In
short, she was given the chance to be in command again, and her
enjoyment was notably increased by the low esteem in which she

held the religious consciousness of her daughter-in-law, the Italian Jewess.

During Passover, there could be very few spectators in the kitchen, which she used like a stage for what was probably her favorite performance of the year. It was Italian Jewry as a whole, I feel sure, that she had in mind in the course of her labors. "This is how things should be done," she meant to say to them, "no half measures here, no deviations from the 'true' traditions, no dilettantish, heretical shortcuts." Left over bread was meticulously gathered and burned; pasta was given away to any Christian within reach; pots of boiling water were poured with a loud hissing over the kitchen utensils; and, in the midst of all this, groans of horror drew attention to the heedless behavior of the uninitiated who happened to stumble upon one taboo or another.

Doing the shopping was another vital part of the ritual, and in Florence Mamulia always dedicated herself to it personally, with faithful old Angiolina in attendance. Angiolina, thin and white-haired, had always been part of the family since its arrival in Florence; she was profoundly devoted to the mistress of the house, and despite being a fervent Catholic, was the equal of Mamulia in her knowledge of Jewish culinary rituals. Avoiding the spotlight, she helped the leading actress in a calm and efficient way. She broke eggs, mixed the dough, poured the oil, spices, and sugar with the timing and skill of a nurse helping a surgeon. At the market she played the part of interpreter, translating Mamulia's approximate Italian into a more fluent language, her strict bargaining demands into reasonable requests.

But Angiolina was one of the many loves we had left behind, and the task of shopping without her help and of doing it in Pau must have seemed insurmountable to Mamulia if in that spring of 1940 she risked the fearful consequences of entrusting me with the job. But I was then in Paris, and how could even the most ignorant person go wrong in the Rue des Rosiers in Paris? I had to go there (by now it was decided), but I had to get exactly what I had been told to, and bring it all down to Pau for our family's Seder. Thus I, who had only a vague idea of the Italian Jewish rituals and absolutely none of the Italian kosher marketplace, found myself making my way one unforgettable morning down the Rue des Rosiers, as profoundly concerned, I fear, about making the right purchases as if the world we knew was going to last forever. My diary is exuberant with respect to this experience. "Powder filled bakeries," says the note for April 21, "noisy matzo factories, butcher shops overflowing with meat, and, everywhere, chickens, chickens, chickens, plucked and sold, plucked and sold, without a moment for breath. The street is swarming with people of all different ages, dress, bearing, all equally intent upon the myriads of counters, discussing prices, quality, recipes. The usual rules seem to have been put aside for this day: the rich deferring to the judgment of the poor who may be more knowledgeable. The merchant broadcasts advice, the *schnorrer* [beggar] puts on a certain dignity. Today charity is owed him; his knowledge of language and ritual make him, too, a priest."

The diary doesn't speak of the trip Alex and I made to Pau, our suitcases filled with purchases, nor does it mention the family Seder held there. Instead, the next note, dated April 28, records the sudden closing of the apartment in Pau and the return of mothers and children to Paris. It was at the end of April, then, that the war so long expected must have become a reality to us.

It's no longer completely clear to me why this event made us reverse the steps we had taken precisely in expectation of the war's coming. However, we were not the only ones to react unpredictably to the situation, and the various lines of action that the Paris refugees were considering at that time all seemed strangely unrelated to the plans they had made during the long months of waiting. Just as the idea of keeping our family far away from a possible "front" suddenly became irrelevant to us, and the need to be together in Paris imperative, so did many of our friends—who had fled from their countries under the pressure of totalitarian persecution—suddenly (and to our eyes absurdly) begin to think of the possibility of going back into the arms of the enemy they had left behind.

Mario, for example, a resourceful Italian businessman, had managed to bring his family with him to Paris a year before, as well as money and some professional activity. He had always boasted that he would go back to Italy only in a particular situation: at the head of French colonial troops, Senegalese! Under the continual, irritating nagging of his wife and daughter even he began to waver. Edoardo, an illustrious jurist who had lost his post at the University of Turin as a consequence of the racial laws, had come to Paris the winter before with his young wife to see the lay of the land. Frightened that the barrier of war would rise inexorably between him and his aged parents, he suddenly decided to go home. At home—it seemed all of them thought—we'll be Jews and that's that. In France we'll be Jews and foreigners, a position critical enough in the eventuality of a French victory, tragic in case of defeat.

My little Hungarian dressmaker came up with still another reason for wanting to go back to her country. She was gentle and brave, and I liked her very much. I was, naturally, very well aware of the fact that if she remained in France she would have to confront innumerable difficulties, but I simply couldn't bear the idea of seeing her sucked back into the implacable world of despotism. "Don't go!" I beseeched her. "What do you think? That you'll be safe from the Germans there?" "It's not that," she answered with a soft smile. "It's that there, no one will try to stop them!"

Even Mother, poor Mother, one evening hesitantly proposed at the table that it might be wise for her . . . after all, she was still an Italian citizen . . . she was wondering . . . perhaps she ought to go back . . . our children could go with her. "Put my children under the protection of Benito Mussolini?" I shouted angrily, and immediately repented my vehemence because my mother flushed and said it was only an idea.

Among all these anguished discussions one of my friends stands out in my memory for the calm and serene way he approached the problems of others, for his faith in the course of action he had chosen, for his confidence in the final outcome of the conflict. His name was Enzo Sereni; he was not a refugee but a kibbutznik coming from Palestine. Although short and thickset, Enzo was endowed with an exuberant and magnetic personality, which made him unexpectedly attractive. Like me, he was born in Rome and attended the Liceo Visconti, but he had graduated before me so that we had never really become acquainted. I had, however, heard a good deal of talk about him, since we came from the same Jewish upper middle class that set a great value on mental gifts, and his were exceptional. What Alex and I discovered immediately when we fell in with him that April in Paris was that these gifts were equaled by an infectious and joyful warmth of heart. Alone in our circle, Enzo was not looking for the best way to escape the enemy but the best way to fight him. During the preceding weeks he had been engaged in a delicate mission, that of bringing as many Jews and as much Jewish money as possible out of Holland before the ax fell. Now that it had fallen, he was marking a bit of time in Paris before his next assignment. If Enzo remained outside of the animated discussions of our group, demonstrating a compassionate understanding for all points of view, he was very clear about what Alex and I should do next: settle in Palestine! I still have one of his poems scribbled on a notepad that bore the letterhead of the "Office Palestinien de l'Agence Juive pour la Palestine, 17 Rue de la Bienfaisance, Paris 8e." Gladdened by our meeting "beyond the mountains of our lost Italy," he encouraged us to rid ourselves of all doubts and return "to the only land that can become a home for the Jews."

> . . . the road of honor there
> leads to Israel. Even if the struggle is
> bloody, there live those who die!

The struggle was to be very bloody for Enzo. A few years later he was one of a small group of Palestinian Jews authorized by the

English to parachute into Axis-occupied territory. Dropped over Northern Italy, he was captured, sent to Dachau, and later executed.

Executed but alive, as his poem says? His land a nation, his name a legend, his memory a sharp pain that brings tears to the eyes of his friends. Dear Enzo, why does all this not seem enough?

16 The Last Car in Paris

Enzo wasn't the only one to think that moving to Palestine should be our next step. Luciana and her husband, who had settled there two years before, thought so too. And so did we. But thinking back, I'm not sure of that anymore.

Since we had obtained the certificates required at that time for permanent immigration; since at a certain moment we had reserved places on a ship for Haifa; since various circumstances beyond our control cropped up to frustrate our plans . . . I've always thought of that particular period in the life of our family as one in which we were helpless and could only resign ourselves to the course of events. But only recently have I come to believe that completely passive moments are extremely rare in life, no matter how extreme the circumstances. I don't know, however, why this discovery, far from burdening me with a painful sense of responsibility, instead sets me free. I only know that after more than thirty years I seem to feel inexplicably relieved at the thought that it was we, not Fate, who made the absurd choice—the war openly under way and the Germans on the point of attacking—to stay in France that spring.

What a spring it was! The weather, ignoring what was going on, was stubbornly perfect, and if there were fewer people walking in the streets, fewer children playing in the parks, it seemed only to increase the blissful unreality of it all. A few steps from our entranceway, Avenue Victor Hugo, almost at its end, opened into the vast, green Avenue Henri Martin, where immense, dark trees benevolently filtered the light of the sun. Entering Avenue Martin with my children, and during the short walk that led to the Bois de Boulogne, I allowed the two older ones to run with their hoops, which they then held in one hand when we crossed the street to enter the Bois, while their other hands rested obediently next to mine on both sides of the little one's carriage. Seated on a green park bench, I did not look impatiently at my watch as I had at the Étoile in winter. Rather I wanted time to stop for a moment and to leave us, just a little longer, right where we were.

There is another Parisian park in my memory of that spring, although we went there only once and I don't even remember its name (I think it might have been the Parc Monceau). It was Sunday morning or early afternoon, and the whole family was going to lunch at some cousins' house. We came upon the park unexpectedly just as we were about to reach the apartment, giving in to the children's desire to go there "only for a minute." It was like walking into an impressionist painting. Children absorbed in their games, toy boats launched hesitantly into the pond, baby carriages, balloon sellers, kites rising into the sky . . . we had to promise our children that we would return later and they would be able to run around to their hearts' content.

Marguerite, Marcelle, and Henri were not really our cousins. Our mothers were cousins, or should I say had been? The relationship had stopped being a living one years before, because Ida had married young, had moved to Paris, raised a family, been widowed and died. Her children were now adults; they had not married and lived together in their parents' old apartment where dark paintings crowded the walls, and framed photographs tried to call attention to themselves on top of the upright piano, on doilies with fringes, and on chests of drawers in the bedrooms. Against this background Marguerite and Marcelle, both women successfully engaged in work, both attractive, full of warmth, and intelligent, shone with great vividness. The only element they had in common with the place where they lived was a veil of melancholy that frightened me, thus protecting them from my curiosity, as well, perhaps, as my love. Long before arriving in Paris, I had heard romantic stories, full of mystery, about their emotional lives, in which prematurely dead fiancés, married lovers, and sick wives who resisted abandonment made sparks in the imagination but at the same time baffled it. Rather than put such stories to rest with its old fashioned appearance, the apartment gave them form, evoking other interiors (Flaubert? Balzac? Stendhal?) where sin could be pardoned but only at the cost of tragedy.

An unhappy love story was also attributed to Henri. Rumors in the family said that he had been madly in love with a married woman who did not want to leave her husband (we asked ourselves why) or to allow Henri his freedom (we wondered about this still more, not without a certain disapproval for the object of such a great devotion). This was the reason, I thought, why Henri rarely spoke and seemed distant and preoccupied. However, he spoke on that May Sunday of the war, but then it was because he had been called up and was about to leave and I, like an idiot, asked him how a man feels when he goes off to fight. "Terrible," he answered, "to be frank, just terrible." That he didn't want to leave was plain; he tried to make his words sound like a witticism, but the effort was unsuccessful because of his smile that did not show humor but betrayed him by its sadness. He had no will to fight, he said, and this time there wasn't even a beginning of a smile, but his face was stiffened in a sort of disdainful grimace.

I was shocked and then annoyed at myself for being shocked. What did I expect, that he would want to go? To go and leave everything, his work, his family, the woman he loved? Weren't his feelings natural? Yes, natural, I said to Alex later, but also tragic. And Alex repeated to me what he had told me for weeks during that period without any special reaction on my part, that one of the frightening aspects of this strange war was the absence of war aims on the part of the French. For the first time I understood perfectly what he meant, and I felt demoralized. Together we reflected on our political convictions and the circumstances that had made them develop. Sadly we came to the conclusion that we had no reason to be proud of our development; if refugees (not all, to be sure) were so conscious of the purposes of the war, wasn't it, after all, because they had been its first victims?

Henri had not experienced it yet. Why should he want to leave his home and risk his life for our sake? And how, how could he understand what for us was clear and unmistakable, that it was also for his own sake? That Sunday lunch with family is one of my last memories of domestic life in Paris. By the second half of May, although the official channels had not been able to transmit to the French people the disaster that had befallen their troops on the Meuse, the general situation seemed serious enough to make us think of leaving Paris. We also began to look for a used car that would enable us to leave on a moment's notice, without having to depend on public means of transport. I remember a heated discussion breaking out one afternoon in a rather deserted garage between Alex and the jovial, big-bellied proprietor. The object of the controversy was a 1935 Buick, somewhat dented but still attractive in appearance, whose jump seats appeared to be a perfect solution to the distinctive size of our family. The seller was boasting that his was "the last car in Paris." "And I," replied Alex triumphantly, "am the last customer in Paris!" We got the car.

From that moment on, matters rushed forward. The first fleeing civilians began to stream into Paris. Centers for the collection of clothing began to spring up all over the city; service counters were set up in all the railway stations. The official bulletins, now transmitted at regular intervals over the radio, were censored; unofficial rumors, however, spread by mouth, circulated unchecked. Poisoned candies, it was said, had been parachuted by the Germans to lure innocent children; mined bridges that were supposed to stop the enemy advance didn't blow up; fleeing civilians had been machine-gunned on the roads.

Then on May 28 a particular rumor made its way from the lips of the milkman and the baker; was repeated with incredulity by the people in the street; and finally took form in the pages of the newspaper . . . the king of Belgium had surrendered to the Germans!

Announcing this on the radio, Prime Minister Reynaud called it an unprecedented act in history. In fact, the king's decision had been taken without saying a word to the commanders of the Anglo-French forces. The effects of the Prime Minister's comments were overwhelming. Consciousness of treachery transformed people's anxiety into panic. "We are betrayed!" Cursing Leopold, the traitorous king, the disoriented French carried propitiatory flowers to the monument of his father, the martyr of the First World War. As if he were a saint to be venerated . . . and begged for favors.

Two days later the car that Alex by force of persuasion had coaxed away from the reluctant seller carried us far from Paris. Alex was in the driver's seat, although his experience there was very limited. I sat next to him. Inside, in continually changing combinations that depended greatly on the two jump seats, were our mothers, the children, and Anne, who had decided to say good-bye temporarily to her "room on the seventh floor."

In my diary the note for May 30 says: "*Arrivederci,* Paris. I know that our troops will stand fast somewhere, that we're leaving only as a precaution, that our apartment remains open, that Alex and I will be able to return next week. *Arrivederci,* Paris. My eyes are wide open to take in all of you. Wide open but full of tears. We leave by way of the Boulevard Raspail. *Arrivederci,* Paris."

17 France Has Nothing to Say

I don't remember anymore what caused us to choose Tours as our destination other than the fact that clients of Alex owned a tannery in Amboise a few miles from there. Could it be that in deciding upon Tours we had in mind not only our safety but also some form of professional activity? As I look back now, both of these expectations seem incredibly naive . . . for these proved to be the days of the retreat from Dunkerque. On June 4, when the last contingent of Allied troops debarked in England, Dunkerque itself fell into enemy hands. These events made Paris the next German objective, and Alex left by car to get rid of our apartment and resolve some matters that had been left hanging.

I would like to go back to Tours some day and see what it really looks like. In those days it was an incredible city where heat, noise, and confusion disoriented the hundreds of refugees who crowded its streets, houses, and hotels. We had four rooms in a hotel opposite the railway station, and from my window I could see the gates of the station from which people incessantly poured out. I asked myself how it was possible for the city to absorb them all.

We did our best to try to arrange a sort of "normal" life that would have some sense for the children. We located a park not far from our hotel, and Anne took them there regularly twice a day, while Mamulia, Mother, and I joined them from time to time. Lunch was followed by an afternoon nap; dinner, by baths and

reading or telling stories. We had a variety of books that would accompany us in all our peregrinations, and we came to put a very
great trust in their affable protagonists (Babar the elephant, Pa-
nache the squirrel) for aid in our effort to weave a stable pattern in
the midst of chaos. Occasionally a question from the children in-
dicated that the pattern was really very fragile. I remember that Simona, who was then four years old, came out one evening with a
very simple but excruciating request for information: "Mamma,"
she asked me, "what does the word 'enemy' mean?"

At least Simona and little Rossella slept deeply at night, imper-
vious to the shouts that came from the canteen below the hotel, the
rumble of automobiles, and the whistles of zealous traffic police.
Not so Daniela, who was seven years old. One night the sound of
the sirens made her jump up, and she bombarded me with every
sort of declaration, both anxious and peremptory. "They're at the
border," she announced excitedly. "Yes, I tell you, you don't know,
that's what the sirens mean. They go off when the enemy airplanes
cross the border. They must be coming here now!" I managed to
convince her, I don't know how, that the sirens only had one purpose, to get people to stay home and not go out in the streets. After
a time she too fell asleep.

Our mothers were, at certain times, more difficult to deal with
than the children. Mamulia would have wanted all of us in the
lobby of the hotel every time the sirens went off, and besides that
she was very upset because we had not heard news of Alex since
his departure. Her inability to speak French increased her fear. My
mother looked down at such anxiety and used her knowledge of
the language to gather every sort of information from the lips of
the maid, the hotel manager, and shopkeepers. Periodically, and
mysteriously, she let drop into my fascinated ear: "Paris has been
bombed," or "Right here in Tours there were five deaths, victims of
last night's raid; that's why there was so much noise of antiaircraft
firing."

Listening to the radio and reading the newspaper, I tried to extract news from the gossip. Notwithstanding the careful language used by both these means of communication, it was hard to be optimistic. If Mother's sources were wrong and Paris had not been bombed, there was still no positive news coming from the front. Not unless one wanted to be cheered by the fact that the enemy had reached the Aisne River "but had not crossed it," or that bridgeheads had been established, but only with "warped" success, whatever that might mean, or because the enemy troops had not been able to cross . . . the Somme, alas, too near Paris to be comforting.

When Alex suddenly returned, we were overjoyed although he had only been gone for three days. Then the news we had awaited in fear for weeks burst upon us: Italy had entered the war! Again Alex picked himself up and went off to Paris. Although his Italian citizenship had been revoked and his passport was no longer valid, my mother, the children, and I were Italians; most of his clients were in the same situation. We needed some guidance with respect to our present situations, or the future. This time he left the automobile with me, although I didn't drive. If he did not come back the next day, I was to hire a driver and leave. Where to? Aurillac, in the Cantal. I have no idea why the Cantal claimed our attention. Perhaps there were friends of friends who lived there? Or had we simply heard that the south-east zone of France was peaceful and off the beaten path, so that it was not likely people would flee there? Be that as it may, once Alex had left I began to pack to be ready for the next move. "Here we are," I said to myself, "seven women alone." That sounded bad. On the radio the restrained voice of Prime Minister Reynaud announced Italy's action: "This is the moment that Italy has chosen to declare war. France has nothing to say. . . ." The next day, the packing finished, I loaded the automobile with our belongings and began to wait for Alex. In the middle of the afternoon, without any sign yet of Alex, we were told that the government was moving from Paris to Tours and that our hotel had been requisitioned. Now we were without a driver or a roof. Armed with the address of a friend of a friend that Alex had left with me, I began the search for both these things.

"A driver?" M. Pernod laughed in my face. "There's not the slightest chance." And yet, despite his brusque manner, he promised that he would try to find us lodgings and, after several unsuccessful telephone calls, he succeeded: three rooms in a private house! I was so happy I would have taken them without seeing them, but M. Pernod said I must go there immediately and settle the matter. Half an hour later I was seated at the kitchen table of a two-story house, simple but comfortable, sipping coffee. Everything had been arranged and agreed upon, and I knew that I should go back to the hotel and liberate my family from its frightening lobby, but the tension of the day had been replaced by a feeling of euphoric relaxation, and I drank happily under the kindly eyes of my new landlady and her family.

"You speak French wonderfully," she said full of sympathy, "but you're not French, are you? Isn't there perhaps a trace of an accent?"

Suddenly I was recalled to reality. Pushing away the cup of coffee, I leaned my head on my arm and began to sob quietly, uncontrollably.

A hand gently patted my back. "Poor thing," the muffled voice reached me, "she's Italian."

18 A Narrow Escape

I will never forget the night that followed. When I had collected the mothers, the children, and Anne at the hotel, given everyone a meal, and arranged things in the new house, I was so exhausted that I couldn't go to sleep. The antiaircraft batteries thundered without a stop, and I couldn't believe the children weren't awake and terrified. I left Mamulia, with whom I shared a bedroom, took a flashlight, and went to their doorway to see how they were. I was greeted with screams and curses. The same woman who had been so polite and understanding earlier in the evening now confronted me in a livid rage, accusing me of using the flashlight to signal the enemy. Was she perhaps too frightened by the air raid to reason clearly? Or did the knowledge that I was Italian acquire a sinister connotation in these circumstances? I turned off the flashlight, hushed the children, and spoke to Mme Renoir in a low and humble tone of voice. "How could I possibly signal the enemy," I pointed out, "when my little girls are right here under this roof?" Shaking, I went back to bed.

The next morning Mme Renoir avoided my eyes, and I went on with my business. I still didn't have a driver, and my agreement with Alex was very clear: if he did not return, we were supposed to leave Tours. There was another name in my address book, that of M. Loos. I telephoned him and he reassured me; he hoped to be able to find me a driver. Three hours later I called again. "He's not at home," a woman's voice said. "Besides," the voice became sharp, "I want to be completely honest; he's too busy helping our French friends to find time for you, my dear lady!" At this point M. Loos himself must have snatched the telephone from his wife's hand. He said he had found no one yet, but hoped that in the afternoon . . .

In the afternoon Mme Renoir, still avoiding my eyes, said she was afraid she couldn't put us up for another night. Then, faced with my obvious dismay, she went to the telephone and surprisingly found us a room in a small hotel somewhere. Perhaps she didn't consider us dangerous anymore, in which case why was she making us leave? I didn't ask her. I went out instead, under a driving rain, dragging along a suitcase for credibility, and my single room at the Hotel Rampart was transformed into two. In an improved state of mind, I went to get my family, and behold! Alex had returned and our trial was over.

With Alex once more at the wheel, we left Tours the next day, and the first miles on the road quickly made us understand the fate that awaited us there: single file at a snail's pace and fruitless lines at gasoline stations. Alex asked me to look at the map for a secondary road; then, not trusting my skill in such matters, made the search himself. He immediately found a road that he said would take us straight to where we wanted to go, in Cantal. Neither our mothers nor I had any faith in his plan. If everyone was going in the same direction, toward Bordeaux, there must be a good reason for it, we thought. When it turned out that the road was delightfully shady and completely without traffic, our apprehension became stronger. When a police officer stopped us and recommended that we turn back because traffic was blocked ahead of us in the city of Loches, we were sure we had made a mistake. Obstinately, Alex went on and the miracle continued; there was no blockage of traffic in Loches. But in Buzancais, which we reached at evening under a pelting rain, our search for a place to sleep ran into the greatest difficulties.

"The best would be a barn, you poor souls," said a sympathetic policeman. A barn? How could one find a barn? A shoemaker who was closing his shop for the night suggested the town hall where straw had been distributed to the refugees. Or we could try M. le Curé, the village priest. M. le Curé came to the rescue! After having entered his house with a certain hesitation, Alex came out and announced proudly that he had two rooms for the mothers and the children. There were no sheets, but what did that matter? And everything was open and aboveboard. The priest had been informed that we were Italians and Jews. I remember that Alex and I slept on the floor somewhere. I don't know if it was a house or an inn. Unable to get the news from the priest's radio, we tried to find out what we could from the rumors in circulation: Paris had been declared an open city to prevent its destruction; the swastika waved over the city hall. It was enough to fill our sleep with nightmares.

The next morning we resumed our wandering. The automobile behaved very well, and I thought with gratitude of our friend, the seller, who had been honest after all. Nevertheless, my heart was in my throat for I knew the poor car was overloaded: we eight, plus our suitcases everywhere, inside and out. Châteauroux, Guéret, Aubusson. Encouraged by the first miracle, we did our best to follow only secondary roads. But it was enough just to come into the neighborhood of a city to find cars, cars, cars, big and small, brand new and old dented ones, crowded with people and things, mattresses, bicycles, tables, and baby carriages tied to the roof, on the hood, everywhere. Needless to say, all the cars were headed south, and if one of them had a flat tire, so much the worse for its unlucky driver. Those behind him, after sounding their horns and yelling, only helped him push his vehicle off the road and into a ditch.

We could do nothing to insure ourselves against flat tires, but we could try to stay as much as possible away from the confusion, and I don't know how, after Feuilletin, the terrible incident happened.

For some time we had made our way along a narrow road, one behind another, and the car in front of us was behaving erratically, going very slowly and then more rapidly, and zig-zagging continually. It was full of men, and Mamulia said they must be drunk,

which made her nervous. Suddenly Alex decided to pass them;
there was enough room on the road and no one was coming from
the opposite direction. Just then the other car inexplicably slid into
the ditch at the side of the road and stopped there. We hesitated
barely an instant, then agreed that we had to stop and see if we
could be of help. Alex got out first, but after a few steps he was
confronted by the passengers of the other car, four of them, who
flung themselves on him cursing and shouting. I can still see
Mother, Mamulia, and me all in the road, pleading with the at-
tackers and succeeding only in making Alex's flight impossible. I
can still hear him cry, "Go back!" and then "Do you want to see
me killed?" Finally his words reached me and gave me the strength
to convince Mother and Mamulia to get back in the car and to do
so myself. All the time I was aware that Alex was trying to defend
himself and escape the blows, but I knew that his glasses had been
broken and he could see nothing without them. Finally he managed to get away (perhaps the anger of those men had waned, or
there were people coming) and he got into the car. One of the at-
tackers, however, was still after him until, hanging onto the wheel,
he was able to push him away with a kick and start the car. I don't
know how he managed to drive, his face covered with blood and
his glasses gone. We were all talking at the same time, now giving
vent to our indignation, now trying to control it in order to reassure the children. Only a few miles farther on we reached the small
city of Courtine. Again, for the children's sake, we made a great
fuss over the big rooms we found at the Hotel des Voyageurs and
the splendid home-cooked meal we were served later. When Alex
slipped away to show his bruises to a doctor and report to the local police, his going was unnoticed. How much had the children
understood, and how much would they remember? And I? Would
I go on seeing forever the blinded man next to me, fumbling with
the wheel, his foot out kicking?

19 A Temporary Paradise

The next day began under the pall cast by that dreadful incident with another visit to the doctor and the police station before taking to the road again. But that very evening found us in Paradise.

"We reached the Cantal this afternoon," says the note in my diary for June 6, "but there are no rooms or beds in Mauriac, our first stop. At the second, Riom, a ray of hope: some rooms at the hotel; more, a casual mention by a shopkeeper of a small house in the country nearby that might be rented. It can't, but we somehow reach an agreement with the owners of one in the immediate vicinity, and in the evening we go to sleep in marvelous beds, between real, old-fashioned linen sheets. I want to praise God, but maybe I'm only dreaming."

That was all for that day, and even if the following notes are packed with all sorts of details about everything from politics to personal states of mind, none makes a complete description of the Meydieu family members. Why? The diary has many gaps of that kind, and when I first picked it up and began to read it, I was often disappointed but never so acutely as this time, because I anticipated the moment of meeting the Meydieus again with all the impatience one feels when turning on the television set and seeing a foggy image. Just another moment and everything will be in focus! But I was left with my defective transmission, and I hesitate to try to force my memory of those times. I can only close my eyes and wait patiently for someone from the past to come back.

The place was only a village really, despite its long and complicated name: Haut Bagnac par Anglards de Salers: three, perhaps four families besides the Meydieus. The gray stone houses, clustered together looked as if they had been set down alongside a strange assortment of barns, pigpens, and chicken coops that remained scattered at random in the grass at their feet. At the top of the cluster, as was appropriate to the social status of its proprietress, stood the house of Mme Peyrac, the widowed sister of M. Meydieu, an energetic and strong-willed woman who on the whole commanded respect; at the bottom was that of her "farmer," Antoine Nougeant. In between was the simple, neat, and comfortable house of the Meydieus, which we shared for a whole month.

I'm a little bothered by the fact that of all the inhabitants of Haut Bagnac I remember Mme Peyrac best, thus conferring the only prize in my possession (a permanent niche in my memory) to this not wholly pleasant personality. If it had depended on her, I'm sure, she would not have consented to our joining the community of Haut Bagnac. Fortunately, however, she did not cast a veto, and we were left to the good will of the Meydieus and their not unreasonable interest—in those uncertain times—in the pecuniary advantages that would come to them from the presence of tenants.

There were many Meydieus living under the same roof, although some of the children who swarmed about the place were added after our arrival, refugees like us. Together with the Nougeant children, they formed a small community apart, to the great delight of our brood.

I can't remember ever having seen M. Meydieu working, or his wife Angeline at rest. He was much older than she, I think, retired from I don't know what sort of work, and now he took things easy. In any case, Angeline took care of the house, the chickens, the pigs and everything else; Antoine Nougeant, the peasant, concerned himself with the little Meydieu farm around the corner. As for Ilaire

Meydieu himself, he stayed comfortably hidden in a corner, a pipe in his mouth and a little beret on his head, seated in a chair beside the oven under the immense hood of the fireplace. Or he stayed "at attention" next to the radio, commenting drily on whatever news reached us in those days.

The radio was on a little table or perhaps a shelf next to the kitchen window, and although the Meydieus had moved to the back part of the house when we arrived, leaving us all but one of the principal, comfortable bedrooms, we all shared the big kitchen where we ate in several shifts which often overlapped. I remember that the room was dark in contrast to the bright sunlight outside, and cool, and that the brass pots and pans shone vividly against the walls. Mme Meydieu (why, why can't I see her kindly face anymore?) was proud of them and so she wanted to bury them to hide them from the Germans. I don't recall anything else about the house except vaguely the room where Alex and I slept with Simona right at the top of the stairs, and the one on the lower floor with its enormous double bed where our poor Mamulia passed the greater part of her days trying to give a bit of rest to her tired heart. What I do see very clearly is the yard, paved in front of the principal entrance, where the chickens were raised and killed, and the children played, some of them only at sundown when their chores were finished. And the toilet in back, a dignified wooden cabin even if malodorous, which was then enhanced with a porcelain bowl in honor of the weak knees of us city folk.

If my diary is as poor in descriptions of the place as it is of its inhabitants, my memory in this case has an unexpected help. I have only to consult the most recent Michelin Guide to find that the area is nine hundred meters high, so that I can—retrospectively—provide another reason that might have moved us to choose the Cantal as our destination. I can also understand why its climate suited all of us so well that summer.

My Michelin Guide, furthermore, gives three stars to the nearby town of Salers, calling it "one of the most attractive cities of the

Haute-Auvergne." How did it happen that we never walked its streets to see its "old dwellings of dark stone, with their sober lines" or enjoy the exceptional view from the Esplanade. Almost every morning Alex and I took out the car, too wide, alas, for the narrow and winding paths that connected Haut Bagnac with the main road. When we reached it, we did not, however, drive to the right to cover the eight miles that would have taken us to Salers. Invariably we turned to the left to the village of Anglards, where I got out to do the shopping, while he went on to Mauriac to the city hall or subprefecture for some piece of business.

Although I tried very hard to concentrate on my errands, I could hardly avoid confronting the endless procession of automobiles loaded with refugees that crowded the road alongside the village. Faces distorted by fatigue and anger looked out through the windows of the cars stupefied and without expression, and I was ashamed at having a shelter and feared that the privilege would not last long. In the evening, seated with the Meydieus around the radio, we tried to get some news, or we passed from hand to hand the only newspaper that someone had been able to find somewhere. One after another, the great tragic events of those days reached to take hold of our anxious hearts.

On June 16 a copy of *Paris-Soir* (then published in nearby Clermont Ferrand) informed us that German troops had entered with heavy tread a deserted Paris. "*C'est dans un Paris désert que les troupes allemandes font lourdement leur entrée.*"

Early in the morning of June 17 the radio announced that Reynaud had resigned, Pétain had taken his place, and the council of ministers had taken decisions weighty in their consequences, *lourdes des conséquences*. Later that day it was the Marshal himself who addressed us. He said he had asked the Germans for an armistice, "*entre soldats, après la lutte, dans l'honneur*" (between soldiers, after the battle, with honor).

Churchill spoke on the eighteenth. "We cannot release France from its obligations," he said, rejecting any possibility of a separate peace. He proposed therefore a union of the two nations.

On the nineteenth Hitler asked to meet with plenipotentiaries. He would decide subsequently on the date and place of the meeting.

On the twentieth the plenipotentiaries left aboard a white airplane, and Pétain explained the difference to us between the situation of 1918 and the present: lack of men, means, and allied help. A commentator favorable to the Germans followed his broadcast, dwelling at length on his words, but failed to convince the little group gathered around our radio. "Why don't they leave us alone with their Marshal!" muttered Father Meydieu, and his explicit, impatient words were a momentary balm to our wounds. Good old Ilaire Meydieu! It would take more than that to deceive the French people! The same day, the twentieth, Alex departed.

He headed for St. Jean de Luz on the Atlantic Ocean south of Biarritz, where some tough Frenchmen were still embarking on English ships to carry on the war there. In the light of what we now know about the German occupation of France and the extermination of millions of Jews at the hands of the Germans, it seems inconceivable that Alex could have imagined that our mothers, our children, and I would be safe in Haut Bagnac, and he free to follow his duty or his dream. At that time I fully shared that dream, and his decision to go on ahead and to enlist was mine too. I would do my duty, I thought, and so free him from responsibility. Conscious of the dangers, but unconscious of the tragic extent of their implications, we were—I believe—proud of ourselves. Did we lie to our bewildered mothers pretending that Alex was making a casual, exploratory trip, or did we brainwash them to get them to share our point of view? I don't know with certainty anymore. Both methods seemed equally useful in the hands of the young to protect their most bizarre plans from the restraining influence of the old. A little more than a week after our arrival in the harbor of Haut Bagnac, Alex was again on the high seas.

20 The Fall of France

It was hard being without Alex at Haut Bagnac just as it had been at Tours, even though the circumstances were completely different. I didn't have to struggle over lodging, and feeding my family wasn't an immediate concern. If the shelves of food products in the stores of Anglards were becoming empty and their owners bitter, I could face these threatening omens without worry and take comfort in the fact that we lived on a farm always supplied with milk, cheese, and eggs. It was harder to maintain the same equanimity in facing the news, and it was here that I felt Alex's absence with an intensity that I had not foreseen. I was so used to having him at my side, he who weighed events with a quiet thoughtfulness, dismissed fantasies with a shrug of his shoulders, and chased away my fears with his laughter, that I was ill prepared for my new role. Now I was called upon not only to face these events alone without the comfort of his support, but to provide that support for our mothers, for Anne and the children. I had to listen to the radio without showing distress, then translate and interpret it with convincing optimism. And the radio gave us no truce.

It was Hitler affirming that the meeting at Compiègne was reparation for a shameful injustice perpetrated by France in the past. It was the signing of the armistice with harsh (so the rumors said) but not dishonorable terms. It was missing Churchill's comments because of the unreliability of our little radio, but it was also trying to catch Pétain's reply. "*Mesdames, Messieurs, le Maréchal Pé-tain vous parle!*"

And Marshal Pétain told us that we must not listen to Churchill, who could decide what was best for his country, but certainly not what was best for France. "*M. Churchill est juge des intérêts de son pays; il ne l'est pas de ceux du nôtre. Il l'est encore moins de l'honneur de la France!*" (Mr. Churchill is judge of his own country's interests, not of ours. Still less is he of France's honor!) With every broadcast the two leaders made new appeals for our loyalty, passionately defending once more their contrasting visions of the truth.

Churchill: "His Majesty's government is struck with grief and amazement. . . . If the German conditions were accepted by all the French, they would place France and all its empire under the German yoke. . . . All the resources of the French soil, its fleet, its air power, would become weapons against France's allies. . . England will carry on the fight, and on the day of victory will take account of France's interests despite the attitude of the Bordeaux government."

Pétain: "Our flag is spotless . . . We have fought heroically . . . The French government rejects every insinuation that aims to separate its actions from the opinions of the French people."

In the little group around the radio we shook our heads with perplexity and disbelief. "Who could have foreseen such behavior by England?" the peasant asked sadly. And old Meydieu: "There's our enemy!"

My God, only a few hours earlier he had asked the Marshal to leave us alone. Today the Marshal's words already have a certain weight. Only a few hours earlier I was cheered by the conviction that the French people were not an easy prey for propaganda. For how long could I go on believing that? I thought of Alex. What would he have said? I could take care of the daily chores, go out in the afternoon sun with the children, gather flowers in the field, talk to the animals. But what could I do with all these goings-on?

"Is the war over?" Daniela asked. "Will there still be rationing of sugar?" I explained that the rationing would go on, and we would be without other things too because we had lost the war. "Don't you think America is awfully stupid?" she continued. "They say it's the biggest country in the world and that we would have won if they had helped us. Why should it just sit there like a bump on a log?" And then as an afterthought: "I think I know why we lost the war! Because we won the last time!"

What could I do but agree? I understood her need to cling to a logical argument, no matter how weird, that would leave her faith in justice intact.

It was easier to handle Dani's questions, which tried to get to the bottom of the situation, than the innocent and persistent day-dreaming of Simona. One evening we heard on the radio that the French government had turned over to Germany all German refugees. Later in bed the words of the English announcer returned to obsess me: "France, which in these very days is sending its refugees to every part of the world, has consigned to torture and martyrdom those who had placed their faith in her . . ." From the bed next to mine came Simona's sleepy voice: "Mamma, are there flowers in heaven?"

21 What Next?

After a whole week passed without news of Alex, I thought that he must surely have succeeded in carrying out his plans and by now had left France. Then one night I was awakened by a knock at the door. I didn't even have the time to be frightened. Through the open window came Alex's loud whisper: "Carlotta, come down, it's me!"

He looked terribly tired and terribly disappointed. They didn't want him, he said; they didn't let him enlist. It was a long story, he would tell me about it tomorrow. In fact, he spoke of it the next day, skipping over some parts, lingering over others. The trip to St. Jean de Luz had gone well; he had tried there to board an English ship almost ready to leave the French coast. When his turn came to be examined, there was a short but intense discussion between him and the officer in charge. "Quite a man, actually," Alex brooded. His regret was intensified by his respect for that man. "I know that he liked me and wanted to trust me. He almost changed his mind. He seemed to have gotten over the fact that I was not a French citizen; he had looked at my documents without apparent antagonism . . . It was probably a mistake to show him the expired and cancelled Italian passport. I only thought it might help to prove that I was not exactly popular among the enemies, but somehow it went wrong. All those Italian stamps . . . there must have seemed too many. He must have thought: why look for trouble? He said he was sorry and for a second I thought I might persuade him out of his uncertainty. But all of a sudden my words were doing no good; they were making things worse . . . He dismissed me with a wave of his hand and called the next one in line."

We were all together around the kitchen table: the Meydieus assented understandingly, although they must have been only partially conscious of the implicit consequences; Daniela hung upon her father's words; Mamulia furtively touched her head to suggest that Alex must be out of his mind. At this point I could only share her point of view. How could Alex be wasting time regretting that he hadn't been able to enlist when our future was so full of uncertainty? Later, when we were alone, I told him the news I had learned from the radio about the French government handing over refugees to the Germans. He was dumbfounded. This action not only destroyed the image of France which had been part of our education, but it pointed to a highly probable danger for ourselves. Today refugees from Germany were being given to Hitler. Tomorrow the Italian refugees could be sent back to Mussolini.

Even if it still took several days to plan our next move, I think it was then and there that we decided to try to leave France.

In the next few days our lives seemed to unfold on many levels. News of the outside world remained our principal concern, but it had become extremely hard to keep up with events. On June 27, a day after Alex's return, French radio suddenly stopped broadcasting. The terrible sense of bewilderment that all of us felt pushed the Meydieus and us in opposite directions. We began to depend exclusively on Radio London; they, on Radio Stuttgart. Old Meydieu came home one evening with the news that Radio Stuttgard was regularly transmitting programs in French, and he announced with a pleased air, "It seems they speak it very well!"

After worry over the news came worry about food. It was up to us to go either to Anglards or Mauriac, which had become accessible once more with the return of our car. Great numbers of troops, half-empty stores, and angry shopkeepers. I couldn't help but compare the bitter women who defended their empty shelves with their warm and obliging Italian counterparts. But actually I had never seen my grocer under pressure. The greengrocer in Mauriac, her face contorted by hatred, shouted at the top of her lungs: "They leave us without gas. Everything for the troops! All right, get yourselves fed by the troops. I don't give a damn!" One might easily have paid no attention to this if it hadn't been for the appearance of the soldiers. It broke one's heart to see them dragging their feet through the crowded streets of a hostile city, with hell still in their faces, trying in low voices to quiet the furious shrews.

Back in Haut Bagnac we almost forgot about them and resumed life at still another level, of the children and the fields, equally demanding in their needs, equally generous of their gifts.

The schedule of activities that framed the day of our children had the same regularity and the same urgency as the routine of the farm. Meals, games, lessons, walks, could not be ignored any more than feeding the chickens, milking the cows, or taking the sheep to graze. Precisely the fact that all this demanded constant devotion gave it a gentle force of discipline. Any threat to their regular flow immediately pushed all other problems into the background. When one morning the little one awoke with a temperature of almost 103°, we became frantic. When one evening black clouds and strong winds seemed to announce a summer storm, the Meydieus were seized by panic. How could one think about something else when the hay in the fields ran the risk of spoiling because of a change in the weather? The Germans? Yes, of course. But the hail?

Alex's return was the cause of great excitement not only for our children but also for their friends. Although I maliciously suggested that his fascination in the eyes of the bigger boys must depend on the fact that he owned the enchanting Buick, I knew that the car was only a small detail. Jean Meydieu, for example, the son of a middle-aged father, probably drew great pleasure from the presence of a young, active, exuberant man. He and his cousin Robert, both twelve or thirteen years old, were always at hand for some little service that Alex might ask for. When (as a reward, I think, for washing the car) he took them to Mauriac for dinner in a restaurant, their devotion became limitless. I had been asked politely to go with them, but conscious of the fact that this was an affair strictly among men, I declined the invitation.

If on this occasion I restrained myself from telling Alex that he was spoiling the boys, I had to show my feelings when, a couple of days later he told me he had shown them his briefcase packed with banknotes. "I told them to look carefully," he said, amused by the recollection, "because they would never again see that much money in their entire lives!"

"That much money" wasn't ours. Both burden and treasure, its presence among our belongings would furnish us one day with a notable benefit as "collateral." At that time, however, it was an immense and heavy responsibility. If taking it out of Paris to prevent its requisition by the Germans had been a wise precaution, carrying it safely and turning it over to its legitimate owners was a task we had yet to carry out and was full of unknown dangers. How could Alex have yielded to the feeling of happy comradeship with the boys so far as to share such a dangerous secret with them?

"Nonsense!" he answered. "Forget that I ever told you!" As always, he brushed aside my concern with a kiss and added smiling, "You want to bet? They will never say anything!" I thought that this time his laugh sounded a little embarrassed, but he was right, the boys never said a word.

On July 1 we celebrated Daniela's seventh birthday with an afternoon snack that brought together all the children on the farm.

Mme Meydieu and Anne had discussed the menu at length, each one trying to put in her own specialty. To make peace, I had one prepare her crêpes, and the other her rice cake. Seated on the kitchen benches, the children enjoyed the food and one another. Dani's pleasure was slightly lessened by the absence of Jean Nougeant, who was milking the cows. We saved his share of the delicacies, and he arrived soon, disheveled and out of breath, to devour them joyfully.

When the group broke up and Jean went back to his chores, Daniela, Simona and I took a long walk on the narrow path that led down to the brook. A red sunset, poppies spread on the ground near the mown wheat, strawberries still green . . . it was easy to forget that all these gifts would not always be ours.

I think that the perfection of that day was of great help in making us see our way clearly through imminent problems. We knew we had to leave France. We knew that in order to do it we needed visas for another country. We had absolutely no idea how to get them. What then? The best place to find them was undoubtedly Marseille, a major city near to Spain and free of German occupation. Should we all go to Marseille? Suddenly the idea of pulling up the children from the paradise of Haut Bagnac and looking for a new way of life for them in a strange, crowded city seemed absurd. We decided that Alex should go ahead once more, study the situation, decide on the next move, and then come back for us. This time, however, he would take his mother with him. She would be able to stay with old Russian friends; she would look for a doctor's advice concerning her diabetes and her heart . . . and she would be spared the excitement of repacking the luggage and making another trip with the whole family. The only serious problem now was to find gasoline for the car.

Gasoline was extremely scarce, and furthermore foreigners were not allowed to buy it. No seller, however, worried about asking for a buyer's papers as long as the price was right. So Alex managed to find someone who knew someone, with the result that at one o'clock one night he was in the right place doing business with the right man. I was entrusted with the job of standing guard at the corner to warn them of anyone suspicious coming. When the operation was finished, I breathed a sigh of relief and felt as if I had carried out a dangerous theft.

Next morning, the morning of July 4, Alex and Mamulia departed. Once more I began to wait.

22 Empty Shelves

This time, waiting was less difficult. After all, I was so happy that Alex was not in England that I could count my blessings. I was also inclined to add to the list the fact that Mamulia was no longer my responsibility and that I only had to discuss things with Anne and Mother. As had been the case in Tours, their sources of information were limited since they never left the farm; even so they gave them more credence than they did me. "In Anglards there's only pork for sale!" Mother announced dramatically. "Pretty soon we'll have no meat!" And if I expressed a less pessimistic view of the matter, Anne shook her head with the air of one who knows better. She had heard on the radio straight from the mouth of This One or That One that "nous sommes à la famine." My answers often were impolite; it's much simpler, alas, to be brusque with one's own mother than with a mother-in-law. Once again I had to put off until nighttime, when I was alone in bed, thinking over the events of the day.

On July 4, the day of Alex's departure, English radio transmitted Churchill's report to the House of Commons on the attack by the British navy on the French ships anchored at Oran. The Prime Minister ended his speech leaving the judgment of this action to the nation, to the United States, to the world . . . and to history. Two days later French radio resumed its transmission. With a new name and a new role, the "*Radiodiffusion de l'État de France*" was the official organ of the French government. On its first day it broadcast a bulletin from Prevost, the Minister of Propaganda, and an order of the day from Admiral Darlan.

"Mr. Churchill has in cowardly fashion ordered the sinking of the very men and ships which, at the time of the battle of Flanders, saved the lives of thousands of Englishmen . . . Our ships had their engines closed down, their guns pointed toward the coast . . . French sailors: sacrificing your lives, you have shown the world France can keep her word . . ."

Should England perhaps have saved those ships and the hundreds of men aboard them out of gratitude to a former ally now in difficulty? Or did it have the right, even the duty, to destroy them in order to prevent the Germans from making use of them at the first opportunity against the free world? And what can one say about the conditions of the armistice with Germany? France had committed itself to keep its fleet inactive. Was the French admiral at Oran right to stick to this commitment and ignore the English ultimatum, or should he have kept in mind that Germany would probably review the agreements on the slightest pretext?

These questions were painful enough to keep me turning in my bed all night, just as historians would ponder them in the years to come. On the other hand, they created no problems for the inhabitants of Haut Bagnac and its neighborhood. The slogan of Radio Stuttgart had smoothed the way: "The English give their machines; the French give their bodies!" From that moment on the French in general knew where they stood. A few hours later the news that in reprisal for the "cowardly English aggression" a squadron of the French Air Force had bombed English units at Gibraltar had everyone nodding in approval.

Other less noteworthy bits of information seemed to escape general attention or failed to hold it, but appeared like painful accompaniments to my nighttime reflections. The first upsetting news, for example, of parliamentary activity in Vichy . . . with Laval suddenly becoming a popular speaker because he proposed the idea of searching out and punishing those responsible for the events that had taken place. Or the unanimous approval by the Senate of a law to abrogate the Constitution and to grant plenary powers to Pétain. Or the regulations that revoked the citizenship previously accorded foreigners, forbade foreigners from entering France, and deprived those already residing there of the "right to move."

Morning somehow swept away these sinister concerns, and my frequent trips to Anglards and Mauriac for exchanges of farm produce were as refreshing to my spirit as they were hard on my bones. It's true that many stores had hung signs outside their doors saying "Closed for lack of merchandise," and those that were open showed mostly empty shelves. But the available storekeepers, surly at first, often succumbed to the pleasure of conversation. A little savoir faire even succeeded in filling my handbag with various articles, though not necessarily the ones I had originally intended to buy.

One morning I went to Anglards with a big plan in mind: a visit to the city hall to secure an official signature for one of the certificates, whose number was always increasing, required by the regulations in force. I foresaw the usual bureaucratic difficulties and was prepared for a long wait in some musty little office. But I was told that the "councilman" authorized to sign my document was a retired butcher who lived not far from there. Luckily I found him at home, dozing in a rocking chair near the kitchen fireplace; he was fat, with white hair, and his eyes immediately came alive when he heard my request. Leaving his chair condescendingly, he invited me to sit down with him at the immense worm-eaten kitchen table and explain my case more clearly. Then, with a great deployment of pens, ink, and blotting paper, he proceeded to affix his signature. If the whole procedure took a bit more time than necessary, it wasn't due to bureaucratic slowness. Besides, the councilman liked a bit of conversation at the right moment, and my condition as a foreigner gave him the pleasant chance to display his authority, benevolence, and knowledge of the world. I think my visit rounded out his day. Certainly it did mine.

I went back to Anglards two days later, on July 14, to take part in the ceremonies planned all across France to celebrate the day. A year before in Paris I had intentionally avoided them because my dread of the crowd greatly exceeded my interest in the proceedings. But returning from one or another of my errands, I had caught a delighted glimpse of a very special "July Fourteenth," one wholly without ceremony. Men and women, abandoning the bistros packed with people, danced in the street, and I found myself a prisoner of their swirls, their foolery, their playful taunts. July 14, 1940, at Anglards was very different. The Requiem mass that seemed to draw the whole city into church did not celebrate the conquest of liberty but mourned its loss. I too went to church, but, as in the years of my childhood, I felt myself alone in the crowd of believers. Unable to share the comfort they took in a familiar rite, I was left without hope to confront the sorrowful company of my thoughts.

That same afternoon our farm lost several of its inhabitants. Some relatives of the "farmer" who lived in occupied Aube had taken advantage of the holiday and come to look for their family members who had sought refuge in Haut Bagnac a month before. They said it was no longer necessary to live apart. Life with the Germans was acceptable, and whatever destruction had taken place in the area had not been their fault but the fault of French troops. As for those who had left their houses fearing an invasion, it was absolutely clear that they were "bad Frenchmen."

At night the sound of the family's noisy and joyful reunion came to us through the open windows. They did not hear the voice of Churchill asserting that London would be defended street by street, house by house. "We would rather see it reduced to ruins and in ashes," he declared solemnly, "than passively and abjectly enslaved."

23 "Don't We Like It Here?"

Soon after July 14 it began to rain. It rained so steadily that it seemed impossible the sun had ever shone on us. I tried to do my part with the children, restless in the house, but Mother and Anne were infinitely more resourceful and endowed with far more good will. I was also responsible for Daniela's rather irregular studies, consisting chiefly of compositions in which she complained of "the departure of my little friends, the farmer's nieces, with whom I had such a good time."

I tried to read but was unable to concentrate on a novel of Huxley's that I had begun weeks before in Paris. Changing to a kind of book more in keeping with my state of mind, I sought comfort in *It's Later than You Think* by Max Lerner. I had begun this book in Paris too, and its beginning chapters had filled me with enthusiasm. Now, however, the reading left me troubled. On the one hand, I was too ignorant of American life to fully understand all that I was reading. On the other hand, events had made me skeptical. On a faded piece of paper still folded into that book, I find some mournful notes: "Everything in this essay is clear, logical, convincing. Yet I can't help thinking that for us, the defenders of democracy, political action is more the necessary conclusion of a way of thinking than a calling, a vocation. Instead, the others, the fanatics (called Fascists, totalitarians, or simply enemies of democracy) seem to act under the same divinatory impulse that presides over artistic creations. They're not only skillful; they have the stars on their side!"

A laconic telegram from Alex announcing his arrival put an end to my perplexed reading. He was surely coming to take us away. Mother and I began to collect all our belongings and tried to think of our next trip. But when Alex arrived on July 21 and asked us if we were ready to leave the next morning, our hearts were very far from being ready. At night, when the bags were all packed, he told us briefly that he had traveled a great deal in difficult circumstances, had seen many people, and had spent much money. The result: visas for Haiti and Panama; transit permits for Spain, Portugal, Algeria. I felt immensely relieved, although we naturally had no desire to settle in Haiti or Panama. But entry to those countries was still available for a certain price, Alex explained, and at that point any destination was better than none. An entry visa for any country carried with it two immediate and invaluable advantages: a French exit visa, that is, permission to leave France, and a transit visa to desirable ports of call such as those in Spain and Portugal.

On July 22, under a driving rain, we said an affectionate goodbye to our friends the Meydieus and to their house, which had become ours for a whole month. When and where would we have another?

The first part of the trip was slow, held up as we were by the rain, by roadblocks, and the children's car-sickness. Extra stops were caused by still another reason: the need to secure French exit visas. Alex thought we had a better possibility of obtaining them in one of the small towns along the road than in Marseille, which was filled to the brim with people in the same critical situation. The matter was less simple than we had foreseen, but in the end we succeeded at the cost of a three hour stop in the town of Mende. All that I will ever know of Mende is the main square lined with trees, or rather that part of it I could see through the windows of the car. So that we wouldn't be seen, Mamma, Anne, the children and I remained inside the car, while Alex tried to forget everything else and concentrate on "flirting" with the stubborn secretary of the local town hall. She got us the visas (bless her soul!), and that evening we slept in Florac, halfway to Marseille, with one less worry on our minds.

The rest of the trip was miraculously without incident. We tried to avoid the sight of abandoned cars here and there in the ditches and not think about the possibility of even a slight accident that would leave us stranded on the road under a burning sun. The countryside was beautiful, and once we left the mountains behind us we ran into wonderful straight stretches of road lined with trees that made me think of northern Italy. Farther on, the country changed again, giving way to an immense plain with marshes that reflected the sun and seemed to intensify the light. To keep the children from becoming restless, Anne would lead them in one of her cheerful series of songs. Digging into her apparently inexhaustible repertoire, she came across two songs in which there were characters with the same names as our two youngest girls. One celebrated the feats of a certain "Cadet Rousselle," and the only part I remember is the refrain, which assures us that this cadet is a good boy!

> *Ah, ah, ah, vraiment,*
> *Cadet Rousselle est bon enfant!*

When she heard this, Rossella exploded in laughter. As for the character who bore the name Simona, she appeared only in a secondary role. The hero of the song was a curate whose activities seemed to lack a little of the dignity we expect from a man in his position.

> *D'ou venez vous si coquet,*
> *M. le Curé?*
>
> *De la foire et du marché,*
> *Simone, ma Simone!*
> *De la foire et du marché,*
> *je peux l'assurer!*

Simona asked how old her namesake in the song was. A little girl like her or a grown-up young lady? I couldn't help but get involved in the plot of this story. The questions they put to us about the curate (had he really gone to the fair as he said he had? and if he had, why the special care about his dress?) was a marvelous diversion, even if useless, from our more compelling worries. Early in the afternoon we arrived in Marseille.

I'm not sure of my memories of Marseille in those last days of July 1940. Not that they are few or faded; rather it seems that they don't make sense. Marseille was as noisy, busy, and colorful as ever; the hotels were full, the streets overflowing with traffic, the stores with merchandise, the restaurants with food. And we, on the eve of another exile, were captivated by its restless rhythm. We ate bouillabaisse in the open; we wandered among the stores looking for things to take with us; we met old friends, all coming from somewhere and heading toward somewhere else. One morning Alex and I even managed to take the children to the sea. I remember that morning vividly; first of all, because our expedition itself was a fiasco. The beach was a city beach, warm, crowded . . . a real nightmare. Then when we went back to the hotel, we found Mother and Mamulia (who was again with us) terribly upset. We had been asked to leave our rooms "because the Italians are coming." Once more Alex calmed everyone, went down to inquire, and came back with the news that the Italians in question were members of the commission charged with supervising the armistice. Then he went out, found rooms in another hotel, and our move was completed by evening.

Nevertheless, our mothers had been greatly frightened, and they became impatient to leave. Alex's observation that a stay of three more weeks might very probably enable us to leave with American visas made them shudder with horror. Their fear was owing to the fact that they constantly saw so many other refugees, some of whom were well known politically. They were sure that one day or another the authorities would crack down on all of us. To increase their nervousness, the next day our new hotel filled up with black shirts. The black shirts made me nervous too, and it was I who insisted that we leave immediately without even having another meal. Surprised at the announcement of one more departure, Simona asked: "Why? Don't we like it here?" We left at the lunch hour, again piled up inside the car. On the way out of the city, Mother continually pointed out automobiles that seemed to her to be following us. It had become almost a habit for me to scold her and tell her how irrational her fears were. The ritual seemed to have a salutary effect on both of us, and I did it again with great vigor that afternoon. Poor Mother! Her anguish on that day in particular was brought back to my memory very recently, in most strange circumstances.

The occasion was a visiting day for grandparents in a New York school; I found myself seated next to another grandmother on one of the benches placed along the walls of the children's swimming pool. She and I had a couple of interesting classes together as well as a general assembly in the school's auditorium. There a young priest in tune with the times had briefly touched on the subject of the approaching Christmas vacation. Perched on the edge of the stage, as if strumming an invisible guitar, he spoke to his young audience in the question and answer style so customary in television shows. His lively, effective, and practical method, which resembled that of a master-of-ceremonies more than a clergyman's, caused a slight confusion among the older members of his audience. I think it was this that brought my friend and me together and led us to speak of children, grandchildren, and our common European past. And it was amid the noisy splashing of the children who were jumping into the pool that her words came to me a little unclearly.

"I don't know if you were ever in Marseille," she asked, and without waiting for an answer she added almost excusing herself, "I never talk of those times, never." Then she went on: "We were there during the war, after the fall of France, and it was there I lost my husband. Purely by chance I and my two little girls were out that morning. I had heard that there was a place not far away where I might find some butter. I don't think we were away more than an hour. When we got back, he wasn't there! They just came, like that, and took him away. I never saw him again."

She spoke without a show of emotion. She was a pleasant old lady, absolutely composed in her appearance, in a simple, well-cut dress, with white hair that shone softly under a small dark hat. I could not tell if, when she spoke of the butter and her short walk, she took comfort from the lucky circumstance that had saved her and her children, or if she deplored it because her husband had been left alone in that tragic situation. I wanted to embrace her, but that would have been out of place in a school gym. I said only, "Yes, I remember Marseille."

24 Perpignan

In my *Larousse,* "Perpignan" is followed by the words, "Capital of the Département des Pyrénées Orientales; Cathedral (14–15th cent.), Castillet (14th cent.), Loge de Mer (14–16th cent.), Palace of the King of Majorca (15th cent.), Museum."

It was at Perpignan that we spent our last week in France, but I have no memories of any of the city's monuments. Not even the beautiful picture of the Castillet in my dictionary ignites a spark of recognition. All that I can recall, if I close my eyes in an effort to "see" better, is the canal (la Basse?) that runs between two embankments on which trees are planted. The trees and the benches traditionally set between them had the effect of transforming the embankments into narrow, elongated parks, where in the course of the day we often sought relief from our suffocating quarters in the hotel across the road. Beyond the open air and the shade, these quais offered a privacy that made them ideal for entertaining our visitors. It's not surprising, therefore, that they have remained in my memory as the only background of the last scenes of our French drama.

Our visitors were many and of various types: some were friends who, as had happened two years earlier in Florence, came to Perpignan to see us before our departure. This time, however, the desire to say good-bye was coupled with the need for a further exchange of ideas concerning the general outlook. Gina and Clara, middle-aged sisters and Jewish, came from Florence like us. One a widow, the other unmarried, they were supported by the income from a small inheritance until the racial laws sent them into a panic. An exploratory trip to Paris where they had relatives had trapped them there when the war came. The general exodus had brought them to Marseille. What should they do now? Stay in occupied France, trying to live on the little capital they had managed to bring out of Italy? Or go back to Florence where they still had their apartment and could count on friends and an affectionate word of support?

Asking these questions, Clara and Gina naturally looked for approval of their nostalgic yearnings. Tired of wandering, afraid of the future, they desperately longed for the comfort of familiar things. What they wanted from us was our blessing, the blessing of reason, so to speak, for a course of action prompted by instinct. How could we refuse it to them? How could we advise our friends to follow the path that we were taking? To flee? How, when, where?

We went back and forth on the quais, sometimes all four of us, but most often Gina (the older and the business woman of the family) with Alex. We invited them in at mealtimes, when the whole family came together in the hotel's dining room. Mother, happy in the presence of old acquaintances and at the chance to speak Italian, did the honors of the house. The children smothered our guests with noisy demonstrations of affection and annoying requests to play, tell stories, take walks. After two days, Gina and Clara left . . . for Marseille, Florence, and the subsequent long years of war, persecution, and hiding places.

Not all visitors to Perpignan were friends. Some of them were business associates, persons connected with Alex's effort to take money out of one more country. It was for the most part the same money that had been successfully taken out of Italy and brought into France two years before. Now it was again exposed to the danger of confiscation; again strict regulations interfered with its transference abroad. During this last week Alex left us twice, once to meet certain people in Marseille, and then in Narbonne. I remember those people only vaguely. A pleasant and courteous visitor (probably a partner in the undertaking) came with Alex from Narbonne and dined with us. "Don't be sad," he said to me understandingly. "You ought to leave France smiling. This Europe has become so disgusting!" Another who didn't have the same courtesy and style, walked on the quai with Alex for hours. When he finally left, I inquired who he was. "Is it something important?" I asked anxiously. "Is he making problems?" Alex shook his head. "No problem whatever," he answered. "His terms are reasonable, and he seems a perfectly honest man. But he's a fool. How can one trust an idiot with a small fortune?" The idiot in this case was a prospective smuggler.

The quai was also the stage for the last scene of my private drama with Pierre. He had just been discharged from the army and came for two days with Jeannette. With them, too, I'm sure, there must have been meals and walks with the family . . . among which I remember an outing with the children when we somehow came to have the open rear end of a tram all to ourselves. I don't remember its destination, only the tram that waggled its tail across the countryside, and its beautiful name . . . *baladeuse,* that is, saunterer, which seemed appropriate to the mood of the afternoon. My meeting with Pierre on the quai took place that same evening.

We had all eaten together, except Alex, who was in Marseille. Then, one by one all went to bed, the children first, then the grandmothers, and finally Jeannette too. I fervently wanted her to go, but felt embarrassed when she did. It meant she trusted me, an idea that irritated me both because it seemed to underestimate my powers as a wicked temptress, and because it blackmailed me into behaving correctly. Not that I considered even for a moment that I, too, might retire upstairs! I had to have a few minutes alone with Pierre. I had a right to them. I followed him outside for a last stroll.

That's all there was to it, almost. A walk hand in hand, interrupted by pauses, during which we sat down on a bench in the darkness and kissed, clinging to one another desperately. Pierre kept on saying sadly and stubbornly, "You have to go because I lost the war." I naturally protested that he wasn't to blame, that we were all innocent . . . and all guilty for having allowed the dictators to come to power. Tears ran down my face, and at the same time, with some part of me, I thought that my leaving was the only possible solution for our relationship.

At a certain point, I don't know why, Pierre took me upstairs to his and Jeannette's room. Was he looking for something? I don't remember. Jeannette was sleeping and blinked her eyes almost smiling when Pierre turned on the light. He turned it off calmly, but in pulling the sheet over her head Jeannette had revealed that she slept in the nude, and I was embarrassed by that. The whole episode had an ambiguous character that I promised myself I would explore sometime or other . . . if and when there was an opportunity to explore it. No more time was left that night; it was completely taken up with good-byes. Early in the morning Pierre and Jeannette departed, and in the afternoon Alex returned.

We had to stay in Perpignan two more days; our departure was delayed by the apparently insoluble dilemma over choosing the right person to carry the money. We briefly considered the possibility of carrying it ourselves in the automobile, but that seemed too risky. Foreigners leaving French territory probably had to get out of their cars one at a time for a careful customs inspection. Besides, Mamma, the children, and I, who had the privilege of holding valid Italian passports, could run into difficulties because of a not wholly irrelevant detail. All our passports bore a stamp that was routine in the period when they were issued: "Not valid for Spain"!

What to do then? Must we make use of an honest idiot or of another man who had made his appearance in the last few hours and seemed full of resources but decidedly a bit shady? Oh, how much

I wanted to tell Alex to let it all go! Just crossing the border safe and sound, all eight of us, would be a miraculous success. How could we have the temerity to risk making it even more dangerous? Nevertheless, I knew how much pressure he had been under during the last few months. I noticed that he coughed now from time to time, a light cough dry and hollow that seemed to relieve his inner tension. And our trial was still very far from its conclusion! Even if everything had gone well, so much more would be required in the coming months. How could I tell him that the money wasn't important, that I was afraid? I remained silent.

We left Perpignan at three in the afternoon on August 9, and a half hour later we were at Perthus on the Spanish border. Our plans were to cross Spain without serious problems and then to stay in Portugal for all the time we were given, for all the time necessary to obtain American visas.

It took three and a half hours to pass through French customs and then Spanish, too long a time for our hearts filled with anxiety, a short time in which to break once and for all the bonds that tied us to the sweet land of France. The Spanish customs officials gave no sign of having noticed the ill-omened stamp in our passports, enchanted as they were with the caprices of our little Rossella. "Me too, me too," she protested noisily, claiming her right to be searched just like everyone else. And she was searched amid benevolent laughter. Then, in accord with regulations, all the gasoline was pumped out of the automobile and we rolled down the hill, motor in neutral, as far as the first Spanish gas station located conveniently at its bottom.

25 Four Days in Barcelona

Entering Spain that afternoon, I again found myself absurdly thinking of Professor Rosi, my history teacher in the last three years of liceo in Rome. He had brought a breath of fresh air into our studies, asking us not to memorize any more dates. Dates like borders, he declared, were words used only for practical purposes and not to be taken seriously. "Remember," he said, pointing his ink-stained finger at us, "that the transition from Medieval to Renaissance is as difficult to define as the transition from one nation to another." I liked Professor Rosi a lot, but that afternoon in Spain I thought he was completely wrong, for as soon as we resumed our trip everything around us became drastically different.

The mules, for example . . . not sturdy like those I had known at Soriano in my childhood but small and black with little dark men on their backs. And the villages . . . which did not display geraniums at their windows, or pergolas covered with vines in their yards, but desperately sad people, who looked straight ahead indifferently outside their wretched, colorless houses. And roads completely ruined, ragged children. . . . Everything pointed to a world laid waste, and the occasional sight of impeccably dressed gendarmes outside an opera house only accented the unreality of all that. It occurred to me that Professor Rosi was right at least about one thing. Our exile had not begun when we crossed the border between Italy and France two years before; it was beginning right now!

I said it aloud to Alex: "Only now are we in exile!" and he agreed. Suddenly we felt terribly tired. We stopped at Gerona for the night.

The following morning found us in a better mood. And the sight of the sea, which we reached at midday, made everything seem more familiar. It was a marvelous sea, marvelously blue. "The same one you swam in at Forte dei Marmi!" I told the children happily. I even got my mother to admit that the town of Badalona, which extended along a bay, with its railway station right on the water, and its cathedral set on a small hill overlooking the town, strikingly resembled Ancona, her native city. . . . When we reached Barcelona, our hearts were a little lighter.

We decided to stop in Barcelona only for as long as was necessary to send our car ahead to Badajoz at the Portuguese frontier. We ourselves would cross Spain by rail, a means of transport preferable by far in a country where we knew neither the language nor the roads. It seemed likely that these weaknesses of ours would attract attention to us, and attention was the last thing we wanted in Franco's Spain. A year before, Franco had issued a declaration of "strict neutrality" in the war, but even then everyone knew whose side he was on. Now that Germany was victorious, it was not inconceivable that the two nations would join officially as allies committed to the same kind of politics. The wisest thing we could do was to leave that country as soon as possible and, in the meantime, attract no attention.

In Barcelona, forwarding the automobile turned out to be relatively simple. Tickets for the train, however, were a different matter. There weren't seats available on the train for Madrid until the following Wednesday, four more days. "Four days!" I wrote in my diary. "But nowadays they can change the face of the world! For God's sake!"

Entrusting ourselves to divine mercy, we began a provisional life as guests of another hotel in another city, exploring hesitantly its unfamiliar characteristics. On the evening of our arrival we discovered two disconcerting features: the hours of meals, and deserted streets that were all lit up. It was ten o'clock before we could sit down to dinner in the hotel dining room; eleven before Alex and I called a carriage to take a ride for a look around. Our request that the coachman take us "wherever you like" did not seem comprehensible to him. However, given that the Italians are well trained in the art of supplementing words with gestures, we managed to convey the idea that we would like him to take us "where he thought best." At that point he proudly carried us to a succession of wide avenues, terribly crowded, the sidewalks filled with the chairs of cafés and glittering lights. After months of darkness, the light came to us like an unexpected gift and, surprisingly, not a welcome one. The privilege of being exposed to neon signs pointing out the merits of Bayer or Galina Blanca products suddenly seemed to us highly debatable, and we were aware of regretting the darkness that had mercifully descended on our misfortunes every evening in France.

When we went to bed that night we were too tired to pay attention to the racket, but the following day, a Sunday, we quickly became conscious of it. Our hotel was right on one of the Ramblas, and under our windows it seemed that hordes of people were incessantly walking in an endless flow. Closed shutters were no protection against the heat and noise. Trams squealed, automobile horns honked, horses' hoofs clattered on the pavement, and over all were the shouts of passersby and the cries of peddlers on foot. Desperately rivaling one another, all of them put their trust in the loudness of their voices and the insistence of their slogans to call attention to their wares, which were as varied as they were unattractive: ice cream, newspapers, shoe polish, toy windmills, lottery tickets, watermelons . . . all with a rhythm that seemed to go on without stop day and night.

Whatever sightseeing we did in those days must have been mo-
tivated by my need to get away from the noise because, as a rule, I
was against going out of the hotel. It seemed to me that by staying
in the hotel we were less exposed to accidental encounters or
mishaps caused by tricks of fate. Alex judged this perfectly sense-
less, maintaining that we were just as likely to get into trouble because of the indiscreet chatter of the children when they received a
pat on the back from one of the other guests in the hotel, as from
going out into the city. "Who knows when we'll be able to come
back to Barcelona," he said playfully, in good humor. He knew perfectly well that I was more worried about leaving as soon as possible than about the chances of our return some day. My passive
resistance, however, wasn't as strong as his ebullience. And so out
we went!

We stopped in a shop or two, and sipped coffee under the aw-
nings on the sidewalks; one afternoon we offered the children ice
cream, then a taxi ride; we saw other plazas, other avenues; we saw
a residential quarter radiant with flowers . . . And all the time I
asked myself what the missing element was that kept Barcelona
from being a truly great city.

I found the answer to my question later when I was almost
asleep, lulled by the swaying of the train to Madrid. Thinking
back, I understood that it was not an absence, but a presence . . .
the constant, tangible presence of poverty. Images I had not been
conscious of and that had been stamped on my memory in the preceding days suddenly appeared to crowd my half-awake mind.
Away from the noisy avenues, from the crowded street corners,
from the sidewalk cafés, there marched a procession of peddlers,
of emaciated women, of begging children . . . grotesque and demanding. I thought of *The Threepenny Opera*, of its realism that
was larger than life. I thought that we, Jews, exiles . . . we were still
privileged. And then I fell asleep.

26 Refugee in the Prado

The two days we spent in Madrid have stayed in my memory, one dark, the other bright, as if they had been painted in two different colors.

The dark one was the day of our arrival, when we climbed to the Ciudad Universitaria where the last act of the Civil War had taken place. We had never seen anything like it, and it was no wonder. We had never before been on a battlefield. The terrain was now covered with grass, and tall, thin trees had been planted, but the peaceful surroundings accentuated the profound desolation of the scene that confronted us. A whole city of houses, buildings, structures of every type, all blown apart, stretched before our eyes, suggesting the idea of a fantastic parade of gigantic skeletons staring fixedly at the sun. They didn't speak of war any longer, the cause we knew of so well; they didn't appeal to our faith, or our convictions. They bore witness to only one truth, death . . . a death that came impartially for five hundred thousand men, all of whom claimed the same pity, the same respect, the same tears.

There were tears in our eyes when we came away at sundown. For whom? For ourselves? That same evening our friend, our good, foolish man from Andorra, arrived safe and sound with the money.

I don't remember the details of this occurrence, only the sensation of relief and the sudden flash of hope, like water freed from a blocked spring. The next morning, as soon as Alex had busied himself again in the city over the money and the problems of our journey, I made a rapid inspection of our little community. Mamulia was giving herself her daily injection of insulin before going to breakfast; Mother had already consented to the demands of the two oldest children and was reading something to them; Anne was in the garden with the youngest. I surprised myself immensely by saying good-bye to all of them and going alone to the Prado. "I might never come to Madrid again!" I said to myself with a smile, and I thought that Alex would be proud of me.

I have never gone back to Madrid, but I can close my eyes and recapture the feeling of that morning, far from everything, beyond everything. And I can almost feel the shock of discovering Goya for the first time.

The little guidebook I used that morning, *Tres horas en el Museo del Prado,* has managed to survive the almost thirty-year interval so that I can still leaf through its pages. One point, underlined in pencil, is an observation made by the author to his *amigo visitante.* The fame of Goya, he cautions, still lacks a "supreme guarantee;" it has not yet been judged by others than those born in the nineteenth century.

A note at the foot of the page written by me asserts angrily, "Nonsense!" and continues expressing the judgments that I made myself. "Tragically grotesque in the *Capriccios;* sparklingly Cezannesque in the *Cartoons;* explicit to the point of horror in the *Disasters of War;* essential and infallible in his portraits; mysterious in the enigmatic *majas* and the saints lost in ecstasy."

I feel quite charmed by my richly colored prose, as one might be for the achievement of a daughter, but I'm puzzled about the reasons that made me lump together the *majas* and the saints. In any case, it's perfectly clear why my second and last day in Madrid should be bathed in my mind in the radiant light of the sun.

The train for Badajoz which we took that evening was very different from the one that had brought us to Madrid. This time the sleeping car was attached to a freight train, so that we crossed one of the most desolate regions of Spain and one of the most poverty stricken, stopping at every little station. The stops shook us out of our precarious beds and subjected us to the insistent cries of children who offered us, at the top of their lungs, peanuts, rotting bananas, stale bread, and warm water. The heat was unbearable, but the sight of a hand furtively reaching through an open window and trying to feel for something to take hold of, decided us to close all the windows. When we arrived at Badajoz, Simona and I had a high fever and we went immediately to bed.

We hadn't planned to stop in Badajoz for any length of time, but our car had not arrived and it seemed mad to abandon it; we could sell it in Portugal. So we decided to wait for two more days. Although we did not leave the hotel, we met many people who were stopping there in transit to or from Lisbon. I remember an enchanting Dutch family (husband, wife, and five children), whose presence at the table next to ours became very important at all three meals, and whose departure left our children in tears. And a Swiss businessman on his return trip home, who spoke of Lisbon as a terrestrial paradise, which made me shiver in presentiment. Might we perhaps be destined to remain outside its gates?

But we weren't. The car arrived on the morning of August 19, and early in the afternoon we climbed aboard one by one in the familiar formation. From a car parked right in front of us a banner (decorated with a black swastika!) wished us bon voyage. Even our peaceful Anne lost control of her emotions for a moment. "*Mon Dieu*," she murmured, "I can't wait to get away from here!"

The Spanish officers at the Portuguese border were much more meticulous than their colleagues at Perthus. Every piece of baggage had to be pulled down from the roof of the car and hoisted back up again. Each of us had to undress and submit to a personal inspection. But finally we were free to resume our journey under the burning sun, and, as God willed, we arrived at the Portuguese customs.

A little man in uniform directed us to a corner somewhat apart from the confusion, where an unattractive and solitary tree offered wretched protection from the sun. While Alex was getting out of the automobile with our passports, the same man went to get a terracotta pitcher at his guard post and brought some water that was cooler and more refreshing than any I had ever drunk. I will never forget that glass of water, or the bench . . . the bench where all of us sat, content to wait there forever.

Once more everything became different. Silent white villages, miniature bullfight arenas, little houses with flowers that brightened the bare landscape, and finally, along the crest of a hill, the cheerful welcoming gestures of our first windmills. When we reached the coast, the sun had long since set. From the deck of the ferryboat that ran before the evening breeze we could see the lights of Lisbon greeting us across the Mar de Paha.

27 A Question of Identity

We were to stay in Lisbon for four months, a period of time long enough to allow us a pause, a truce. But in my memory the four months are a single, interminable moment filled with anxiety.

Our arrangement itself at the Avenida Palace Hotel, far from alleviating anxiety, increased it. The hotel faced the Praca Restauradores, sun-filled and windswept, and our rooms were spacious, actually luxurious. They were also an absurd drain on our limited financial resources. But the hope (at that time a certainty) that our visas for this or that country were at hand prevented us from looking for an apartment and gathering our things once more to proceed with domestic life as we had done in Haut Bagnac. Instead, each one of us began to build his or her own personal nest that seemed durable in a world around us that lacked all permanence.

Mother and Mamulia followed a routine of meals, short walks, and naps that seemed to restore their physical energies at least, if not their mental tranquility. Anne took the smallest children to the park twice a day, kept their things in order, and found great satisfaction in criticizing the hotel's kitchen. Daniela went to the Lisbon French School and seemed not to be troubled by all that she was asked to do, including the study of Portuguese; at that point anything was better than continuing to play with her sisters! Alex and I devoted the greater part of our days to the full-time project of looking for a permanent solution to the question of our family's future.

We had transformed our bedroom into an office furnished with a typewriter, stationery, and telephone. This was my place. Alex went out to visit consulates, police commissioners, travel agencies . . . in search of a million things: travel permits, proofs of citizenship, money exchange, ship passage . . . and so on.

We were on one of these ships, the *Nea Hellas*, just a few days after our arrival, to say good-bye to the Strausses, friends whose departure saddened us although we had known them for less than a week. But time seemed to have its own special laws in those days. I had never before been on a transatlantic liner, and at first I was surprised by all the ways it resembled the ships I had seen in films. Only after a little while did I become aware, with a sudden shiver, that something was different. There was no confetti thrown here, no elegant women breathing with an ecstatic air the scent of bon voyage bouquets, no people sipping champagne; the *Nea Hellas* oozed a gloomy exhaustion. It was enough to read the names on the backs of the chairs to understand why. Rabinovich, Weil, Fano, Arias . . . all lucky ones who were departing, and departing in comfort. What possible use could they have, however, for the many salons, the gym, the bar, the swimming pool? Their voyage had begun; there was no way of return, and no lighthouse before them.

I remembered with a sense of relief that I didn't have to leave with them; I wouldn't have to look into those empty eyes during a long voyage. When the loudspeaker announced, "All visitors ashore," I took Alex's arm and hurried to the gangplank.

Of course, this was the first departure of refugees that I witnessed. I experienced quite different feelings when some time had passed and our situation became more tense, the need to escape more pressing. In those first weeks of September, I could still allow myself to think I would be able to choose what ship to leave on, and what country to go to. We wanted to go to the United States! And all our efforts in that period were dedicated exclusively to that end.

Alex had gone to speak with the American consul several times and had drawn up an accurate list of all the official requirements. They were numerous, all apparently tending to confirm the reliability of our European past as a guarantee that we would not become a burden to the community in the United States. However, since Europe was at war and communications were uncertain throughout the world, the difficulties facing refugees in transit in obtaining the necessary documents were sometimes insurmountable. For hours and hours I pounded out letters on the typewriter addressed to friends and relatives, especially in New York, with requests that went from a simple testimonial, authenticated by a notary, to the all-important "affidavit" that would place the responsibility for our future on the shoulders of whoever acted as our guarantor.

Since one refugee was hardly qualified to guarantee another, neither my brother Guido nor my uncle Giorgio, who had landed in America some months before, could be of help. Our only hope was an old friend of Alex's, a man named Max Ascoli, whom he hadn't seen for ten years. I remembered him vaguely, having had dinner with him one evening in Florence. He had just come out of prison, where he had served time for anti-fascist activities, and was just about to leave for New York thanks to a providential "Rockefeller" fellowship. Would he remember us? And would it matter to him? In any case, we had to try. A letter went off addressed to Max with a request for the "affidavit;" another to a common friend with a request to urge Max on; another to my brother with a request to urge on the common friend.

The fate of all our correspondence was uncertain in the best of cases. Once, our letters didn't even get to leave Lisbon because the transatlantic ship *Clipper,* which carried the mail, had mysteriously gone aground; at other times the answers arrived late due to odd accidents (the common friend explained that Max, incredibly! was on his honeymoon); at yet other times our correspondents did not grasp correctly the nature of our requests and sent us the wrong papers. These cases were particularly frustrating, and I thought of them as dialogs between the deaf. In one of the stories from my childhood a deaf person asked, "Are you going fishing?" "No," answered his deaf friend from behind the fence around his house and with broad gestures of denial; and then he shouted, "No, I'm going fishing!" "It doesn't matter," said the first shrugging his shoulders. "I thought you were going fishing!" Yes, that's how to describe it, the story of two deaf people.

To make things worse, the American consul, a young, elegant man of prosperous appearance, who seemed friendly at first and wishing to be of service, began to enlarge his initial demands with the unthinking cruelty of a blackmailer. No sooner did we manage to secure a document, than he discovered that another was needed. Not that the expression "another" was ever used; the second demand always seemed to come from some element that was missing in the first. All the same, he stifled our hopes by requiring of us a new, necessary task.

One time we had to furnish the proof that my father was the owner of a famous jewelry shop on the Ponte Vecchio in Florence, the "Settepassi Company." I don't know why that should have mattered. It must have had to do in some way with our reliability, I suppose. In any case, it took days upon days to obtain a notarized testimonial from a trustworthy witness in the United States certifying that, in truth, my father had been the owner of the store. "Mmm," said the consul, "I see." Then he came out with a request for further documentation, this time confirming the fact that my father's company was well known. Strangely enough, the answer to that request came from a wholly unexpected source: the little Tauchnitz edition of a book by Aldous Huxley, *Brief Candles*, which for some reason had followed me all the way from Paris. One evening as I was reading in bed, I happened upon the following passage: "When she was dressed ('she' was the heroine of the story), she went down into the city (Florence) by car and spent an hour in the jewelry shop Settepassi. When she left, she was taken for a princess on the Lungarno."

We greeted this discovery with excitement and decided that, if our hardships ever had a happy ending, we would certainly let people know, in a perfectly casual way, to be sure, that we owed our good luck to Aldous Huxley! Thanks to this help, the matter of my father's business was successfully put to rest . . . leaving the American consul free to unearth different kinds of demands.

While we were occupied with our personal battle, the war in Europe was going on. The refugees had many ways of following its developments by means of a vast assortment of newspapers and periodicals coming from every country and written in every language, the reports of which—often contradictory—were the subjects of lengthy discussions.

Two reviews that we usually read in Paris, *Gringoire* and *Candide,* were engaged in conducting intense anti-Semitic and anti-English campaigns. No longer interested either in style or humor, their sickening obsequiousness to those in power disgusted us.

Paris-soir, once familiar, reported that Gamelin, Mandel, and Reynaud were under arrest in some remote castle and were conducting a "life of expiation," while an investigation of their actions was in progress. Who were their judges? the Lavals, the Bonnets?

The English newspapers spoke of the English Air Force bombing military objectives in Germany, of cities and villages that were being destroyed in England. The German papers wept over the victims of English raids against helpless civilians and boasted of having hit military objectives in England.

Gradually as the weeks passed, two possibilities seemed to emerge slowly from the different versions that bombarded us every day. England might be on the point of striking back and, in fact, of surviving; Germany, not having obtained the quick victory over England it had foreseen, might use Spain, perhaps Portugal, in order to occupy Gibraltar.

England's resistance was encouraging us to hope that our future life, the life of our children, might be worth living. "You see," Alex said passionately, "if our people win, life will be good, it will be worth living. If not, what good will it be to live? What difference will it make to have taken or to have missed the last boat from Lisbon?"

But there was a difference, naturally, and at the end of September, with the American passports always within reach and always eluding us, we began to take steps to acquire visas for Brazil, and travel permits to Panama; we began to consider a treasure the only thing, alas! we were actually in possession of: visas for Costa Rica.

One afternoon Anne came back from the park completely distraught. Daniela and Simona had made her spend a dreadful quarter of an hour, she complained; they had argued noisily from the minute they had left to take Daniela to school. Simona expressed herself very properly in self-defense. "We were playing consulate," she explained, "and we could have had a really good time! But Daniela always wants to be the boss. She never lets me be the consul, *elle me ne laisse jamais faire le consul!*"

28 We Had Come Too Far

It bothers me that I can remember so little of the city of Lisbon. Now that Portugal has become fashionable, I constantly hear talk of people buying houses there as an investment or as a permanent residence. I'm always about to say: "Portugal? I know it well. I once spent four months there." But I don't, because what do I really know? I only have isolated images of Lisbon (la Praca do Commercio, the charming neighborhoods of Esposicao, the Casino of Estoril) and vague feelings about its inhabitants. The language barrier made our contacts with travel agents, postal workers, and news vendors quite barren. And we rarely met a Portuguese who spoke English or French and who could enlighten us about the habits and customs of the country. An occasion of this type, a casual meeting with a young, good-looking lawyer and his delightful wife led to a not insignificant confusion in our initial vision of Portugal as a "free country."

The four of us had dinner together at Estoril, and I had appreciated the food and the casual, pleasant conversation. Later the young woman suggested a turn around the Casino, and I enjoyed this part of the evening less. Standing at a green table to allow our hosts to try their fortune at *chemin de fer,* watching later on at another table so that Alex could observe more closely the erratic reactions of a compulsive gambler . . . were both equally tiring. When, long after midnight, it was suggested that we go to the bar, I was overjoyed. I indulgently nestled against the cushions of a divinely comfortable sofa. With every sip of tea I became more and more sleepy and gave a distracted attention to the words of the young lawyer next to me, who with every sip of whiskey became more expansive. It was only gradually that some of his words penetrated my sleepiness and made me look at my companion with incredulity. He was talking about "tyranny," "freedom of the press," "religious conformism," "imprisonment," and he clearly meant what he was saying. When we were on the point of leaving, he helped me put on my shawl, and let a last, impassioned declaration drop in my ear: "The answer is not to die obediently; it's to live rebelliously!"

During our return home we were all silent, but I was aware of seeing the Estoril-Lisbon highway with new eyes, as one of the grandiose accomplishments of the Salazar regime. I thought of the Italian roads recently repaired, the trains running on time, the swamps drained. Was it possible? Was it possible that Salazar, whose liberal views—exalted in the press, engraved on the walls of the Exposition—had won our respectful admiration, was a potential Mussolini? That the newspapers, whose opinions on foreign affairs we enthusiastically approved, were carefully avoiding all dissent concerning internal affairs? That a country that opened its doors so generously to all exiles, was forcing its own children into silence, suffocating their independence of thought with prison?

In the following days I pressed Alex for the well-informed and imaginative answers I was used to expecting from him on every occasion, but he had none. Strange! We were quick to recognize a note of discouragement on Hitler's part when, in a public statement, he referred to victory as a success he would achieve "step by step." We had no trouble deducing from Mussolini's promise to the Italian people that Greece would be beaten "even if that might require two weeks, two months, or two years" the probable fact that he was suffering a defeat on the Greek front. We were able to formulate hypotheses, if nothing more, on the many and contradictory actions of Russia, and on the recent elections in America and

Roosevelt's victory over Willkie. And yet our ability to make up
our minds was drastically diminished when it came to events taking place right under our eyes. The operations of the Portuguese
government remained as mysterious to us as those of the consulates, the embassies, and the legations on Portuguese soil.

Our wearisome experiences with bureaucracy were made even
more troubling and nerve-wracking because of those undergone
by many people whose paths crossed our own. Among them were
often relatives, friends, friends of friends, who looked for us when
they passed through Portugal on their way to other countries.
Carlo, my dearest cousin from Rome, whom I had seen for the last
time in Switzerland just before the war, stayed in Lisbon for three
weeks waiting to embark for Brazil. The young Italian wife of a
German art historian, whom we had once met at a reception,
stayed with us for three days during her journey, with two little
children, to join her husband in New York. A professor of philosophy from Turin, in Portugal for a conference, stayed for fourteen
days looking into the possiblity of permanent emigration. However, the majority of the people we saw were acquaintances we had
made in Lisbon, or in the hotel, or in the synagogue, or the various
offices we had to visit every day.

In the synagogue where I sat upstairs with Mamulia and Daniela, it was easy to distinguish which women were Portuguese and
which were foreign. The first had the indifferent and calm look of
people at their ease and at home; the others, the timid, embarrassed manners of uninvited guests. During the services there were
those who could not control their sobs.

Mamulia and I rarely talked to the other women, but when we
met Alex after the services, we invariably found him in the company of old or new acquaintances. We all walked together in the
streets, exchanging remarks, sometimes arranging to meet again.
In this way we shared lives, extreme situations, and hopes that
made our own all the more intense. When someone's turn came to
leave Portugal, his departure upset us, not only for the loss of pre-

cious ties and renewed worry about our own fate but also because of the arbitrary nature of the forces that controlled all our futures. A few days were enough to create a community of several scattered families. Then suddenly some visas—owing to the whim of a consul, the distraction of another, the corruption of a third—flung one family to the United States, one to Brazil, one to Argentina, like leaves driven by the wind. People who had never heard the word "equator" since elementary school found themselves listening anxiously to fragments of information about the climate of equatorial regions, which—they were assured—were worthy of the Côte d'Azur. A few days later, full of trepidation, they were en route to Quito.

At the beginning of October, from the moment when all our various documents were finally in order and duly handed over to the American consulate, we began to wait with increased confidence. We even went so far as to reserve our crossing on a ship that was supposed to leave for New York within the month. Our faith was rewarded. In the middle of October, the fifteenth to be exact, a call from the consulate informed us that our visas were ready and summoned the whole family for the completion of the official ceremony: signatures and oath-taking. We also had to take with us medical certificates confirming that we were all in good health.

We walked on clouds all day long. When we left the doctor's office after an examination that seemed endless, I kissed him in gratitude. When we went to bed, Alex said to me, "Sleep well, my dear! This is your first American night!"

But we had underestimated the American consul! With great care and fuss he examined our Italian passports, then raised his head with a questioning look. These passports . . . naturally, we needed the approval of the Italian consul in Lisbon for a trip to the United States.

We were thunderstruck. Didn't he know that we were fugitives from Italy and only with the greatest difficulty could we turn to the Italian consul for anything? Didn't he see that our passports were stamped "not valid for Spain," which made our presence in Lisbon illegal so far as the Italian authorities were concerned?

So sorry! The consul could do nothing. Only the Italian authorities could validate an Italian passport for travel to the United States. Notwithstanding all our protests and pleas, we had to leave with empty hands. "*Gamze' letova!*" Alex said in Hebrew as we went out: even this is for the best! He continued explaining to us how unreasonable it was for man to concentrate his thought only on a certain course of action. What does man know about the fate reserved for him? Absolutely nothing! Maybe by means of the ill offices of the wicked consul, God was really protecting us now from some terrible misfortune that would have happened to us on American soil. Isn't that so? I could only think that I was about to be ill, and I would have wanted the children not to be there so that I could abandon myself to despair.

We had no choice. We had to go to the Italian consulate. But how? We had heard it said that the Italian consul was a humane person, that whenever possible he tried to simplify things, to help people in difficulty. Nevertheless, we couldn't dare to present our request like an ordinary piece of business, risking a refusal that would forever destroy our chances of success. We had to find a way that would attract compassionate attention to our case. Unexpectedly, Mother had an inspiration.

Purposely ignoring me, she turned to Alex: "I have a childhood friend," she said in a convincing tone of voice, "a marvelous woman. We were close friends for years. Her brother Renato, Renato Bova Scoppa, is a career diplomat and a kind man. Carla knows all about him; she also knows that right now it so happens that the brother is no less than minister plenipotentiary in Portugal. I have repeatedly suggested that we make ourselves acquainted with him, but Carla has always rejected my proposal, replying that we're not dealing here with a procedure that we can call to the attention of the Italian government or its representatives. Now . . ." and this time she turned to me with an air of reproof, "an idea is not necessarily bad just because it comes from one's own mother! It seems to me that at this point it's perfectly legitimate to get in touch with him . . . Look, you don't have to do it. I can do it! I can write him a note (after all, one of the Italian passports is mine) and ask him to put in a good word for us at the Italian consulate . . . What do you say?"

What could we say? Neither Alex nor I had much faith that Mamma's past, romantic friendship could still endure, nor that an Italian diplomat "of Aryan race" would have the decency to do what he could on behalf of a Jew in trouble. But we had no alternative; we allowed Mother to write the note. And we began to hope again.

It was at that time, I think, during the last part of October, that our visas for Brazil arrived. They had been procured thanks to the intervention of my uncle Carlo, one of my mother's brothers and the black sheep of the family. Years before, having taken his degree in medicine and having practiced for a certain period on and off, he had set out on the reckless path of gambling and women. His brothers, proud of his intelligence and good looks, paid his debts for years. Finally, they agreed with a certain relief to his plan to move to Sao Paolo in Brazil where he had good friends who were fabulously rich. It had not been easy for us to appeal to Uncle Carlo's family feelings, since we suspected they were slightly if not entirely resentful. But we had done it, and to our amazement his good will and his connections had accomplished miracles. We had Brazilian visas!

God, how hard it was to accept the idea of Brazil as our final destination, to persuade ourselves that this too was for the best! On the other hand, Serrano Suñer, the Spanish Interior Minister, had made several ill-omened trips recently to Germany and Italy. He was perhaps working on a plan to allow Germany to make use of Spain in order to occupy Gibraltar, in exhange—so the rumors ran—for a free hand in Morocco? We decided to accept the Brazilian visas.

I don't recall if the children were with us that time although they must have been, and the lack of drama on this occasion could have been owing to the fact that we were getting used to disappointment. And there was indeed disappointment once more, although of a different type. It wasn't the Brazilian consul who refused us the visas; it was we who gave them back! When we already had pens in hand to sign the final documents, we noticed one of the guarantees we were required to give. We had to affirm under oath that we were not Jews!

The consul was very friendly. In the face of our consternation, he patiently explained that it was only a formal declaration, that it had been added only recently to the standard forms to calm the fears of a few alarmists worried that the influx of immigrant Jews might reach excessive proportions. "It would be mad to take it seriously," he told us, "to risk the future of your family for an irrelevant detail!" But we could not take his advice.

In some strange way, we were too tired, too discouraged to do it. We had come so far, both in spirit and in space. Florence, Nice, Paris, Tours, Haut Bagnac, Marseille, Perpignan, Barcelona, Madrid, Badajoz, Lisbon . . . all that wandering and for what? To settle in a country that, pro forma or not, closed its doors to immigrant Jews? And to go there denying precisely the identity that above all else had driven us into wandering?

We excused ourselves to the Brazilian consul and took our leave. Later in the hotel we tried to explain our decision to the children as best we could. Once they were in bed, we went to talk with Mother and Mamulia. Both were downcast, though in different ways. Remembering the time decades before when she had crossed the Russian border on foot to enter Germany, Mamulia took a pill (was it the third or fourth that day?) for her heart. "What else could we do?" we asked again and again. "It would have been like jumping from the frying pan into the fire!" Mamma said nothing, and I knew she was thinking of her brother and the letter she would have to write to him, trying to explain why we had thrown away the fruit of his labors by refusing the visas.

In the end, she wrote the letter. Uncle Carlo never answered, and only some years later did we learn that he had been very angry and had said, "What else can one expect from one's relatives?" Of the entire family, only my cousin Carlo, who left for Brazil a few days later saw him again. He died in Sao Paolo soon after the end of the war.

29 The Consul

The validity of our passports was extended to the United States at last, and with a promptness that left us dumbfounded. Was it all owing to Mother's powerful "connections"? Or was it in part the result of the Italian consul's humanity? Probably both. When Alex went to the Italian consulate to find out the fate of our request, a clerk, full of himself but friendly, whispered in his ear, "I told the consul that he really didn't have the right to grant you the extension, but . . ." And that very evening, before we had time to reflect on the implications of his words, another less important employee of the consulate delivered the passports to our rooms with their validity extended to the United States. "I was told to be careful with these documents," he confided to us in a low voice. "They concern people very highly regarded by the embassy!"

Both of these assertions might have been suggested by these gentlemen in the hope of some financial recognition of their good will. That did not prevent Mother in any way from taking exuberant pride in these events. I thought she was about to kiss the messenger!

Everything had gone so smoothly that our passports were back in our hands at least a week before the date of our ship's departure. Was it possible that we would leave with it? Keeping our fingers crossed, we took the precious passports to the American consul and . . . were told to come back in three days! Three days? It would be the Friday before the departure set for Sunday. What did it mean? Was everything in good order or wasn't it? Had the date been chosen with the intention of granting the visas, or only to tell us once more that something was lacking, to place another obstacle before us?

At the appointment on Friday we learned with dismay that the speed with which the extension of the passports' validity had been granted had raised suspicions about our political integrity. Italy, after all, was a nation at war. Instances like ours, it was thought, should be examined with care . . . especially in the case of refugees. We had ourselves recognized this when, only a few days before, we had insisted that it was impossible to satisfy the consul's demands. How could we explain coming back so soon having fulfilled all of those demands? The consul was simply perplexed. He had to telegraph Washington for instructions. In the meantime we were free, naturally, to provide any pertinent document that might help throw light on our political convictions, to show our condition not only as victims but also as enemies of fascism.

This time Alex did not say, "This too is for the best!" Nor did he bow before the mysterious ways of the Lord. He was angry and explicit. "One day," he said, shaking his head with incredulity, "one day someone will tell the story of these 'waiting rooms.' It will be too late for those who fall by the wayside to benefit from it, but it might bring a sort of catharsis to those who survive."

Alex, since he was the only one who had actually sat in all the waiting rooms of our pilgrimage, had personal knowledge of the extraordinary situations of those "who fell by the wayside." He had been witness to what I had only heard described. The old man who died of a heart attack right on the bench where he had waited patiently week after week; the young woman who had killed herself the evening after she received another no; the family that had gone "home" because it had become financially impossible to wait any longer in a foreign country . . . they were all protagonists of tragic stories to me. To him they were people. He had talked in Yiddish with the old man; in German, with the young woman. He had walked the streets with the father of the family, sharing his agony over the final decision. What writer could do justice to their fates?

For once it was I who tried to channel Alex's suffering into the relief of literary speculation. It would have taken the pen of a Kafka, I suggested, to depict the world of visas in all its surrealistic absurdity; that of a Dostoyevsky to render the nightmare of the petitioners' struggle for survival; that of Proust to enquire into the distant roots, the hopes, the fears. At that time I didn't know that my only consolation after all would come not from a novel but from a musician. I didn't know that ten years later I would be seated at the piano in my house in Larchmont while tears blurred the score before me of Menotti's *The Consul.*

"Tell me, Secretary, tell me. . . ." My children would sing the words with me, only partially conscious of their meaning.

"Tell me, Secretary, tell me . . . have you ever seen the consul? Does he speak? Does he breathe? . . . I ask you for help and all you give me is paper! What's your name? Magda Sorel. Age? Thirty-three. Color of eyes? Color of hair? Single or married? Religion and race? Place of birth, father's name, mother's name. . . . Here is my answer: My name is woman! Age: still young. Color of hair: gray. Color of eyes: the color of tears. Occupation: waiting . . . *waiting, waiting!*"

I too was thirty-three years old that November in Lisbon. But my hair was still brown, my eyes not yet injured by tears. And I had Alex! Alex would get us out of any difficulty.

In reality Alex was at his wit's end. He telegraphed my brother to inform him how best to deal with the consul's telegram to Washington "for instructions." Maybe Guido could find someone (would it be absurd to try Max Ascoli again?) who might testify that we were not Fascists?

In reality, we did not expect a positive answer; we would have been grateful to receive any kind of answer. On November 9 Guido sent us some unexpected news: the American consul in Lisbon had asked his colleague in Florence to resolve the problem of our political identity!

Our first reaction was optimistic. What could come from Florence if not the truth? And yet "truth" was a complex word, its destiny inevitably at the mercy of a thousand circumstances, a thousand interpreters. Better give it some help. We too could write or telegraph to Florence and ask some friend for helpful material. There was an article published in the Fascist journal *Il Telegrafo* a few weeks before Alex left for France . . . that would really be perfect!

When we telegraphed Piero Calamandrei, professor of law at the University of Florence and a highly respected friend, asking for a clipping of the article, we did it with certain misgivings. Could the request get him into trouble? Maybe if it was written in professional style, like the inquiry of a client or a lawyer, danger would be avoided. And naturally our friend was free to ignore it. But he did not! The clipping arrived by return mail, and its contents were even more pertinent to our political ideas than we had remembered.

Dated August 18, 1938, it had been written on the appearance of the first issue of a law review edited by Alex and aimed at examining and commenting on the decisions of the Court of Tuscany. The *Telegrafo* article began by acknowledging that the work had been done with great skill and that the review could be of inestimable help both for lawyers and lay people. The review could, in fact, be considered admirable both for its aims and for the manner in which it pursued those aims, if . . . if its editor in chief were not a man with the name of Alessandro Pekelis! "Regrettably," the journalist of *Il Telegrafo* went on in a typically Italian convoluted style, "it is upsetting to see a law review, the purpose of which is to help judges of lower rank to know the Court and the Court to know itself, in the hands of Professor Pekelis, Russian by birth, Jewish by race, Zionist by choice, whose lack of warmth toward fascism (he is not a member of the Party according to the official list of members for the year 1938) is testified to by many manifestations of solidarity with everything that, in the past, has been hostile to the Revolution."

God bless you, Calamandrei! The article served its purpose. On the twentieth of November, after a ceremony that lasted five hours, we were officially granted American visas.

"We have them!" says the entry for that day in my diary, "we have them, with the red ribbon and everything! With so many uncertainties behind us, so much unknown before us . . . how can we be so happy?"

30 The Crossing

We had to stay in Lisbon for another month, forced to delay first by the lack of places on departing ships, and then by the postponement—week after week—of the sailing of our ship, the *Serpa Pinto*. For some reason my diary contains only one personal note for that entire period: Daniela's first scholastic success. She was promoted to a higher grade, called to the blackboard, and pointed out as an example to her comrades . . . and my mother's heart exulted! Except for this one subject, all the other entries are political in character.

Reading them now, I am fascinated by the passionate intensity of the diary's author and by her knowledge of events. The passion is a quality I can still share with her, because the years have contributed little, alas! to slow my reactions or govern my temperament. But that is all. I feel long before I understand, while she seems to understand everything! About the significance of Molotov's visit to Berlin, for example, or the presence of Weygand in Morocco, or about the effect of topography on the war in Greece. Most especially, she has news, suffers feelings, and agonizes about France.

When Jean Zain, ex–Minister of Instruction, was arrested and accused of "desertion in the presence of the enemy," she wrote that "all of Pétain's previous glory will be insufficient to cleanse his name of this awful stain"; when a demonstration of French students provoked the closing of the Sorbonne for three days, she greeted the dawn of the resistance; when Laval resigned and was arrested by order of the French government and then liberated by Abetz, the German ambassador, she welcomed with joy the defeat of the German policy of collaboration in France.

One day a whole page of the diary is dedicated to an article that appeared in the review *Gringoire*. Signed by Paul Lombard, it was written in the form of an open letter to the Jews and listed for their benefit all the reasons the French had for resentment toward them. First of all, they were guilty of having invaded all possible fields of activity, commercial, professional, or artistic. Moreover, they had failed to demonstrate a proper gratitude for the "hospitality" offered them. And finally, they had had the effrontery to transform the French into crusaders and had dragged them into the war! France had had enough of the Jews, M. Lombard concluded. He could no longer swallow their nomadism, nor the readiness they had shown to fold up the tents they had just finished unfolding!

In a militant tone the diary called him to order. "This is what *Gringoire* and its supporters cannot excuse: the capacity of the Jews to suffer and at the same time to set out again with new strength; their stubbornness; their scandalous tenacity in wanting to live and wanting to see their children live. They don't know, or prefer not to know, that thousands of us fall by the wayside for lack of physical strength, lack of courage, lack of money (yes, money)! They know nothing about the depth of our nostalgia, our regrets. But we won't be the ones to tell them! We can't allow ourselves to waste time in words. A pause, no matter how short, can condemn us forever. We have to go on. We have to restrain our tears, hide our anguish and bitterness deep in our hearts, grit our teeth. That will be our only revenge. That will be our only source of pride in the midst of so many humiliations. We raise our heads and go on. Let *Gringoire* and its readers think of us as ambitious, rich, indifferent. For this error we humbly thank God!"

There was, after all, more than one personal entry in my diary for the month of December 1940.

We left Lisbon on the afternoon of the twentieth-eighth, and the crossing took twelve days. I remember nothing of those days; I spent them all in the upper bunk of a small cabin, where I suffered violently and hopelessly from seasickness. Every now and then Alex came in; he told me the children were behaving like old sea dogs, that Mamulia had made some friends, and that the first-class passengers were as snobbish and arrogant as if they were on a cruise in peacetime. Or he suggested that I come out on deck for a breath of fresh air. I tried it once, only to be frightened to death by waves that seemed bigger than the ship and was almost swept away in the accursed tossing of the deck. I didn't go out again until the last day of the voyage.

I will never forget that day! It was a beautiful day, sunny, serene. The sea was so calm that it seemed unthinkable that waves could have disturbed it; and so blue that one never wanted to see another color. The ship proceeded without a tremor, calmly, and all the passengers were on deck basking in the winter sun and admiring the sea gulls. With their almost motionless wings, their whiteness that shone between sky and sea, they surrounded the ship like an honor guard. I remember that someone said, "Sea gulls! They foretell that land is near. We'll arrive soon." I remember thinking, how was it possible that they foretold the land; they seemed so supernatural, celestial. I hadn't yet seen them as I would some years later on the beach of Long Island, hovering over the asphalt streets with shells in their beaks. I hadn't yet seen them drop the shells and then dive down and seize the broken ones . . . or defend them, if perchance someone approached, with the warlike air of a lioness protecting her cubs. I would learn that the seagulls in reality belong to the earth and that, if they ever foretold anything, it was earthly passion and not heavenly bliss.

I remember little of the last hours of the crossing. I remember only that, when the formalities had been completed, it was too late to disembark and we spent the night at anchor at some point in the harbor.

I remember that from the deck of the *Serpa Pinto* we looked longingly at the shore opposite us and couldn't tear ourselves away to go to bed. I don't think I saw any of the famous sights: not the Statue of Liberty, nor the lighted skyscrapers, nor the city's skyline. Only the dark shore and along it the moving lights of a myriad of automobiles. I could not tear my eyes away, fascinated and frightened. Was it possible that those streets would become familiar to us too, that we would have a house, that we would return to it by car at the end of the day? Shivering with cold, I silently wished that the night ahead might last forever.

Part Two
December 1946 to August 1947

31 Five Years Later

When the telephone rang, it was not yet day. As usual when I was wakened suddenly, my heart started pounding. I felt for the lamp and my slippers in the darkness. The telephone rang again. Maybe it was Alex from the airport. I thought impatiently that it would wake the children and ran barefooted to pick up the receiver.

But the voice that answered was unknown and uncertain, a man's voice. I thought it was a mistake. But he was calling me, about Alex. My eyes were still half closed, and the words reached me through sleep as if through a fog. "A forced landing . . . we think the passengers are safe. . . ." The voice became more distinct, more confident, in a series of hurried and urgent questions. How old was he? Was he returning from the Zionist Congress in Basle? What party did he represent? How many children?

I answered mechanically: "Forty-five years old. Yes, he was coming from Basle. Delegate of Poale Zion, yes, Poale Zion, the Zionist Labor Party. Five children." As I spoke, the anguish of the past tense the man was using for his questions wrenched my heart. When I came to five children, the voice asked incredulously, "How many?" I repeated, "Five." He gasped and then controlled himself and said in a jolly tone, "A fine family!" I asked, "Is it certain that the passengers are all safe?" "That's what we think."

Then the voice was gone. It was finished. In a second, while I was asleep in my bed, everything was finished for me.

Waiting until late in the evening; the familiar sound of the bus that stopped in front of the house; running to meet him happily or with a dignified pout; going together to the kitchen at midnight to tell one another the events of the day; climbing the stairs arm in arm to our bedroom; walk softly, the children are sleeping; stop reading, turn the light off, I'm sleepy. All of it over, finished.

And that insistence that I read his briefs (because, if you want to, you give me a lot of good advice), and my lazy evasions (you know this is a bad time for me, I have to give the children their baths). And that stroll on Saturday through the streets of Larchmont, admiring the house we would like to have, with its garden a little bigger than ours and nearer to the sea. And the plans for the future (when we have American citizenship and admission to the bar . . . when Haim will go to school and I will have a half day free . . . when they'll be big enough to leave them with the maid and I'll accompany you on a trip sometimes).

A strange, remote voice on the telephone, and everything was over for me.

But I didn't take it in that morning. I dressed, combed my hair, put on lipstick and powder, telephoned friends, and the airline. No one could tell me anything definite (we'll let you know, wait, don't go away, we'll call you back), and all the time I thought that Schura was coming home (all the passengers are safe, we believe), and I would put that lying reporter in his place. I only had to keep calm, control my nerves, get the children up, prepare breakfast, send them out. I would tell him all about it, showing off a little, and he would be proud of me.

Instead the house was soon full of people. They were in the front hall, and the study, and the playroom. Why was I up, moving around? I should go into my bedroom and lie down. I didn't know yet that I would never again rest. I only knew that I wanted to be there, among the people and the confusion and the talk.

I told everyone very clearly and precisely that they must not worry about us because Alex had taken out an insurance policy just the day before leaving. Every now and then someone would come up to me, take me aside, and whisper: "These are delicate matters; they'll end up believing you're richer than you really are. Don't talk too much about these things with strangers." But I didn't know who the strangers were; they all seemed friends to me and I couldn't remain quiet.

Daniela was very efficient, much like her father (remember, Dan, if I die one day you will take care of Mamma, you're strong like me). But the younger girls cried, and the little boy, profoundly interested, asked: "Mamma, are you a widow now?"

Then it was evening, the end of Sabbath, the first of a long series of Sabbaths I would spend alone. Almost all the visitors had gone. On the mantle I had lighted a *yahrzeit* candle, and the trembling flame that illuminated Schura's photograph in fits and starts made him look alive and mysterious.

And then it was night, and then it was morning, and that was the first day.

32 Widow

Immediately, as I recall, people began to talk to me of travel. There was a lady who knew me slightly and had a house in Bermuda. She let me know that she would be very pleased to have me come there; she had so few interesting guests.

Travel in order to forget, just like in the novels after disappointments in love. But in the novels the heroine meets—on the most beautiful of melancholy voyages—a new and more worthy lover, or better yet the first, now seeking to please instead of being haughty. But I wouldn't meet Schura ever again, and certainly not in Bermuda. So I answered with a shrug of the shoulders, and the kind lady thought I was not very grateful and gave up trying to help me.

Then Anne, our old French nanny, took the matter up when my mother was already embarked from Europe to join me. "When Madame will be here, why don't you take a little trip to Italy?" This angered me again. A little trip, for what? What did I have to say to my friends and relatives, who would welcome me with open arms and tearful eyes? Nothing. Just the word "back" was hateful to me. Back, go back. To what? To the time before Schura, to school years, dancing parties, piano lessons, trips to the mountains. Sixteen years and my first silk dress, eighteen and graduation from the liceo, twenty and my first concert. Pretty, rich, respectable . . . She will make a good wife. The old ladies looked at me warmly and thought that maybe . . .

But I married a "Russian," a man they considered clever but who certainly "did not make a good impression": loud, aggressive, and to top it off, penniless. I married him with a bit of fear at the bottom of my heart (he wanted so many things of life, and so much work both from him and from me). I married him because I couldn't help it; he was so far above all the other men I had known, I couldn't let him go.

And now they wanted me to go back, to the years before, the Carla before. I hated them and I hated her, that's all there was to it.

So I stayed home. It always snowed or rained. I went out in the morning to shop, and almost immediately I was ashamed. People I knew pretended not to see me, fearful perhaps of talking to me. People I didn't know lowered their voices at my approach, with a knowing look. Others stopped. "Don't take it so hard," they said. "Crying doesn't help."

It grew dark early in the afternoon. The children were all at home, bored, fighting among themselves. Sometimes I played the piano to quiet them. I had dug up some French songs for the littlest girl; there was one, "The Wooden Horses," with an easy, commonplace, fairgrounds rhythm that made me physically ill.

After dinner I took the youngest ones to bed. Haim always wanted to chatter. He asked, "Will you get married again?" I tried to give my voice a reassuring and decisive sound: "No, of course not, don't worry." But his little face twisted in a grimace of dislike. "Too bad," he said crossly. "Why too bad?" "I would have a papà again, and you wouldn't cry anymore."

He didn't want me to leave the room; he held me with a thousand questions, always about death (where did I read that children between four and a half and six years are especially interested in the idea of death?). "Is Papà now with Nonna Rosa? And does he see everything we do? If I pray, maybe God will make him come

back right this minute?" "No, he can't." "Why not? He can do anything." And then suspiciously: "Mamma, do you believe in God?"
I beat about the bush: "Well . . . I believe, I don't know how to put
it, in something beautiful, and good. . . ." He interrupted me, anxious and implacable: "I want to know the truth. Do you believe?
Yes or no?" "Yes." Relieved, he sank down on his pillow.

33 Becoming the Man of the House

Then Mother arrived and a new life began, a strange new life in which I became the man of the house, going into the city to meet the lawyer or to White Plains to see the judge, and returning home tired in the evening, just in time to kiss the children and put them to bed. I found them very restful after a day of work and saw (as often happens with men) that Mother was a little unfair to them, too easily irritated or rigid; they were so good with a bit of patience and common sense.

Then summer arrived. Workmen took down the storm windows and put up screens. Ladders leaned against walls, buckets of water, hammers and nails. Haim motionless for hours watching the work. The gardener came to weed the garden, to bring the shriveled geraniums up from the basement in boxes to the early sun. We went back to living on the veranda. Sometimes in the evening friends from the old days dropped in. I got up to serve drinks. From the kitchen, I used to hear his voice louder than the others. "It's not polite," I told him after the guests had gone. "Give the others a chance to talk." He hugged me, saying, "Nag! Pedant! That's how I enjoy myself."

Now the guests can talk at their ease, but it seems they don't have anything to say. When they leave, I go to the kitchen to wash the glasses and empty the ashtrays. The drain is leaking, as before; there's the same moisture stain on the wall above the sink; if I turn,

I see my face in the mirror and I fix my hair; I turn out the light on his desk, the desk terribly in order.

Yes, I think it was the summer that convinced me, with that inexorable new beginning, that revival of trees and flowers. Under the radiant sun it was no longer possible to hide; our house became transparent, and so did those of our neighbors. One lived in the garden or the street. Every evening at six the bus from the station arrived bringing the men from work; at every stop a group of them emerged and spread out to the nearby houses. The happy shouts of children: "Daddy!"

When the letter arrived from my sister in Palestine with a plan for us to meet in Italy, I shook my head again, saying, "It's crazy, I don't want to, I can't," but inside I already knew I would go.

34 Goodbye, Again

The porter who helped me out of the cab at pier 88 spoke Italian. He told me I could entrust my luggage to him and would find it in my cabin on the ship. All the people around me were speaking Italian, as if we were arriving rather than departing. An unusual and colorful crowd: heavy middle-aged women in print dresses, arms full of purses, packages, and flowers; overheated men running busily in every direction, greeting one another, exhibiting a confidence that they must have had difficulty feeling.

I, for one, was frightened to death. Our ship was tied up next to the Queen Elizabeth, and it looked fearfully tiny. On board, I was at first unable to find my cabin, so thick was the crowd. While I tried to escape, worry about my cabin mates grew to the proportions of a childish nightmare. But here, seated on a bunk, was the sweetest and most fragile girl I could have hoped to find. Her questions, the discouraged look on her face, made me feel strong and protective. Together we went to look for our missing luggage and for deck chairs.

Around us the crowd was becoming frantic: people calling to one another, journalists snapping pictures, the Polish crew trying hard to direct traffic, and towering above us the Queen Elizabeth, indifferent and majestic.

Only much later did the loudspeaker begin to send out its urgent demands: "All visitors are requested to leave the ship," and in small groups, reluctantly, people began to obey.

Then, as the decks were still swarming with people leaning out and waving handkerchiefs and crying and calling good-bye, the first passengers were beginning to gather in the tiny second-class lounge and to exchange the first words and smiles. As if, while certain ties were loosening, they felt the need to form new ones for reassurance.

The large families sit heavily and close together around the same tables, the mothers worn out by the frenzied work of the last few days, the girls wary, smoothing their soft hair after recent visits to the beauty parlor. The father comes and goes wrapped up in the serious problems of getting everything arranged: luggage, deck chairs, a table for meals.

The "singles" are few; everyone seems to have found a companion already. My friend from the cabin has taken off her hat and a mass of blond curls frames her pale, gentle face. She seems very young, but I see she has a wedding ring on her finger and imagine that she's going to join her husband. No, the husband died two years ago in an automobile accident. She's going to study French and perfect her Arabic; her ambition is to work as a missionary among the Arabs.

I'm dumbfounded and don't quite understand. These are great matters for someone so fragile and in reply to so casual a question as mine, and the words are said in a simple, almost distracted tone. Around us they are speaking Italian. On our couch two women of a certain age are exchanging their histories in loud voices, and every now and then they smile at us, almost inviting us to take part in their conversation. One of them, fat and placid, with a dark dress brightened by showy gold pendants, has not been to Italy for twenty-seven years.

"You know how it is," she confides hesitantly, "you put it off and put it off . . . then the war came. . . . Even now, I don't know if I'm doing the right thing by going; I left my son at home alone. . . . He says he'll get along very well, but these men, you know . . ."

The other is a Waldensian, a strait-laced old woman with white hair pulled back in a bun filled with metal hairpins. She speaks with the stiff and refined manner of her people, and with an almost professional goodness and charity.

Hearing that Anne, my missionary friend, is intending to debark at Cannes, the fat one takes an interest.

"Are you French?" she asks solicitously.

"No," answers Anne with the brevity of the timid.

"Italian?"

"No."

"What, then?" as if all possibilities had been exhausted.

"I'm American."

"Oh," in utter surprise, and then warmly, reassuringly: "How nice!"

Perhaps I'm in a peculiar state of mind, but that "how nice" touches my heart. I easily intuit the past of that ordinary woman, landed twenty-seven years ago in America, years of uncertainty, of humiliations never completely swallowed. And suddenly the sense of security, of relaxation coming from the fact of finally belonging, on this ship, to a majority. Isn't it touching that, from the height of this so recent security, she instinctively hastens to reassure the outsider, the foreigner?

At the little bar one of the Polish waiters occupies himself behind his bottles. Some passengers begin to approach, the first cigarette, the first cigars. A young blond urges a trembling old woman solicitously, "Drink, Mamma, drink, it will do you good. And don't cry."

Suddenly a scream transfixes us all. It's a tall, elegant, well-preserved lady with a heavy stomach, putting her hands to her head. "For the love of God!" she cries, and we all ask ourselves what could have happened. "For the love of God, don't shake a martini!"

We sit down again, slightly embarrassed but reassured, without understanding at all what happened. The Polish barman is surely most embarrassed of all as he continues to shake his cocktail with conviction and smiles a stupid, innocuous smile.

Now the lady is really infuriated. She gets up and her bracelets rattle menacingly up and down her thick, bare arms. She snatches the bottle from the barman repeating her indignant, "Don't shake a martini," and then thrusts it back into his hands leaving him more than ever confounded. "Just forget it," she exclaims unhappily, shrugging her shoulders and seeming to call upon all of us as witnesses of this terrible event. Then she sits down with her martini glass shaking in her fingers and nervously lights a cigarette.

We have stopped talking; only here and there a cough. Then the conversation begins again quietly.

Beneath us the floor begins to move. I want to go above to watch and be alone, but I don't know where to go and I'm still afraid, afraid to see New York and familiar things drop inexorably into the distance.

I should have a newspaper somewhere. Here it is in the pocket of my jacket. But it's not a newspaper; it's a comic book, one of the familiar, silly "Donald Ducks" that circulate in the house. Now I understand what Haim wanted when he ran after me at the last minute.

Ciao, Haim. Ciao, my little ones.

35 The Purser and
Mrs. Hutchinson

At dinner time we're already at sea.

Anne and I sit at a little round table with an elderly lady whose hair is carefully protected in a white net. Her name is Mrs. Hutchinson, and she tells us she is going to Italy to study.

"You probably know my teacher, Sig. Lanfranconi; he's the one who built that immense arch in one of the big squares of Milan. You don't know him? You never heard of him? How odd!"

I see that the lady is not only disappointed but also a little suspicious. Who knows, perhaps I am only pretending to have been born in Italy. In response to her stare I almost begin to blush, and I'm greatly relieved when the purser asks permission to sit at our table.

He is one of the few Italians in the crew, tall, thin, with gray hair and glasses and a certain air of distinction. He sits down and asks if all is well with us and if we need anything. Anne smiles without answering; Mrs Hutchinson is happy to have someone to tell of the various mishaps that have occurred. Milk, for example. Perhaps the purser could get her some milk; she is used to drinking it every day, and the Polish waiter seems not to understand. Of course, right away. The purser is delighted to put on a show with the hybrid German waiter, which results in the miraculous appearance of milk on the table. Mrs. Hutchinson drinks and relaxes.

At this hour my children are also eating. All except Simona, who is on her way to camp in Vermont. Everything has surely gone well;

Mother has promised to talk to the driver. But I should have asked
her to telegraph me with news. Nonsense, it would have just been
another five dollars wasted.

The purser and Mrs. Hutchinson go on talking with the impersonal politeness of worldly people. "May I pour you some water?
Should I ask them to bring another portion of dessert?" Above the
clinking of silverware, the chatter of table companions, and the
steady racket of the orchestra, their words reach me half audibly
and I have stopped trying to follow them.

But I catch one suddenly that makes me prick up my ears. Trieste. The purser is talking of the Yugoslavs and Dalmatia. He says
that he cannot go back to his home in Dubrovnik; he would be
killed. He describes the pain and bitterness of the Italians there
(the wars of independence, so much suffering, and now we're back
at the beginning, even worse off than before; a hundred times better the Austrians than the Yugoslavs). Aroused, his banal features
assume an unexpected nobility.

Mrs. Hutchinson conscientiously cuts her slice of veal and seems
wholly unprepared to deal right off with such subjects. Uncertain,
she makes vague objections.

"You see, everyone looks at things, how should I say, from the
point of view of going back to his own home." She takes a sip of
milk and hastily adds important words. "One must look at things
from a historical point of view. Don't you think so?"

Who knows what history is according to her? And if it really is
the result of these little, individual states of mind, these infinite
personal problems?

I ask what is happening in Trieste.

"They came, you understand." The purser drops into Italian to
unburden himself better. "And how they came! But by God's will
the Allies chased them out after forty days."

His voice became fearful like that of a child frightened by rob-
bers.

"They said they'll come back, it's just a question of time, but
they'll come back. You see, Madame," he speaks to Mrs. Hutchin-

son in a persuasive tone of voice, "you Americans have done so much good in the world." He is reminded by the old lady's distracted look that she doesn't understand Italian, and he continues in his clear, slightly awkward English. "You have helped the whole world so much. Don't abandon us now; don't abandon Trieste. Otherwise they will return. And the peace treaty, you see, it should have been signed immediately. Immediately, while your troops were still in Europe. Look at the Russians. They have understood and are not going away!"

Again Mrs. Hutchinson smiles rather enigmatically from her coffee cup.

"We have too good a character, you see," she tries to explain. "When the fighting is over, we like to go back to our daily business and give our enemies a pat on the back. We're real sports, aren't we?"

I don't know if the purser understood this reply. He shakes his head in discouragement.

"Trieste," he says by way of conclusion, "Trieste will be the spark of the third world war!"

Through the porthole I see the line of the horizon slowly fall and then rise.

I feel a sort of discomfort. I look at Anne. "What do you say we go straight to bed?"

The purser holds Mrs. Hutchinson's chair, then ours, bows, and is the last to leave.

36 Seasickness

I never had a weakness for Gertrude Stein or, to tell the truth, for Joyce either. Yet I think about them constantly during these tumultuous days. It seems to me only that urgent, breathless style could render this accumulation of elements that takes one's breath away.

They say that in first class there are only a few dozen passengers and an immense lounge. But in second and third there are several hundred of us, and the two small lounges put together can hold fifty, more or less. Thus at all hours and in all sorts of weather we are always outside and on the minuscule open spaces of poop and prow the deck chairs are tangled like the threads of a strange, coarse cloth. We're stretched out en masse; the wind sweeps us and the sun dazzles us. Nauseating smells come from the kitchen. Every now and then a contorted face asks, "May I?" an elbow pokes into our ribs, a foot stumbles between our legs, and finally two convulsive hands manage to catch hold of the railing. Fat, pimpled girls strut about in light colored pants; mothers of families who have long dreamed of these restful days lie dazed with suffering; youths in sport shirts try the ping pong table. Buried in the crowd, in the shelter of a smokestack, a little nun, enervated by seasickness, looks like a wax doll in the window of a religious goods shop. One cannot look at the sea, or think, or suffer alone; there's no room for any of us; there's only room for the herd. Calls mingle above our heads; right and left, conversations run together.

A puff of cigar smoke ("and now, you understand, I've sold the business"); a whiff of smelling salts ("I tell you, you're all right, Sister Rosa, get up, get up, we'll be arriving soon"); the sweetish odor of suntan oil ("what really gets me is the price they're making me pay for a crossing like this"); the tinkling of a glass on a tray ("I worked for more than fifty years, now I want to buy me a house and sit in the garden under a fig tree").

And the loudspeaker, stronger than all the rest, that deafens with its announcements to the passengers. And the gramophone that croaks old Italian songs. And in the evening, the tables of the dining room up against the wall, bingo, rhumbas, movies. And at night, in the too small and too crowded cabins, fiddling with the fans, resignation to the open door on the corridor, the discomfort of light in the eyes, and finally sleep, oppressive and restless.

How many days? One or ten, they were all the same. Where I came from, where I was going, were not at all clear. On the map hung on the wall, the little flag that marked our progress never seemed to move. According to the weather or the sea, people repeated vague phrases to one another: "This is the gulf stream; tomorrow it will be calmer." Or: "It's nothing, it's nothing. They call it the Biscay wind. It only lasts for two days."

And then one evening against that infinite gray a vague line was traced, half blended with the sea. And that night, on both sides of the ship, rows of lights were lit. And the next morning a calm, blue, limpid sea, and the Spanish coast very near, reddish, with snowy mountains and tiny, white villages at the base of hills.

As if at the touch of a magic wand, what had seemed to be a small emigrant ship became a tourist yacht. Swimming pools appeared and bathers; white hats with visors and varicolored scarves; shorts and bathing suits.

The gate to the first class deck opened benevolently, and benevolently people looked into one another's faces and smiled. Only the lovers, who had triumphed, indifferent, over the nightmare of the preceding days, now walked around uncertainly or stopped in corners holding hands silently: they were afraid of arriving.

37 It's Not So Simple

Cannes, our first stop, is still some hours away. I, too, like the young lovers, am not ready to debark. To forget my anxiety, I join a group of people talking quietly in the sun.

There is a university professor of Italian origin, a young scholar of antiquities on his way to save the treasures of Europe, an important businessman in advertising, a college teacher and a radio journalist who is traveling in order to learn about Tito and the state of Yugoslavia.

We watch the crowd below gathering in the enjoyment of a sense of well-being from the sun and the imminence of arrival, and ask one another what will come of the meeting between these Italian Americans and the country from which they have been absent for so many years.

"I'm afraid," the old professor says as he carefully cleans the lenses of his glasses.

"Afraid of what?" the others ask, almost in chorus.

"I don't know. Of their return. They have thought about it too much and have formed too many illusions."

"I don't understand," the teacher interrupts. "If they had to leave, and for the most part, from what I've heard, in order to look for bread, they won't have many illusions."

"That doesn't matter, it doesn't matter. Each of us has to give a name to our own unhappiness, to tell ourselves: if it weren't for this, I would be happy. And to think that somewhere there's a remedy, a sort of magic formula to cure our own particular condition. Which can take, mind you, the most varied forms, sometimes just a phrase or a slogan, sometimes a person or a country."

"How's that? No, excuse me, I don't understand." This time it is the journalist who interrupts with a slightly ironic smile. "Nevertheless, it's simple," the professor continues with mild insistence. "For these people, for example, Italy has become, through distance and imagination, something miraculous, infinitely sweet, familiar, and protective. If it rains, ah, the Italian sunshine; if someone is rude to you, ah, Italian courtesy; if a son wants to get married too soon, ah, Italian women. Now they expect to take hold of the dream . . ."

Someone says, "It will be enough if the Fascists don't come back. . . ."

"The Fascists come back?" The professor doesn't know whether to be surprised or angry. "You Americans are sometimes really incredible. What do you think these people here are now, liberals? They're Fascists, I'm sorry to say, Fascist to the marrow. It seems a paradox, but after having lived for twenty years in Mussolini's Italy, do you know where I met the first real Fascist? Not in Italy, but right here in America, when I got off the ship."

"Go on, professor," the correspondent protests irritatedly. "Don't exaggerate. You'll end by saying there were never any Fascists in Italy, and never any Nazis in Germany. Who then made all this mess? Did we dream it all?"

"Don't get upset, Signora; you're right also. Fascism is too complex a phenomenon to be exhausted in a definition or a paradox. But I assure you that there is a part of the truth in my point of view. How can I tell you: in an Italian living room before the war it would have been in bad taste to speak well of fascism."

"But then, go on . . ."

"You're right, Signora, you're right. I know what you're going to say. It was shameful to have put up with, to have smiled, to have ignored. . . . But it remains a fact that those who believed in it, in fascism, were very few. . . ."

"And the Italian Americans, then? Who could have taught it to them, according to you? Did they learn it from the letters they got from home?"

"From letters? Please, don't make me laugh. From the letters of Neapolitan peasants? They learned it from propaganda, first of all: the radio, the trips for Italians abroad, the clubs—all of it well done, have no doubts, according to the rules. From propaganda and from you Americans."

"What next! We taught fascism to the Italians? Professor, don't ruin the sun and the sea."

"Mah! Signora, as you wish. When you put your head in the sand like the ostriches, it means you'll pull it out in the next war! You want to know how you pushed these Italian immigrants toward fascism? By beginning to respect them only when Italy was Fascist, when Balbo made his transatlantic flight, for example. Before that they were nothing, dirt, at the bottom of the social scale. From that time on they became people. And then they too began to look with respect at those who had restored their halo. They, too, believed in the Empire. . . . But who can tell what they will find and what they will make of it. . . ."

"If it's as you say," the student of art history smiled with interest through his glasses, "if it's as you say, now they'll open their eyes. They'll see the ruin that fascism brought to Italy, the evil done by the Germans . . . they'll understand, they'll go back to America with a feeling of gratitude . . . no?"

"Yes, of course," the professor says, giving a start. "Or rather, let's hope so . . . I'm afraid that it's not so simple. . . ."

No, it's not so simple. Anne gets up with her French book; she hasn't done her exercises today. When she has left, the correspondent asks who she is and comments, "Pretty!" I explain. I'm a little proud of Anne, I don't know why. Perhaps because she shows me that it's possible to be very unfortunate and yet draw strength from it, and then who knows, one day I too. . . . But the journalist laughs loudly: "Why the Arabs, good God? I wouldn't be surprised if what she's looking for is a handsome Arab husband!"

She goes away laughing, to take a walk up and down the deck before dinner.

Who knows why she's going to interview Tito? How will she be able to understand Tito and enlighten us ordinary folk on the subject, if she can't understand Anne?

38 Homecoming

We arrived at Cannes early in the morning. A launch came from the shore to take off the passengers landing in France; we didn't even know that we had such beautiful people on board.

Anne, too, departed, holding tight to a card with the address of her friends in Paris. "Imagine, what if I don't find anyone in Nice?" and she smiled nervously. "Do you think my French is good enough to get me to Paris?"

The beach was gray and deserted. The massive row of immense hotels with their shutters still closed looked like assembly plants or prisons more than worldly gathering places. On the promenade the carts of the streetsweepers stood open waiting.

Almost all the passengers were awake by then. They held on to the railings, looked with sleepy eyes at the Côte d'Azur, and repeated respectfully, "How beautiful!"

Then the ship started out again, and we settled down to wait. There was nothing else we could do; we were too nervous to talk or read. I had written that no one should take the trouble to come and meet me; I would go alone to Florence. Who knows if they had taken me seriously! Was it possible that I would find no one in Genoa? And my sister? Better not think about it! Perhaps she was still in Palestine or at sea.

And then someone said, "Here we are." And again, vague but unmistakable, we saw the coast. Genoa, the last Italian city when

I was leaving nine years before with the three children. At the frontier the Fascist customs officers did not have a brutal manner, but they searched through everything, even the baby's diapers, and I felt my heart beating. So many things had been told us. About people who had been arrested, for example, on the pretext of money being found on them. But everything had gone smoothly for us. And at the first French station Alex was waiting, alone at night. Before boarding our train, he had stopped for an instant with his hands to his mouth, perhaps to thank God. It had been a moment of happiness, at the turning point between the anguish of departure and the unknown that awaited us. Perhaps that's all we have a right to: moments. Who had put into our heads the idea of wanting more? Maybe when we understand this, we'll be at peace.

Now the houses can be made out on the hillside. Somewhere all the way at the top, there must be a hotel with long corridors, and verandas facing the sea, and green bathrooms. I think it was called Miramare. We went there on our honeymoon and spent whole mornings on the terrace of our room. Except that Alex didn't yet know yet that I'm unhappy if I don't have my breakfast as soon as I get up in the morning; he never called for it, and I didn't dare ask him to.

We're not moving, waiting for the pilot. Here and there small boats of all kinds approach and move away again. Someone murmurs, "Contraband cigarettes." How is it that everyone knows about it? Yet nothing happens. Finally, the pilot jumps from a launch and climbs quickly up a rope ladder.

Now we're really at the entrance to the port. A tiny beach on one side is swarming with bathers. Trams are bowling along the corniche. Ships' hulls not completely submerged, we proceed cautiously through the rusted wreckage. On a wall in large black letters the first Italian words: SMOKING PROHIBITED. Impersonal houses crowded on the hill and the first awful craters. "Look," someone says, "the bombs." "What bombs?" a curious child asks. "What bombs do you suppose? Ours, stupid."

There are precarious houses, and one can see the insides of rooms with the paper hanging from the walls; an old iron sink remains oddly balanced in a corner. Now we are truly stopped, at rest in the middle of the port, we don't know why.

We're all on deck, handbags tightly in hand, coats on our arms, silent and tense before those last few interminable meters. Suddenly, very near, the sounds of a festive march burst out. It's the ship's orchestra standing on the second class deck. I want to stop my ears; I try desperately to think where this has already happened to me. But maybe it hasn't happened to me; maybe it's only the background music from old French movies. *Pépé le Moko* and the player piano that's set off at the moment of the crime and drowns out everything with its vulgar, triumphant, inexorable rhythm.

We go forward by centimeters. The wharf is black with people. As long as they don't tumble into the water! Now we're so close we can almost make them out one by one. Stretched out from the railing in the effort to recognize our own, we're still united by a thread.

"Do you see that one, that little boy dressed in blue?" The voice shakes: "It's my brother's little boy." And then a shout goes up: "O Giovanni-i! It's me, Giovanni-i!" We're docking, just touching the wharf. My heart stops. Right here, a few meters from me, I can almost touch him, it's Alex's brother. He's come to meet me after all; I won't be all alone, I have someone to call to. I scream "Brasha!" at the top of my lungs.

What's happening? Doesn't he hear me? Why then is he looking me right in the face? Why doesn't he make a gesture of greeting, or something of the kind. Brasha, it's me. No, now he's looking away. Good God, he hasn't recognized me; I come back and they don't recognize me anymore.

I lean back against a column. People are pushing me away from the precious place in the first row that I had been guarding all day for this moment. Past the people in front of me I look into the sea of unknown faces, too upset at first to notice a tender, familiar smile.

Still it touched something in me because I remember it and look for it again. Where is it? There. It's a woman leaning against the railing; she doesn't call, she doesn't gesticulate like the others. She stands still and looks at me with a fixed, somewhat mournful smile. Who is it? I'm in despair, who is it? Yes, yes, I know, it's Aunt Lilla. Is it really her? And did she recognize me? Is that smile really for me? There's so much pity in that smile and so much sadness, I want it for me. I raise my hand slowly, slowly; maybe I'm mistaken, I'm afraid. She too raises her hand. Someone pushes me aside yelling. It doesn't matter. The gangplank goes down; people hurl themselves at it furiously; the porters first, let the porters get off! It doesn't matter; I can lean back and cry. I'm home at last.

39 Tuscany and Luciana

Lilla and I decide to spend the night in Genoa and leave the next morning, she for Rome, I for Florence.

We take a taxi to the hotel: a sense of mortal danger as we go careening madly through the narrow, crowded streets, slipping in behind a wagon, the driver desperately blowing his horn. We can only follow his exploits as if participating in a drama, and we draw a sigh of relief at the door of the hotel, as if to say, "What luck, we've made it!"

I look down from the window at the swarming piazza, a round one, it's been so long. . . . I hadn't been aware of missing the piazzas. Trucks . . . several small ones, open, empty; people run and climb in, filling them to the brim, and the overflow hang outside in bunches. And the trucks speed away. Songs. They're singing: "Little girl, *garibaldina*, tra la la, you're a star to us poor grunts."

The Fascist hymns are abolished, and there has been no time or energy yet for a new music. So they go back all at once to the songs of twenty years ago.

On the train to Florence I can't tear myself away from the window. On the hills the pale green of the olives alternates with the dark of the cypresses; in the gardens the oleanders are all in bloom. The ruins are already being covered with green, becoming part of the landscape.

The desolate, half-wrecked stations contrast with the glorious countryside everywhere, and the profusion of flowers from the hills to the sea. But they hardly interrupt my pleasure, almost as if man in his decline gives way, without bitterness, to nature. A girl flaunting strange dress (one shoulder bare, the other sheathed all the way to the wrist) sits up straight in order not to muss herself; I remember hearing her say that she was traveling on a mission. It would be thrilling to see her suddenly disappear as a result of the machinations of a bald man with a hard face and a monocle fixed in his eye. But, alas, nothing happens except that his face contracts suddenly into the rhythmic chewing of gum.

Next to the window two dirty priests mumble litanies from their wrinkled little books.

An old woman in a blue silk smock sits uncomfortably with her hands in her lap; they are big, rough, knotted hands that contrast with her slim body and seem not to belong to her. At her sides are a man and woman who seem vaguely familiar to me. "Mamma, are you comfortable like that?" Mamma is too much in shock to understand or answer. She only raises her gray head timidly toward her daughter-in-law's hat, a blue hat dripping with cherries. In the entire car there are only three women with hats. But of course I know them; they were on the ship, too, that's why, and only the Americans are wearing hats.

The man smiles at me. "We're in Italy, Signora! Are you also going back on the same ship September 16?"

Going back? I don't want to go back; I don't want this to be a parenthesis that ends and cuts me off from these flowers and that sea forever.

Pisa, Viareggio. My sister will be in Florence; so I was told, it was certain. I had seen her last in Paris, nine years before; I left for the mountains, since one of the little girls had been sick and had to recuperate there. Then came the sensational announcement of the Russo-German pact; that meant war, and I returned posthaste. But Luciana had already gone to Palestine.

We've left the sea; now it's just country and hills and cattle and piles of straw. When I was a child I thought that I would like to see the straw being cut some day. I thought: "It must be cut by a giant with a great big knife." I thought: "They look like the beginnings of a cake."

Empoli. Such familiar names that it seemed I had never stopped pronouncing them. The Tuscan countryside. I'm in the Tuscan countryside. Over there is Florence and up above it is Fiesole. What's different about it? It's like always. And those houses are already the suburbs. The level crossing, I recognize it: it's Cascine. And this is the station. My God, it can't be; on this very platform Luciana is waiting. In a minute I'll see her; in a minute her face will be familiar to me again. Stop the train for just a minute, I'm not ready, I don't want to. But the train is already stopped; the people are getting off, hugging one another. I hear my name called. Luciana's face is contorted, how odd, and she's not alone. Three, four people are with her, friends, relatives. She's crying. "Don't cry," I say judiciously. "I'm happy, don't you see? Very happy." She hugs me and the others hug me; maybe I should take off my hat, it's ludicrous to go around with a hat.

We walk in a group in the familiar station. Luciana explains to me that she is already settled in a friend's house and there's a bed ready for me.

"No, no!" I cry in horror. "Thanks, but I don't want to. I want to go to a hotel." I must have cried out too loudly because my brother-in-law Mario says reassuringly, "Do just as you wish, and only go where you like." He talks to me as one talks to children and mad people, in a loud and firm voice. And like them I calm down.

It's a nice hotel, right on the river, and a nice room, a room where I can be alone.

40 You and Your War!

I am definitely settled in the hotel to the great indignation of my relatives. They can't understand how I can bear it. "If I had to come back after nine years and live in a hotel," one of them said to me, "I would feel terribly bad. It would really depress me." Nevertheless, I now understand that this is absolutely the only way for me to come back. Looking at things from the outside, with a certain detachment. Knowing, without consciously thinking about it, that at one time Alex and I fell in love here, we had a home and work and recreation.

Besides, from the very first moment when I opened the window on the Lungarno, I wanted passionately to stay in this particular room. The river glistening under the sun, and the men intent on their fishing, their legs deep in the water, and the line of the hills sharp against the sky. The walls on the opposite side of the river are covered with slogans: MONARCHY IS LIBERTY, LONG LIVE THE CUCKOLD KING! NO FREEDOM WITH PRIESTS IN GOVERNMENT. The dripping paint of the huge black letters stands out against the white like a page in a messy child's homework. There is almost no traffic on the Lungarno. A constant flow of bicycles, few automobiles and some motorcycles. It must be the latter that make such a terrible noise, which is somehow related to the saving of gasoline, I've been told. However, it doesn't matter. At night, going to bed, I can still hear the people singing from the river below, and I wake early in the morning with the sound of horses' hooves on the pavement. The peasants come to the city in their little automobiles with provisions for the day. It's still dark and lights are on here and there, but a few men are already fishing, and the cypresses begin their fantastic embroidery work against the sky.

I rise early but don't manage to get dressed. I relish the pleasure of being on terra firma and having within reach so many dear ones. When the man knocks to clean the room, I'm always there with the newspapers on my knees, and the poor fellow starts to withdraw in fright.

"Come in, come in, you don't bother me."

"May I? I'll be quick, Signora, thank you." And he sets to work, while I try to be in his way as little as possible.

"The signora comes from America, right? You can tell by the suitcases! How lucky, how lucky! You didn't have to go through what we went through here!"

For him it began with the campaign in Greece, he tells me with a sort of pride. Was it terrible? No, not so terrible.

I'm astounded! Hadn't it been a crushing and chaotic defeat, with huge losses?

"Beh, it wasn't exactly like that. Sure, we retreated, but not because we had such big losses. The matter, you see, was this. . . ." He leans on his broom with one arm and gesticulates sententiously with the other. "Common soldiers and officers, you see, got along pretty well. And when we began to go home on leave and saw the same people who had preached war having a good time on the home front, then we got smart and decided to get out of that mess any way we could . . ."

"What could you do?"

"Oh, you'd be surprised at the things you can do to save your skin! One by one we made out we were sick, and with the help of some decent doctor we really managed to get better. Once you were in the hospital the worst was over, you had it made. One way or another you could stay there indefinitely. . . ."

I'm a little out of practice, I'm afraid, concerning the means of passive resistance, and I can't persuade myself of the fact that, while a bloody expedition was under way in Greece, the Italian government could pay for the food and lodging of deserters from its army. But he seems quite sure of what he's saying, and when a maid comes in to make the bed, he hurries to finish, afraid of being deprived of the climax of his speech.

"When my turn came," he says, starting to sweep again, "when my turn came to go home on leave (and keep in mind that my Company had gone down from a hundred and forty to sixty men), I asked myself: why should I be more stupid than the others?"

As might have been foreseen, the maid seized the chance of having a new audience.

"You and your war!" She pushes him aside with an impatient gesture. "To be on a battlefield is nothing! The enemy attack and you counterattack. So what? But to be in your house, trapped, as we were . . ." Trembling and rapidly making the sign of the cross at the memory, she turns to me. "If you had seen this place, Signora! And the Germans telling us we had to evacuate the city, but to leave everything just as it was because it was only a precautionary measure. God help us with their precautions! Who would see anything again? As soon as we were gone, they came, the Fascists and the Germans, and they took everything they could and blew the rest up."

Later on, going out with Luciana, I can see for myself what they blew up. I ask her to follow the Lungarno, and as we walk arm in arm under the fiery sun, she reminds me of a Florentine proverb: Only donkeys and Englishmen go out in the midday sun. She's right; every sensible Italian avoids the sun in July and looks for the shelter of the narrow, shady streets between the ancient buildings. But I've been deprived of this sun for so long that I can't give it up right away. Besides, it seems that the heat doesn't bother me at all. I must have stored up enough cold and shade to last me for a while.

The Santa Trinità bridge no longer exists, but somehow, I don't know why, it hurts me less than the Ponte Vecchio, which had been formally respected. In fact, in a certain sense its whole meaning has been distorted and mocked. One can see now that it does not have an independent existence (perhaps it never had any architectural beauty) and that part of its significance came from the old houses on one side that stuck out above the water, and from the little church and shops on the other side. Now at both ends there is nothing but rubble, clean rubble, neat and well swept. The bridge, all alone in the middle, with its ancient jewelry shops intact, looks like an old dusty toy about to fall to pieces.

A passing woman, all bent to one side by a heavy bundle under one arm, points to the Santa Trinità bridge with a gesture of her shoulder. "They did it out of spite! It didn't do them any good. And half an hour later the English put up a bridge of boats. . . . I tell you, out of spite . . ." And she waved her free fist in the air threateningly.

I couldn't help remembering her words along with others, spoken by different people in different circumstances, but with the same feeling. And I had to ask myself if these tragic ruins couldn't have a mysterious, positive aspect. In fact, the Florentines seem to be even more sensitive to the damage to their monuments than to the harm suffered by their population. As if, having learned from time immemorial to accept man's death, they were wholly unprepared to face it in works of art. So that if some message must come to humanity by means of war and about war from Florence, it must come through its ruins. That morning, however, I could see no hope in those ruins. We departed hastily from the bridge as from open wounds.

41 The Terrace Is Empty

We strolled toward the center of the city, stopping from time to time to greet someone. I had forgotten how things are done in a small city and that to go out on errands is like paying visits. At first I found these meetings exciting ("it's fantastic that you're here again, stay for a long time, you must come and see us, we have loads of things to tell you"). But then the exchanges become less superficial, more personal, and unexpectedly they aren't light-hearted anymore, nor even an adventure.

The first is a friend of Alex's, a lawyer, and the joy of our first greetings end quickly. "Yes, we're working again. I'm on my way to court right now. But I'm quite willing to admit, our hearts aren't in it. Nothing seems to make sense. We've got rid of a dictatorship, and what's facing us now? A choice between two others: communism or the church! As a Catholic I shouldn't be concerned, but you know me: "a free church in a free state." The idea of priests in the government scares me to death! Not to mention the Fascists, many of whom have got off scot free, after all. You don't know, you've just arrived. Just wait and see. The problem with this country of ours is that no one is completely a bandit or completely a saint. So that every single Fascist around us has some tiny good action to his credit. Either they warned a Jew of a raid about to take place, or they passed some valuable information to the English army, or God knows what else. And the Allies swallow it all! As if those irrelevant gestures at the last minute could redeem a whole shameful past."

A little further on, another old friend, Nino. "You remember," he asks us, "how proud I was of avoiding military service because of my bad eyesight? No, I've forgotten that you couldn't remember because you left before the war. Well, let me tell you, if there was another war, I'd immediately volunteer! Death on the battlefield? So be it, pazienza! War is nothing. After all, what can happen to an individual? A bomb and you're dead. Or you can counterattack. But to live as a civilian, in this war inside the war! A nightmare, I tell you; you always have to run away and hide. The airplanes over our heads, and even worse, the Germans all around us. . . . No, it wasn't only the Jews, everyone, all of us were hunted: one because of his draft status, another because they wanted him for work in Germany. Believe me, we were all in danger. A friend of mine in Milan (it's true she was Jewish) didn't get undressed for nine months. When she heard of the liberation, what do you think she did? She put on her nightgown, that's what! Oh, I could talk about the Germans for days on end. I wish someone would tell the Americans about them; they seem to like them a lot. Oh yes, it's really like that. You ought to hear the American soldiers coming from Germany! I know all about it! They say they're so well behaved, honest, disciplined, that sort of thing. You're an American now. Tell them. They don't know that the German has two faces!"

Nino leaves us, enraged at the Germans, the Americans, and me, I fear. Instinctively we resume our walk at a faster pace, crossing the Piazza del Duomo and heading toward Via Cavour, far from the center of the city. But we're destined to have another encounter.

Someone takes hold of Luciana's hand from behind, a tiny, wrinkled, old woman. It's the serving woman of a friend who was deported to Germany at the age of eighty-four. She holds Luciana's hand and cries.

"How often I thought of you, Signora *mia!* And poor Signora Daria, God rest her soul; she always spoke of you and the children. She always had the picture of your older ones on her chest of drawers. What a terrible thing, Signora mia. I can never forget that day; I dream about it at night. Because, you see, the police had warned us. There was a man there who knew us, a very nice man. And he told us, 'Go away, hide yourselves, they're going to make a round-up.' But how can you go away from home, just like that? And go where? And then the good-hearted signora didn't believe in the danger. All right, she said, I'm Jewish. But I'm so old. What do you think the Germans will do to an old woman like me? Do you know what I'll do? Bolt the door, and that's that. But the bolt, Signora, didn't last a minute. The trucks were downstairs. Even the neighbors heard her screams."

Luciana grips my arm. "Now," she says firmly, "we take a carriage; I'm tired." I follow her quietly, with gratitude.

The creaking of the carriage on the pavement is pleasant, and so is that sudden jolt when the wheels go over the tram rails. It's like returning home together, so many years ago, when neither of us was married yet. How good everything was! What did we think about then? I remember that I thought a lot about books, or rather novels, but—let's be clear—novels of the highest class: Tolstoy, Stendhal, things like that. In those years I devoured them and then noted the titles conscientiously in a certain shiny, black notebook. Sometimes, if I was in the mood, I even added my equally conscientious comments.

And right after the books, the dresses. These also mattered a great deal to me, and acquiring them at that time demanded not a little sacrifice. It was necessary to go round from one shop to another for the material, then to choose the style from one of the various albums, and finally to try on, try on, try on. . . from the seamstress to the dressmaker, there was no end to it. We did the errands as a group: my mother, Luciana, and I; Mother vigorously at the head, omnipotent, I more inclined to sacrifice (wanting to look attractive . . .), Luciana reluctant.

And the dances, how I loved them! Of all my passions, as I recall, the least fervent was perhaps music, to which I devoted an enormous amount of time. Determined to get my degree with the highest grades, I sat at the piano up to four or five hours a day. Yes, I remember, the degree was very important.

Our carriage makes its way slowly through the streets. I don't know why Luciana has such an embarrassed air and why she's talking so fast, as if she wants to distract me from something. What is it? Oh yes, I see, we're approaching the house where I once lived, in which the children were born. Soon I'll see the terrace over the garden where the children played and we had dinner in the evening; the garden full of geraniums and with a big gardenia that Sandro gave me every year for my birthday. When the children were in bed, I waited out there in the dark until he came out of his study. Sometimes it was very late, the clients refused to leave, and I fell asleep on the chaise longue. He woke me with a kiss, but I complained all the same. I said, "I'm certain there's not another woman in all Florence who waits so late for her husband." He always answered, "On the other hand, I happen to know three. The wives of the three who just left."

We're almost there; I pretend to Luciana that I'm listening to her, and at the right moment I will turn quickly and see the terrace, the geraniums, the big, white gardenia, and Sandro, I'll see Sandro.

It's just an instant. But I have time to see that the terrace is empty; there are broken rods in the railing and a pile of bricks in a corner.

Next to me, Luciana has stopped talking.

42 Hero or Pig?

We had dinner with our cousins, but not in their house; that had been sold some years before at the beginning of the racial campaign, in the fear that otherwise it would be confiscated. Now they live with a friend, a lady of eighty years, in a house crammed with old, black furniture, with a little courtyard in back completely filled by an immense, shady fig tree.

"I'm sorry, but we have to eat quickly," said one of the girls. "Some people are coming after dinner." She looked at us timidly and explained that on the way back from work she had met two or three friends in common. "What do you want? By now everybody knows that you're here; they ask where they can see you; if I didn't tell them it would look as though I wanted to keep it a secret."

We forgive her, eat hurriedly, and clear the table. Soon the dining room is full of people, all around the table, under the silk lampshade with hanging tassels. The lady of the house is in a corner sewing.

There are various women. Gianna, who has not married during these years, has lost her parents and continues to live with two faithful maids; she embroiders, reads, plays the piano. And Raffaela, elegant as always, hair streaked with gray, skin well cared for, nails perfect. There's a friend of my brother-in-law, a man of forty, bachelor, Aryan. Always an anti-Fascist, he has done much good in the last terrible years. My cousins owe their lives to him and recall the episode with gratitude.

"We were in his office," they tell us, "about a matter of taxes. Whenever we had some problem, we went to bother him. Well, that afternoon while we were there . . ."

"Signorina, for heaven's sake," Camillo interrupts in distress. "Don't begin again! By now everyone knows that story by heart! While a German battalion was passing on Via Cavour that afternoon, a bomb was exploded . . ."

My cousin is implacable; she takes up the story again, but in haste for fear of being interrupted.

"Yes, a bomb was exploded, and naturally the building where we were was surrounded immediately, and the SS began to search all the apartments from ground level up. No one could come in or go out. Documents in hand, everyone was closely questioned. . . . We . . ." However often she had told the story, my cousin shivers again. "So far as documents went, we had nothing. Some old identity card that told we were Jewish, and the false documents that had been promised a long time ago and were never ready."

"And after all," her sister interrupts with a smile, "even if our papers were in perfect order, I think you as well as I would have fainted at the first direct question!"

"Probably. So all in all, if they had fished us out, we would have fried! Well then, he . . ." and she made a gesture to Camillo with her shoulder, "he put us in a room and closed the door. We heard him answer in the darkness; you remember, Lina?"

"Yes," says Lina. "First we heard a metallic voice in German: '*Ist sonst noch jemand da?*' And then the obsequious voice of a Fascist official translating. 'You understand the question, lawyer. Are you sure there's no one else in the apartment?' You are responsible, take note: it's a question of life or death!' And then Camillo's voice, calm, almost jolly: 'I'm perfectly sure. There's no one here except me and my secretary.' A hero, let me tell you!"

"What overblown words!" Camillo mutters in irritation. "Sometimes you don't have a choice: either you're a hero or a pig. What should I have done? Open the door and say: 'Here they are,

take them, all ready for Auschwitz and Dachau, just help yourselves.'"

"Go on, go on," Lina interrupts in a brusquely affectionate manner. "You know very well that there are always ways to avoid getting actively involved and staying at peace with your conscience.
Or if not, I would like to say that Florence today is still full of pigs."

Camillo grunts something that resembles a disagreement, but
the girls pay no attention, still tense with the memory of that fatal
day.

"And all that time, you understand, there was the door. We let
the secretary out, who probably was too terrified to betray us. But
the door! Up to now I still can't explain how it is that they didn't
see the door."

"They saw it," Camillo says, "but they didn't give it a thought.
There are several doors in that room; they might have thought it
was the entrance where they came in, or the one to the library. . . .
Even great schemes get lost like that, over a nothing. . . . And don't
forget that they never found whoever it was who set off the
bomb . . ."

Like good hostesses the girls go from one to another, bringing
out some pastries made at home and even some American Nescafé.
They explain that it came from a boy in Cleveland, who had been
in Florence with the army of occupation and now was back in
America, in college.

"He says we saved him from depression that winter, and every
month he or his mother sends us a package."

It's a pity to drink in one evening the jar meant for a month, but
probably we would have disappointed them all the more by refusing. I don't even have the courage to say that coffee keeps me awake
at night.

My brother-in-law fires a barrage of questions at Camillo, and
the other answers with a mixture of modesty toward a stranger
(after all, Mario is now definitively settled in Palestine) and spon-
taneous trust in a friend.

Political confusion. He doesn't believe we Italians are capable of taking anything seriously. The same scandals as formerly, the same people in office.

Indifference? Yes, supreme. No one has trust and so all end up being uninterested.

What is the stronghold of the monarchists, the conservatives? Strange to say, precisely the South where there is the most poverty and oppression. How can that be? Mah, a sort of feudalism. They vote as the proprietor votes, not so much out of fear as for a strange sort of fidelity; they identify with the proprietor and his rank. If he wins, they imagine that they too have won.

"Probably," he concludes, "the reasons are as usual many and complex. But it's a fact that for now, in the uprisings in the South, the socialists are the ones taking the lead."

"The same explanation holds as well for the monarchists, I suppose," Mario says thoughtfully. "Are there many of them?"

"More than the monarchy deserves, you can be sure of that. Do you know the latest joke? That even De Nicola, the president of the Republic, is a monarchist! How such an institution (which at best is useless and at worst criminal) can still have supporters, God only knows!"

"You're naive," says Lina, who is behind us with a bowl of *biscotti* and has caught the last few words. "You're naive and have no imagination. I remember when I was six or seven and listened with my mouth open to the maids talking about births in the royal family. And later the excitement at every wedding of the princesses, who, God knows, married badly, poor things! And standing for hours at the door of the Opera House mostly to catch a glimpse of the heir apparent and of Maria José. The monarchy in Italy? It's a cheap substitute for romance novels, for the movies, for—what do they call them in America?—'comics.'"

I'm sure that Lina is right and that Mussolini must have understood all that long ago and made use of it as the emperors made use of the circus games, the famous "circenses."

"For that matter," says Lina quietly, "do you want some proof?" And then loudly, "Amelia, Amelia, stop your embroidery; tell us about the king and queen."

Amelia is the old mistress of the house in her eighties and the widow of a general. Some years before, she was an ardent and trusting Fascist, and even now, although her sister had been deported and she herself, having been warned, had miraculously escaped, she had been heard to state: "I can't say anything about Mussolini; he did nothing to me."

At Lina's call she raises her eyeglasses and begins to dream with her work in her lap. "Ah," she says deeply moved. "Her Majesty the Queen was courtesy personified. I always remember that lunch at court (I must still have the menu somewhere) and the dress she wore with the sash over her shoulder! I bowed down to the ground and my heart was beating hard enough to break. Ah, the sounds of the 'Royal March'! Even as an old woman they make the tears break out on my skin as if I were twenty. Just wait," she interrupts herself and Lina gives me a nudge with her elbow. "Just wait, I'll go look for the menu . . ." and she makes her way heavily up the stairs.

The conversation has now become general, but Mario won't allow it to fall apart uselessly. He's impatient, anxious to find out more and insists on drawing out Camillo whether he likes it or not.

"What do the Italians think of the Allies?" he asks. "Is it just my idea, or is it true that often even the common people differentiate between the English and Americans?"

"Perhaps, yes," Camillo admits, smiling, "you may be right. It depends especially on the zone, on the strategies of the commands in this or that region. In Florence, for example, the English let the partisans clean the city out, and then they came in with them. That's why you'll even hear them made fun of: yes, yes, it's all clear, nothing to be afraid of, come on! And then, no doubt, it's a matter of character, of temperament. . . . Look at Rome, I heard vicious things said about the Americans for the way they get drunk, and there's no denying that when they get drunk they're capable of doing some big . . . beh, after all, the people have easily forgotten these excesses, but not the coldness, the 'aloofness,' of the English!"

"And then among the American soldiers there are many of Italian origin, aren't there?"

"Yes, that too, naturally. . . . But I don't think that's a very important factor. It's that English way of acting, reserved, to themselves. . . . I don't know. I still remember one day, after an air raid . . . it was right here in this neighborhood, in Piazza Savonarola. We found an English lieutenant with his leg smashed, losing blood. . . . We didn't know what to do with him! Beh, we tied the leg as best we could, found a truck, I don't know how, a broken down armchair thrown out of a nearby house, and away we went with the poor lieutenant looking for a hospital or the English lines. The nearest Italian hospital then was at Careggi, but you could forget about that. I can't tell you how we ran around! That poor guy must have seen stars; he was gritting his teeth, but I remember that in Piazza dell'Annunziata he looked up at the Della Robbia putti and said, 'Beautiful!' Beh, finally we found the English at the Hotel Excelsior; I think they're still there. There in the grand salon, a group of officers were having tea. You can imagine, half an hour after a raid, tea? We put the wounded man in a corner; no one got up. Wounded? all right, we'll see to it. Finally one of those officers gave him a cup of tea!"

God knows I don't feel tenderly toward the English, for their conduct toward Palestine and many other matters. It must be a sense of justice (and I feel almost angry) that makes me ask, "But the wounded man, the one who gritted his teeth and admired Della Robbia, wasn't he English, too?"

The arrival of Signora Amelia, who cries out triumphantly, "Finally, I've found them," drowns out my question, but I think that Camillo understood it, for he looks at me seriously and then his face lights up in a smile.

The menus circulate from hand to hand. They are dated 1902 and invite the General and Sig.ra Coen to a lunch at court in gilt lettering embellished with flowers. There is a list of twenty courses, and etiquette required (Sig.ra Amelia gravely explains) that one taste all of them.

I wonder what would happen if now, when my turn comes, I tore up the card with its flowers and the list and all they represented. Instead, I pass it dutifully to my neighbor, who dutifully admires it.

I suddenly become aware that I'm dead tired and think of my hotel room with longing. While the guests are saying good-bye (we'll see you again, won't we? you won't be leaving us just like that?) and then again at the door, when I am taking my leave (yes, tomorrow morning, I'll call you as soon as I get up) all I can think of is the moment when I will be alone. It takes a little patience, I tell myself; I'll think about the whole day and surely everything will make sense.

But later, in my room, I try to think and I can't. The more I reflect on things, the less sense do they make. And once in bed, everything begins to come back to mind in a distorted way. The Fascists smile behind their desks, while everyone bows down to them. The woman on the Ponte Vecchio shows her fist, while the bleeding, young English lieutenant says he's sorry, it's not his fault. And right there on our terrace, with a cigarette in his mouth . . . is it you, Alex? No, it's the waiter; why the waiter? He keeps on smiling and waves the menu of the Royal House toward me. And over everything else those words keep echoing in my ears, louder and louder, "Even the neighbors heard her screams, *even the neighbors heard her screams. . . .*"

The next morning I can't get out of bed; I have the strange sensation of drowning.

"What is it?" the hotel maid asks from a great distance.

"What is it?" my sister asks from very near, her voice filled with fear.

I want to say that I don't know, but it's very hard, so I give it up and let myself simply sink, down, down, down once more.

43 No Jews in the Phonebook

Not much time must have passed before I came back to the surface, because my brother-in-law was on the telephone looking for a doctor.

"Signorina," he said impatiently, "Signorina, look and see if you can find this number. Dr. Pisani, yes, that's right, Pi-sa-ni! What? Is he Jewish? No, he's not Jewish."

And turning to my sister: "She says the Jews were removed from the telephone book for 1940, and the new one hasn't come out yet. But Pisani isn't Jewish. What could have happened to him?"

"He could be dead; he could have gotten a professorship in another city, forget about it. Call someone else, but hurry up!"

My sister's voice is tense, anxious; she must be very worried about me. Who knows what's wrong with me? My head is spinning, and I feel myself sinking down again, and I can't think. Why have I come here? Why must I talk to all these people? Perhaps I'm losing my mind. Or maybe I'll go on understanding things like this, halfway, and people will think I'm crazy and put me in an asylum. With much kindness, and much affection, and much firmness, like in *The Snakepit*.

Oooh! If only they would stop talking, if they'd only get it over with. I would like to be at home, in my own bed. To die, but in my own bed. But I won't be able to. I'll never have the strength to go

back: to get out of bed, pack my bags, the tickets, the crossing. . . .
I'm so tired. What does he want now, this nuisance? "Breathe
deeply, more deeply, that's it. Your knees, relax your knees, that's
right, completely. They say I'm worn out? A sea voyage, so many
people in the last few days, so much talk? I don't understand the
temperature. When did it go up, at night?" I don't answer them;
I'm tired and I can't make the effort to answer.

"It's what is called a nervous breakdown. Calm, naturally, before all else. Peace and quiet, no excitement; a little bit every day.
No, it's not necessary for her to stay in bed."

That man is crazy; I can't even get up, I feel like I'm dying. Thank
goodness, he's leaving. Now I can rest for a minute and then explain everything to Luciana.

But when I come to the surface again, it's almost evening, and
Luciana is in an armchair near the window watching the sunset.

I call her softly; she gives a start and immediately gets up. "You
have to take a spoonful of this right away," she says with an authoritative air and hurries to uncork a bottle ready on the chest of
drawers. It's pleasant to feel myself raised by her arm under my
shoulders; I've slept well. But what is this blackish liquid with the
strangely familiar smell?

"Shhh," I say, half closing my eyes. "I remember something,
wait, I want to guess, I remember our mother . . ."

"Lie down, don't fuss," Luciana interrupts me severely. "You
don't have to remember the least thing. First you give us an awful
fright, and then you want to get poetical about smells. No, my
dear," and the brusque tone softens in the word "dear," relieving
the tension. "No, my dear, it's not Proust's madeleine, just, alas,
'Giovanni's' nerve medicine!"

I break out in such hard laughter that a gleam of concern is
again visible in Luciana's eye, and then it changes to a smile. Because at bottom she knows as well as I, that if they're giving me
"Giovanni's" nerve medicine I can't be very sick. I was right: our

mother used to take it when she was overtired by the spring cleaning, and we children were also allowed to taste some spoonfuls
during the time of examinations.

I laugh and Luciana shrugs her shoulders indulgently and begins
to arrange her jacket and purse.

"You're not going?" I ask, trying to hide my concern.

"Of course I'm not!" Luciana answers with decision. "Tonight
I sleep here for sure and maybe tomorrow too, until you're feeling
better. And then we'll see about taking things more calmly; we'll
go to the country, think it over there. . . ."

Too perfect to be true! No neurological clinic, no visitors, just
Luciana and me and all the things we have to tell one another ac-
cumulated over the years.

Dinner is brought to my room on a tray, and she is of the opinion that I shouldn't eat too much, and I reply that it's just as if she
were Mother. Hasn't she gotten into step with more modern theo-
ries? Doesn't she know that when you've got a case of nerves, you
must take nourishment?

Later she stretches out in her chair and yawns happily: "We'll
convalesce together," and we recall and quote at the same time, in
romantic fashion, lines from an old poem of D'Annunzio:

> Were you ever convalescent
> in a slightly misty April?
> They say that nothing, nothing in the world
> is sweeter . . .

We go on reciting, one here, one there, verses from the past. We
can't recall a complete poem nor agree in our appreciation of an
author. But we enjoy ourselves and we're laughing when, a little
later, we wish one another good night.

44 Last Minute Anti-Fascists

The next morning I've recovered. I get up without delay and Luciana decides to go home for a moment in order to change. She leaves me with strict orders: "If the telephone rings, don't answer it; and above all, don't read. It will tire you out." She gives me a kiss and leaves.

Ever since I reached the age of reason, that is, since I was five or six years old, I've known that at times of sickness reading is considered one of the worst crimes a person can be guilty of. That she might try to prolong her illness and the distress of her family by any means is taken for granted. But she can limit herself to the simplest contrivances, like turning down the cover and pulling up the sleeves of her nightgown, or resorting to other more refined measures (of which children are the masters) like forgetting to take her medicine at the proper time or pretending that a poultice burns. It's also common knowledge, even if not yet scientifically proven, that every boring activity is healthy, and every enjoyable one is more or less unhealthy. Thus to do homework, for example, can somehow help a child get better, while playing the "Game of the Goose" or reading can easily cause a fatal change for the worse.

So Luciana's recommendations do not surprise me at all. I am only deeply saddened to see that she has passed over—in the course of the years—to the enemy camp, that of the adults. For a moment I even consider the idea of instructing her in two or three of the fundamental principles of modern education, with particular emphasis on the case of the sick child and his increased need for both moral and physical comforting. How can she ignore in such a pathological manner, I ask myself, a sick person's need for security?

But Luciana has already gone, and besides I am too occupied in finding out if I have all the necessary instruments to carry out my treacherous plans of disobedience.

But I calm down quickly because on the table, apart from two or three newspapers probably left there by Mario, there's also a book, *Let's Talk About the Elephant,* by Longanesi. I had taken it from Lina's library; she had warned me: "I don't know if you'll like it." But it didn't matter. I remember having read almost in secret, during a bout of the Spanish flu, a long and rather boring book, and thinking about it afterward for a long time as if it were the most passionate novel. I don't recall the title, something like *Around the World by Automobile.* If that could be attractive enough for an influenza, maybe this one would do well for a nervous breakdown.

I begin with the newspapers. Articles on the ratification of the peace treaty (have we served the cause of peace, or betrayed sacred Italian traditions?); others on the estate tax, a summary of a speech by Truman, photographs and reports from the Graziosi trial (the music teacher who has or has not killed his wife).

Then I begin to skim the Longanesi book, a diary of the months of German occupation and the Allied liberation. On the first page, a brief quotation: "Let's talk about the elephant; it is the only large animal of which one can speak openly nowadays without danger."

From the first page on I realize that I must not let myself be irritated by the mordant tone toward people or things I respect, because in this display of intelligent and extremely shrewd malice there is something profoundly interesting.

I ought to know who Longanesi is, but I don't remember very well. On the inner cover it says that he edited *The Italian* from 1927 to 1946. If he could edit a review during those crucial years, he must have been a little bit Fascist. More than a little, some say: a hard-line Fascist. Take it easy, say others; he also had moments of generosity, and in the period of racial persecution, for example, *The Italian* came out with a quite courageous article against the concept of racial differences. What did the lawyer say the other day in the street? The trouble is that, in this blessed country, no one is all bad . . . and a small good deed is enough to restore virginity!

However, from the book one can tell that yes, he was a Fascist, and that even now he's still very angry. But he's too intelligent to confess it to others and too proud to confess it to himself. So he prefers to assume the arrogant tone of one who says: Fascist, well, so what? We're all a mass of scoundrels and fakes, Fascists and non-Fascists, liberated and liberators! And naturally, he's not totally wrong.

Speaking of a friend, he says, "He considers himself anti-Fascist because fascism didn't take notice of him." And of another, "He has little faith in himself and a great deal in the United States."

He compares American gum-chewing to a cow with its cud, and asserts that "he eats American canned meat but leaves on the plate the ideology that accompanies it."

He depicts Sforza and his son Sforzino in pitiless brush strokes; then, stamping his feet like a capricious child, he declares that "he has no ideas at this moment, only antipathies."

Reading this book and considering the particular state of mind of the author, many things are cleared up for me. The American soldiers who squandered much of their popularity by drinking too much. The people of Naples to whom no one gave a thought for years, for centuries. The ex-professors come back from exile, hated by the last-minute anti-Fascists.

Who knows if these men on the margin, these spectators, when they are as intelligent as Longanesi, constitute a force or not. The critic as artist, Wilde wrote. The critic as political force? When all's said and done, it's the eternal response of intellectuals. They say:

we don't *act* directly, but we influence the minds and therefore the hands of others; we don't take sides, but we create the partisans. It remains to be seen if one can influence the opinions of others without having one of one's own. And also, if a certain form of cynicism may not be only apparently informative and impartial and if it doesn't end up, rather, by driving the boat in one direction and one direction only.

There is an expression, maybe only one in the entire diary, that unmistakably deprives me of the serenity I am so proud of. It's Longanesi's wife who says, speaking of the war: "My God, think of all the new cripples we'll have! They're so repulsive, poor things!" What is this supposed to be? The cult of unpleasant sincerity? Or only the refusal of that famous homage that vice is supposed to render to virtue. To hell with it!

When I hear Luciana's steps in the corridor, I put the book back on the table without regret. Legs stretched out, eyes closed, the nerve medicine in plain sight, I hope to be the perfect image of innocence.

45 Culture Clash

There are not many people to be seen in the streets. The institution of summer vacations seems to have lost none of its popularity, and if one inquires about this or that middle class family, one is told that they are at the seashore or in the mountains until the beginning of September. For the entire length of our visit, that is. Men are about, and from time to time an elegant woman comes in from the country to run some errands.

But hotels, restaurants, and travel agencies are overflowing with English and American tourists, seasoned now and then with a sprinkling of Nordic women who travel in tight little groups that sit down and stand up as one at a signal from their guides.

The Americans are often young and anxious to do their duty as tourists. In the heat of recent days, however, they have had to spend some very difficult moments. As I leave my hotel, the complaint of a young blond comes to my ears: "One more church and I give up!"

On this first day, obedient to the doctor's orders, I have only one appointment, with an American lady introduced to me by friends in New York who is here on business and for whom I must play the hostess. It's strange, as soon as I see her: elegant, simple, direct, I feel a curious sensation, as if I had found something precious and alive. It's easy to talk, easy and relaxing. I even go back to English with pleasure, although it's often hard for me and seems a hindrance to the full expression of my feelings. Today, I don't know why, English carries me back to my home and my children, and I give myself up to it with the same sense of relief that she evidently does. But as for showing her some typical haunts, that's another kettle of fish; I've been gone for so long I don't know anymore where one can eat well or which restaurants are fashionable. Let's see . . . ten years ago the most elegant street in Florence was Via Tornabuoni, and the cream of good society used to walk there at this very hour. I went for an aperitif to Doney or Casoni or Procacci. Yes, at Procacci we used to eat certain *panini* garnished with truffles; the smell would meet us in the street. "I like the word *panini!* Garnished with truffles? Let's go and try them."

Gertrude is amused and I go along, though without conviction. In fact, it's not very likely that just those sandwiches have remained the same where so many things have gone to ruin. But the little shop is still in its place, and behind the counter the two clerks are only a little older and their alpaca jackets are more shiny than ever. And the sandwiches, wonderful to tell, are exactly the same as those I remember and have exactly the same taste. The only detail that's different is the price, which is incredibly high. Not, however, for our American dollars, nor, it would seem, for the pockets of the boys and girls standing and chattering on the threshhold. How old can they be, eighteen? nineteen? The girls are lovely, dressed with taste, their legs bare and a sort of monks' sandals on their feet with laces that pass between their toes. They toss an English word out among every ten of Italian: "Really, Consalvo, it would be a good *match.* Then make them give you an *allowance,* and everything will be just right."

Consalvo, Cosimo, Vieri . . . one hears the names of the old Florentine aristocracy, but those who bear them are well-turned-out young men in immaculate shirts and with handkerchiefs puffed out of their breast pockets. They laugh and talk in loud voices in a somewhat clumsy effort to reconcile inherited self-importance with the inexperience of their age. When they separate, they no longer climb—as they once did—into a handsome Lancia or a glittering Alfa Romeo. "Want me to take you home on the Vespa?" And the Vespa is a small motorcycle that looks like a toy and has a little space on the saddle behind the rider.

Outside, on the opposite corner of the street a small group of older youths stands chatting. They have that air toward passing women that I had forgotten, self-conscious and simultaneously tense.

Gertrude points to a tiny automobile at the curbside with barely room for two. "I know it," I say, "it's a Fiat Topolino. A nice little car, don't you think?"

"It's not the car I'm looking at," Gertrude explains. "It's the driver. The two just don't go together!"

She's right, for, seated at the wheel patiently waiting with a newspaper in his hand, is a magnificent chauffeur in an elegant navy blue uniform.

"Do you see," Gertrude continues, "when the owner comes back (in fact, I feel sure it can't be a man), the two of them will hardly be able to get in the car. Are people too lazy to drive themselves, or is there some other reason?"

"I don't know. I haven't thought about it. As for the car, I don't think people have much choice nowadays; there can't be many automobiles on the market here. Servants, on the other hand . . . I think they can have as many as they want and cheaply too. So, why pass up the opportunity?"

"But in so tiny a contraption, if you go any distance the driver must be more of an annoyance than an advantage. I would bet that it's not a matter of economic convenience but of dignity. I would bet that for them it would be undignified to be seen driving. . . . Where are you taking me? Not too far, I hope. I'm dying of hunger, you know!"

"I'm taking you to Giovacchino where we can eat in the open, even if the "open" is only the sidewalk; but it's a quiet street, and I like the place a lot."

But when we arrive there's not a free table outside, and the inside rooms near the kitchen are burning hot. We hesitate uncertainly, when a young man, dark and attractive, gets up and says, "May I?" and switching to a slightly halting English, offers to share his table with us.

"May I offer you . . . my table is too big for just one person."

Gertrude accepts with enthusiasm. Maybe she has some doubt about my authority concerning Italian things and wants an opportunity to talk to a real Italian. I'm still looking over the menu, and she already is directing a barrage of questions at Signor Biagi on a variety of subjects. Signor Biagi, thirty-five years old and an accountant, answers as best he can, smiling and wishing to please, but not without a slight embarrassment.

"Explain something to me, if you please." Gertrude has the menu in her hand with both the English and Italian versions. "We're in a country still suffering the effects of a long, harsh war, and full of hungry, unemployed people. How can you justify the presence in this menu of dishes like ravioli, fish, steaks, and strawberries? And with whipped cream, no less! And the price of the meal? A dollar! How can that be? Any restaurant in the United States would charge, let's say, at least three dollars and a half for a meal like this!"

"But Signora," our accountant protests, "a dollar is worth seven hundred Italian lire! For us it's a lot. Very few people can afford that."

"Not exactly few," Gertrude replies doggedly. "Some of the patrons here may be foreigners, but many of them seem to me to be Italians! Beginning with you, if you will excuse me for saying so. You come here, don't you?"

"For heaven's sake, Signora, I'm here by chance." Signor Biagi turns to me. "Explain to her, Signora, that I'm here by chance. I always go home to eat, and the majority of people do as I do. Today I was late and I have to go back to the office right away, and so there it is. But it's not the rule, for heaven's sake!"

I try to explain to Gertrude, who doesn't look convinced.

"What do you say about that?" she resumes, indicating a poor, gaunt woman shuffling in a pair of slippers from one table to another, her hand out in a habitual gesture. "I'm sure that no fewer than three or four beggars will come around before we leave. Yesterday one of them asked me for some bread. Just bread, she said, and when I gave her a piece of bread, she kissed my hand!"

"An outrage!" a lady at a nearby table exclaims in a loud voice. And turning to her companion: "At least, if the truth be told, fascism did away with this sort of thing. There weren't any beggars!"

"You mean begging was prohibited. Or are you so naive as to think that fascism did away with poverty?" They go on arguing in lower voices until the waiter, arriving with our sole, makes an impatient gesture. "I've told you a thousand times, woman! We don't want you here. Go on, I'm sorry, go away."

The woman sneaks off. But as soon as the waiter departs, there she is again on the attack with her mournful sing-song. Gertrude opens her purse, without, however, letting herself be diverted from her investigation.

"Come, tell me," she demands of poor Biagi, "what is your government doing about all this?"

"Our government is very poor, dear lady." I think our friend is beginning to feel annoyed. "*Very poor,* and . . . how can I put it? *Non ce la fa!*"

I have to translate the expression for Gertrude and reject one after the other the various versions that come to mind. "Can't cope, can't manage, can't make it?" Who knows? *Non ce la fa,* that's all!

Gertrude understands but insists: "Well, what about the community? Why don't the community organizations do something?"

At this point, and in spite of my sympathy for our new friend, so unprepared for this kind of sharp dispute, I can't belp but feel a little proud of Gertrude, the American Gertrude. Because the Americans, it seems to me, don't suffer from the European malady

I remember so well, that of waiting eternally for the State to do something and shrugging their shoulders in commiseration when it doesn't: there, you see, they're good for nothing! As if the State were something outside of us, not emanating from ourselves, either to our credit or our shame. I don't think I have many illusions about the community. I know that much of the time it means only a futile game of small interests and small ambitions, gatherings at one-thirty in the afternoon with the promise that "dessert will be served," ladies in elaborate hairdos, tiresome reports by the treasurer and the chairs of this or that committee, motions made, seconded, passed. Perhaps at the bottom of all this there is a spark of human solidarity or of individual initiative that arouses the official organizations and prods them. Sometimes the whole thing is simply ridiculous and nothing more, "lip service" (how do you say "lip service" in Italian?) to supposed American ideals that leaves you unconvinced. And yet it's not useless, it's better, much better, than not trying, not doing anything. Because that "lip service," that abstract "homage to virtue," creates in those who give it, a sort of obligation, or rather a more or less conscious desire to live at the level of an order of ideas much above themselves.

But Biagi shrugs his shoulders. "The community," he repeats with barely concealed irritation, "the word itself has no meaning here, at this moment in our history. It implies many things that don't exist in Italy today. Independence, for example, since economic aid, of which we have a great need and which we receive from abroad, can't help but turn into a political bond." Here a meaningful look at Gertrude which she does not catch. "And security! No one is secure in Italy today, with the exception, perhaps, of those who work in the black market, and it would be naive (to use a euphemism) to expect that they would act with civic responsibility. As for the others, the aristocracy, the upper middle class, do you think they feel secure? Nonsense! They know very well that the ground all around them is mined. They don't trust one another; they're afraid of the future. According to circumstances, it's easier for them to perform, if necessary, some occasional act of charity, and even that . . . not so much out of a sense of duty as because they hope to gain some credit for it in case the proletariat ever comes to power! But as for civic conscience, or group initiatives, I'm afraid we have other things on our minds. We have other cats to skin!"

Biagi's English is hesitant, and the passion he puts into the discussion is more of a hindrance than a help to him. On the other hand, Gertrude has her defects along with her qualities as an American. Her wish to know more than she does and, if possible, take action in consequence is undoubtedly genuine, though it sometimes shows a surprising indifference to the many shadings of the information she receives. Thus she abandons without conclusion the argument about "community" and goes on to that of "taxes."

"All right, let's look at your 'government is poor.' What do you say about taxes? Certainly there are many people who are able to pay them. Do they? How does this business work?"

"A painful subject, isn't it, Mr. Biagi? It seems that from the merchant to the housewife everyone is upset about taxes."

Biagi agrees, thankful for my help. "Yes, that's right. A small shopkeeper, who even had his shop cleaned out by the Germans, is infuriated to hear talk of war profiteering. And the bourgeois, under the burden of inflation rebels at talk of taxes on his inheritance."

"Unfortunately," he continues not without melancholy, "the same people who complain of the government's inefficiency, for example in the field of social welfare, don't understand that it involves first of all a financial problem and one that is very serious. Or maybe they understand in theory but forget when it's their own money that's at stake."

On the opposite sidewalk three guitar players are tuning their instruments and then strike up an old Neapolitan song. Slowly, slowly, the words come back to me, I don't know from where:

"*. . . facite, tazza a caffè parite, sopra tenete o' zucchero e dentro amara site . . . tra ra ra la . . .*" ([something] you do, you're like a cup of coffee, sugar on top and inside you're bitter . . .). Songs are the worst. One can bear an old photograph; creased and yellowed, it brings nothing to mind. But a song can evoke a world. An arm around your shoulders and a cheek rough with unshaved beard and a deep voice, gay and off-key.

"It must be something profoundly rooted in Italian blood," I say hurriedly in order to hide my distress.

"I don't know about that. However, it is profoundly rooted in Italian law! The law foresees tax evasion and takes action in consequence of it. It's not a simple matter, I assure you." By now, Biagi gives up English altogether, intent on unburdening himself rather than informing. "It's taken for granted that no one will name a correct amount, and for this reason taxes are set very high. So we arrive at the paradox that whoever tells the truth will end up paying more than the law intends. What then? One must lie, but not too much. I say it again, it's not simple. The fact remains that every time I have advised a client to tell the truth (for example, where there are minors involved), our declaration has never been accepted and the amount in question was doubled. Once that's understood, the will to tell the truth is gone."

Now the guitar players are circulating among the tables with a little dish. They must be satisfied with their take, because they favor us with an encore.

They played the first song with a distracted air, all the while exchanging comments among themselves. But now that they know they're being heard, they must feel themselves clothed in a new dignity. With their heads bent over their instruments, they sing in low voices.

On the sidewalk opposite, the passersby stop with interest and respect. On a corner a blind man dreams, his eyes wide open to nothingness.

We get up, we separate. My companions go back to work; I slowly to the hotel. Florence is asleep. Every day at this time the whole city gives itself up to the afternoon siesta: stores closed, shutters pulled down, passersby scarce. Even the horse cab drivers sleep on the back seats of their carriages, and the horses, their faces buried in bags full of hay, drive away the flies with a sweep of their tail and a lazy motion of their collar.

Coming from outside, the entrance of the hotel is an oasis of shade. But a harsh voice breaks the peace. It is a massive lady pouring her indignation upon the head of the doorman. I catch a word here and there ("simply disgusting . . . a real shame") before the virago finally decides to follow her husband into the elevator.

"What happened?" I ask the doorman, while he gets me the key to my room.

"It's those damned Greeks! The lady is right, but what can I do about it?"

I don't understand a thing. What do the Greeks have to do with it? The doorman explains patiently and carefully that there are young men, mostly of Greek origin, who are called that, and who traffic in various illegal goods.

"There's always a gang of them, right outside here, on the corner, who pester people with offers of every kind: American cigarettes, currency, and even worse! I assure you, the lady is right, more than right; it's a scandal, but tell me, what can I do about it?"

As I head toward the elevator, I see him pick up the telephone receiver. "The police," he mutters, shrugging his shoulders, "As if it matters to them!"

46 La Selva

Whenever, at home or during the voyage, I had imagined my meeting with Luciana and our gradual getting to know one another again and living together, I always saw "La Selva" as the setting. I don't know why. "La Selva" is a beautiful villa belonging to Luciana, or rather to her husband's family, but I had never really lived there. Perhaps from afar it looked to me like an oasis of peace, outside the round of chance encounters, balanced between the world I was getting ready to leave and the one that was waiting for me and making me slightly afraid. Luciana had warned me: "You won't recognize it. It's been badly damaged. First it was used as a forwarding camp by the Germans: they held Jews there who had been rounded up and were waiting for deportation. Then it was bombed by the Allies. And for two years now Polish DP's have been there, waiting for visas and their final destinations. Last winter they were so cold they burned the shutters and chopped tree trunks on the parquet of the living room."

We arrived one afternoon, rather late. The taxi followed the familiar lane upward between the cypresses and stopped in the open space behind the house, in the midst of gigantic pines. At the threshhold of the kitchen Augusta and Pietro met us to take away the suitcases, grasping our hands in embarrassment and emotion. Here and there, seated on the low wall of the chapel and on benches against the wall, the DP's watched us without curiosity.

"You see," said my brother-in-law, showing me the facade riddled with holes, the empty windows, the clothes stretched out to dry on the iron gratings. "What did I tell you? There's nothing left but the garden; I've had it restored, who knows, in case we decide to sell the house. So that a buyer can at least get some idea!"

At that point I suddenly ran to the garden and remained there breathless: I hadn't remembered it being *that* beautiful! Broad, sloping down in flowery descents toward the fields below, not separate from them, but rather completed, continued in the line of the hills. Solitary old villas cloaked in cypresses, farms hidden among the olive trees, and here and there a square of dark, freshly turned earth.

We stayed for a long time, seated without talking on the stone steps, our backs to the house where little by little the lights went on. Children were still playing on the balconies or persisting in their last tantrums before going to bed. Then the moon came out and the spell became more profound. The children quieted down to sleep, and in one of the corner windows of the top story a woman began to sing. It was a simple, monotonous song with the wailing intonation of Jewish melodies, and it suddenly seemed to me that I wouldn't have been able to endure a different one against the background of the pure Tuscan night.

47 If This Poor Kitchen Could Talk

The next morning we decide that we must absolutely take advantage of these days to rest. Under a pile of furniture that fills my room all the way to the ceiling we find two old deck-chairs. We drag them out, ignoring Augusta's protests who would like to wash them at least, and stretch them out in the sun. The Poles, occupied with their housework, watch us diffidently from the balconies. Seated at our feet, the dog waits upon our decisions. Giulietta, the housekeepers' little girl, hair newly combed, has already taken off the shoes her mother had made her wear in our honor, and chatters without stop.

"Aren't you going to play with the other children, Giulietta? Aren't you going to look for eggs?" No, it's not time yet. She prefers to consult us with her sensible manner. "There's a Jewish lady [*ebrea*] who would like to have the keys to the garden. Should she give them to her?" Because the garden in front of the house is enclosed and belongs to the gardener who grows carnations and chrysanthemums there for the flower shops of Florence. Giulietta explains to us that the *ebrea* is studying medicine and needs quiet; there are too many people in the house and she can't work there.

I am struck by that word *ebrea* in the child's mouth: ten years ago it did not exist in Italy. The young telephone operator had also used it the other day; I was looking for a number that wasn't in the phone book, and the operator asked: "Is he a Jew [*ebreo*]? Because the Jews were all removed from the phone book some years ago and the new one hasn't come out yet." Only natural. Nevertheless, I can't help but think that, even if what they tell me is true—that anti-Semitism doesn't exist in Italy, that it was only a matter of foreign pressure—the word represents a new fact, and this fact, I'm afraid, will remain. I wish Gertrude were here who—I don't remember anymore in what connection—said with conviction: "Why do they call them the 'Jewish people'? Judaism is a religion; I don't understand what that has to do with the word 'people'!" Who can tell what Giulietta and the telephone operator are thinking? Nothing, I'm sure. They are just giving voice to hints that have sprung up around them. Still, I very much doubt that these hints have nothing to do with religion.

However, we promise Giulietta that her question will be given consideration, and we finally have peace. We read, we talk, we dream.

At one we eat in Augusta's little room, with the shutters closed to protect us from the sun and flies. In a corner, on the oven, there is a picture of the Madonna with a lighted lamp and faded flowers. A glass case along the wall holding the "good" china; a table covered by a fringed cloth and pen and ink for the bailiff when he comes; an uncomfortable couch of red plush.

Pietro seats himself lazily in a corner, ready for the plate of soup he will be served with later and for the afternoon siesta. He has a peaceful life, Pietro: he takes care of the house, a bit of orchard, some errands. His blue eyes still laugh in a face burned by the sun. Augusta, on the other hand, is on her feet from morning to night and never rests. Like all the women from around here, she is missing many teeth. She runs from one chore to another and has no time for fine sentiments. Pietro likes to talk to and goad his wife. There's no lack of subjects. The older daughter, for example, who married an English soldier and now talks of going to live in England. Augusta weeps despairingly at the mere idea. And Pietro, in the choice and almost pompous language of the Tuscans: "Don't cry, come on," he tells her. "Or didn't you, too, marry as you liked? Now it's their turn. And they'll travel. I would have liked to travel also, not just spend all my life at Ponte a Ema." He turns to us and explains that, after all, a man's happiness is in his family; he uses important sounding words in a clumsy way: "The family is everything to him. It's happiness to him, it's conversation to him, it's affinity to him. Understand, Augusta? Ah, you don't understand the existence of life, let me tell you!"

No, Augusta doesn't understand; she keeps going between us and the stove, thinking of England and shaking her head. She wants me to eat; first of all, one must be healthy. Don't they eat in America? "Yes, they eat, but not like this. Not so much pasta. How can one face a chicken after a dish of pasta like this?" It's certain one can, and her face becomes so anxious, that I feel a warmth at my heart. It's so strange for me not to have anyone to take care of; here it's the others who take care of me as if I were a child. A lump comes to my throat, and I can't stop the tears running down my cheeks. "Come, come, for heaven's sake. That's all we need . . . ," Augusta mutters grumpily, but her eyes are full of tears, and she dries them surreptitiously with a corner of her apron. How can she cry for me, she who has suffered and seen so much suffering? They say the Italians take everything lightly, that they have forgotten the war and the defeat in their haste to live. But they don't say: "Don't get upset!" They have a place for suffering and for tears. As it says somewhere in the Bible? There is a time for sowing and a time for reaping; time to enjoy and time to weep, time to live and time to die. . . . Perhaps simple people are nearer to divine wisdom. As for me, it does me good to see someone suffering with me. I dry my eyes and smile at her first.

"Come on, tell me something, Augusta; It's been so many years since we've seen one another! How did you spend them?"

"There's not much to tell, Signora. We went through hard times from beginning to end. At first we weren't badly off, but we could see the suffering of all those other poor folk; and then we also had to run away because of the bombing. There was no peace. . . . If this poor kitchen could talk! Why did so many come to me? For a little water or milk, or just to sit down for a minute to cry. Do you remember Signora Passigli? That little, dark one; she never was very healthy, and she was pregnant, too. They were all well hidden, really well hidden, out in the country with very good people. One day, to her misery, she gets a terrible toothache and goes down to the city to the dentist with the idea of having it pulled. And didn't it pop into her head when she passed her house to get some stuff that she needed? God wanted it that the Germans should come in at just that minute. They ask: "Signora Passigli?" And she, poor thing, didn't know what to answer but, "It's me." So they took her and sent her up here. Every evening she came here to cry. Her belly was getting bigger, but she didn't give it a thought. All she thought about was her littlest girl out in the country. She said: "Augusta, what will happen to her? If I go away for a minute, she calls Mamma. That day, because I was going to the dentist, was a calamity; she threw herself on the ground! If I wasn't there to give her her food, nobody could. And if I didn't cook the semolino, she didn't want it; she said the others always left grit in it." She said, 'Augusta, where will they take us?' By then we knew that from here they were only sent to one place, to die. What could we tell her? Once her husband came, but he couldn't even give her a kiss. If the Germans saw that they knew one another, he would have been taken too. He came under some pretext, I don't know any-more what: they looked at one another and that was that."

"And then?" I ask with an absurd hope.

"And then nothing. Did anyone have to tell them where they were going? Every week a truck left, and you had to stop your ears not to hear the screaming. But not her; she didn't scream. She just sat on the bench, I can still see her; her back resting against the side of the truck. She held her hands on her stomach and looked at me."

48 Letters from Home

It's mail time and we are both immersed in our letters. We read quietly, respectful of one another, but from time to time an exclamation or a comment escapes our lips. "Listen to this . . . incredible . . . I must answer right away."

My older children hardly ever write. One is at camp in Vermont, and I have the impression that she is too happy to go into details; happy people have no stories to tell. The other is in a *chevutza* in Connecticut, and her life, for its part, must be too turbulent to write about. Now and then two hasty lines ask for my reaction to some new project (I don't want to come back to the stupid life of Larchmont, can I enroll in the New York School for Music and Art?). Generally I spend the night lying awake thinking about the matter and my responsibilities; if I can, I talk about it with someone I think has some authority on the subject. Finally I answer, not without a certain caution. But my letter is hardly gone when another one arrives (the proposal for Music and Art is abandoned; she wants to go back to high school skipping a year, could I write to the Dean of Girls and ask her about it?).

Rossella, who is nine years old, writes more often than all the rest and with many spelling errors, because her need to tell the latest news is such that she's forced to go beyond the level of her third grade competence. Her father used to call her "the reporter," and in fact one sees that she is happiest when she can tell me about some important event, even if it's not at all pleasant.

"Yesterday morning Haim refused to go to day camp. When the bus came, he hid under the table; the counselor came in and talked with him but he wouldn't come out. And his friend the postman came and went under the table, but even so Haim wouldn't come out, and I had to go by myself. Maybe Haim was still a little sick because he vomited the night before and Grandma says he has a little temperature."

I don't think that Mother had read the letter, or perhaps she didn't understand it, since her knowledge of English is modest. However, here I am brooding over Haim's illness, the money wasted on camp, and Mother's labors at my house. In the last paragraph a cheerful note is sounded: "Bye, Mamma, I hope you're having a good time there like we are here."

My sister's children in Palestine write much more often. At first enthusiastically about life at the seashore, the pool, invitations to the houses of their friends. Then a bit out of sorts because their uncle won't let them go to Tel Aviv anymore for fear of disorders. Terrorists have killed two English sergeants in reprisals.

I ask Luciana what the children think about politics. "They don't think about it much. When you're there, you think less; this also happens to us grown-ups." She tells me that a year ago when she brought the children to Italy for a month with their grandmothers, Myriam had asked her, "Mamma, what is this word 'Zionism' that I keep hearing all the time?" Myriam was eleven years old, and in Palestine she had never heard Zionism spoken about!

Often Luciana's letters come from Tel Aviv and Jerusalem. Those from Tel Aviv are from Gualtiero, an engineer also of Italian origin. They are full of a profound melancholy: this terrorism is destroying the very essence of the Jewish spirit; it is contrary to its traditions and history; nothing good can ever come from it. Those from Jerusalem are from Paola. Paola is twenty and had left her studies to join the English army; now she has resumed them, attends the University of Jerusalem and lives alone in a tiny apartment. She almost always writes in the evening, because from eight o'clock on there is a curfew and she must stay at home; she is bored and complains. Sometimes two or three friends come to keep her company; then they make themselves as comfortable as they can in order to sleep in the living room, but much of the night is spent in discussion. They are Communists, and just the other week Paola wrote of her wish to join the party; everyone is so stupid, they cry and do nothing, but the Communists at least bestir themselves; they fight. Today's letter is not so high pitched: she has joined the party . . . but now that they've caught her, they're transferring their propaganda activity to some other potential member; life is absolutely boring. . . .

Gad's letters come from a kibbutz. Gad went to Palestine on a tourist visa ten years ago and remained illegally. He can live like that, lost in the crowd, but he can't leave, can't come to Italy to see his mother.

I know his mother, too. I went with Luciana to visit her a few days ago in a little apartment at the top of an old Florentine *palazzo*. A single room crowded with heavy pieces of furniture one on top of the other, a thousand pictures in black frames; yellowed lace doilies on the armchairs, the table, the buffet. On a small table a youthful face smiles through eyeglasses. It's Gad's younger brother, killed in the Val d'Aosta fighting with the Partisans. This summer his mother hopes to go there to visit those places. Refined and courteous, Signora Sarfatti is wholly enclosed in her world of memories and mourning. The conversation turns to Amelia Rosselli, who lost three sons, the first years and years ago in the First World War, the others victims of fascism. I say that Amelia is in the mountains and, I don't know how, has managed to take with her a bedspread and cushions to spruce up her little room in a *pensione*. Signora Sarfatti is astonished. "How can she? To move for reasons of health, well all right. But how can she interest herself in such trivialities?"

As I listened to her I thought that it took great strength to remain like this forever, on the edge of the abyss without ever falling in. Isn't she afraid of staring forever into the void? Doesn't she ever want to escape its attraction by turning away her eyes, rushing in the opposite direction? How is it possible to renounce all interests, all the pleasures of life, and go on living?

"Don't think about Haim anymore," Luciana says. "I bet that it's only a little indigestion. I'm sure by now he's all better."

49 Sunset in August

In the afternoon we don't dare go out. There is an orgy of sun outside and we prefer our rooms with their closed windows, thick walls, and very high ceilings. We write, talk, sleep. Sometimes I think that time is passing and we've told one another almost nothing. But it's nice to live like this, as if it weren't just a parenthesis but our real, habitual lives to be spent together always.

When we hear the rustle of water on the plants, we put our heads out: it's almost evening and Ugo the gardener is watering the flowers, his pants rolled up over his hairy legs, his feet bare. "Let's not talk to him," says Luciana, "or he'll never finish." But it's he who talks to us, pouring out all his stories. Poor fellow! The people of the village must be tired of listening to him by now, and then they have suffered more than enough themselves to care much about Ugo's captivity: in Bulgaria after the armistice; in Dresden working in the munitions factories (whoever resisted was sent to be slaughtered); the fire bombing of Dresden (it seemed like day, but there were 250,000 dead, and many of them were prisoners like me).

Mah! He escaped, returned to his work, he can't complain. But his brother came back with a bad heart. "Ah, Signora, I know I'm shameless, but if you could send me a little streptomycin from America! They say it works miracles. There no one worries about the amount or the cost. You should send as much as you can. And

I mean if you advance the money, we'll resell it and pay you for what my brother needs. . . ."

Because there's everything in America, the panacea for every ill: penicillin, sulfa, streptomycin. These names pass from mouth to mouth, repeated with awe. No one thinks about the need for a medical prescription, of the correct dosage, of different uses according to different cases. They are like talismans: just to have a small piece, you could touch it and be saved. And then, naturally, the idea of dealing it on the black market. Everyone says that in the end it's enough to have an idea, to know the right person, and fortune will be there instantly, money in heaps, just the way Tizio or Sempronio did it, easily, without sweat, between morning and night.

I promise that when I go home I'll talk to my doctor and find out all about it, and then I'll have an answer for him. Pietro rolls up his hose, puts away the watering cans. "If I'm not needed for anything else, good night, ladies."

Sunset takes a long time in August. The sun has already gone down, but the hills give up their mantle of light reluctantly. Crickets are chirping in the ditches. The moon suddenly rises from behind a black clump of trees.

Augusta has come to call us to dinner and instead she sits down on the stairs with a sigh. From a window behind us an accordion timidly tries a melody and then stops awkwardly, staying on the same note. "It's the groom," says Augusta. "They were married a week ago because she got her visa, a visa for America. She left the other day. If they're married, maybe now she'll be able to call for him."

The accordion tries once more, the melody rises little by little, then breaks in a sob.

50 Displaced Persons

Luciana says it was noisier last year, but more cheerful, more co-hesive: a community. They had a chief, a common dining room, meetings, all on the model and in the spirit of a real kibbutz, a real Palestinian settlement.

This year half of them (precisely those destined for Palestine) had gone to Rome. Those remaining are destined for America; they generally have relatives there and are waiting for visas. Augusta, who knows everything behind the scenes, tells us that the truck from the Joint Distribution Committee that brought fresh supplies of food has not arrived for some time. Now the refugees get three thousand lire a month for each person, something like five dollars. They have dismissed the cook for the common kitchen and now cook in their own rooms on shared hot plates. "But they don't cook much," says Augusta. "They go hungry a lot."

I'm upset at not having a common language with them and search desperately among my memories for some words of Yiddish or Russian, all of which hardly brings a glimmer of a smile to those tired faces. I feel especially unhappy with the children, who regard me gravely with serious eyes. There are a few who speak Italian by now. A middle-aged man with a listless child in his arms tells me that his wife won't come out here. "This panorama," he says, pointing with a disconsolate gesture to the countryside around us. "She misses the forests of our country."

A woman still young, with a slight squint in her dark eyes, speaks a dreadful but rapid Italian, as if afraid of losing her interlocutor before unburdening herself of some of the fullness of her heart. "Without work," she says, "the men get nervous. And we women? Look . . ." and she points to her patched dress and torn sandals. "Is this a life? I'll soon be old, and it's five months that I haven't even gone to Florence."

I ask, mostly to show some interest since I already know the answer, "Is there really no work to be found?" "Just imagine! There isn't enough even for the Italians. And they already look at us with an evil eye!"

One morning while we are having breakfast we hear a terrible uproar and hysterical screams of women at war. "Mah!" says Augusta. "Before there were a lot of them and they lived four families in a room. Now that they all have rooms of their own, they can't get along anymore."

What a shame. I remember what Luciana wrote last year when she was here for the first time. Heroic stories, escapes from concentration camps, days spent with partisans in the woods, dragging oneself up from a pile of corpses after the hail of bullets. Last year they must still have been living with those memories and with hope. But day after day misery and boredom kill the memories and nothing remains but impatience and rebellion.

That young woman with the dark eyes. The men without work who become nervous. Augusta tells me that her husband beats her. I think of the book by Crum that came out last year; he said there was no time to lose, that we mustn't let this human energy be wasted. What have we accomplished in this year?

I listen to Augusta who speaks, in the same tragic and monotonous tone, of events at the time when the villa was used by the Germans for those sentenced to death; and events now, apparently woven only of boredom and sadness. She's right. There's no difference. There are only gradations of suffering, and not enough to excuse us. In the same setting we treat the same people cruelly. The methods and intentions differ. But what does it matter? The conclusion is the same. They killed their bodies, and we their souls.

I told my brother-in-law that perhaps it would be good for Luciana and me to leave for Ancona a few days early; the aunt and uncles write so impatiently! He wonders at the change of plan: "But wasn't it only yesterday, when we walked to the church at Baroncelli, that you said it would take force to make you leave this countryside?" "Isn't it allowed to change one's mind?" asks Luciana nervously. "Of course, of course." Mario never loses his good humor, but he still questions us with his look. I don't know what he sees in us, but he doesn't say, "I told you so!" Thank God for that, at any rate.

51 Mussolini Liked the Jews

The motor coach from Florence to Bologna is not one of that princely, late model which has been described to me; it very much resembles the crowded, uncomfortable buses of an earlier time. But it's nice, like being at home. It can't leave on schedule because one of the passengers, a lady, is having a coffee and takes her time. The conductor laughs, gets impatient, sounds his horn; finally the lady arrives out of breath and we leave.

We follow the highway as far as Pistoia with its beds of dusty plants. Then up along the Porretta road. There's no time for heat or tiredness; it's all an adventure going up through these mountains and across the wooden bridges. Cows gravely swinging their tails, sheep clambering up steep paths, stone-breakers at work under the fierce sun, and everywhere buses, jeeps, trucks loaded with wood. Then at top speed down to Porretta.

Stop. Change of driver. The new one is more irritable. He swings us from side to side, heavy as we are, shouting curses at whoever won't let us pass. When there's no way to carry on a discussion out of the window with his rivals, he's constantly turning toward us, much more interested in what's happening inside than on the road. We're all rather surprised to arrive safe and sound in Bologna.

We get out to wait for our connection and dash into a church for shade. I have a silly, childish fear of the unknown city under the hostile sun, and I linger in the cool aisles, calmed by the murmur of the litany and the silvery tinkling of a little bell far to the back.

We go to eat under the arcades. "Have you understood," Luciana asks, "what all those people are doing in the street?" and she points to the groups crowding the sidewalk and overflowing into the road. "Mah! They're doing business, making deals, so far as I can tell." I don't know why I want to legitimize in some way their heedless behavior, but in truth it isn't clear at all. Because it seemed that actually no one was coming from any direction: they're all there, on their feet, talking.

We leave in another bus even more crowded, hotter, and more uncomfortable. It's the only one and we'll be in it for another five hours. A Milanese traveling salesman brandishes a bottle of cognac, asking everyone: "Do you feel bad?" He also sings a song he regards as extremely witty and continually repeats the last stanza: ". . . Eulalia Torricelli . . . di Forlì!" A woman with a child on her arm eats bread and mortadella. A workman in overalls declares importantly that he comes from Egypt. The ticket taker, dark and unbelievably young, pushes his cap back on his head and asks, "Signora, am I mistaken or haven't I seen you somewhere before?" Every now and then a sudden braking throws us against one another. The heat is at its peak.

When we've told each other everything: where we come from, where we're going, and we've exchanged family photographs, etc. (this is my daughter, she's called Rossanna, yes it's from *Cyrano*, I had literary dreams too when I was young), we fall by chance into a political discussion. We pass by Forlì, Mussolini's home town, and someone says, joking but not entirely, "He was a great man, let me tell you!" Another sings a rhyme: "*Se Matteotti vedesse la luce, griderebbe viva il duce!*" (If Matteotti came back from the dead, he'd cry out, Long live Il Duce!) Then, despite Luciana's look of disapproval, I ask timidly, "I would be interested to know . . . I've been gone for so many years . . . what you think . . . ?"

They all fling themselves at me at once as if a bomb had exploded; they interrupt one another, get angry. The ticket taker is nearest to the one who screams loudest. He tells me how he was "worked over" by anti-Fascist groups who advised him to hide in order to avoid being conscripted into the labor battalions being sent to Germany. But someone squealed and he was caught and sent to Germany after all. "When I came back, I found the Republic." His voice pauses ironically on the last word. "I looked for my old friends, the ones who had filled my head with so many fine words. When I saw how they laughed at me and how things were going now that we were "free," I said to myself that I had been a fool and I raised my hat to Mussolini."

And the traveling salesman: "I don't have political opinions, and my job is to dish out white, red, and black. But I know that I used to collect my money in the south and bring the exact same amount back to my company in the north. Now, if I don't want to be robbed or knifed or I don't know what, I have to do everything through a bank."

And another, a tall, muscular man with a violent air: "We're sitting on a powder keg, on the threshhold of a civil war. The Communists have all their cells and are armed, let me tell you. I belong to a different organization, I can't say what, but you can be sure we're armed too, and it's America that's arming us."

The women keep quiet and look at me: one from a seat behind me with curiosity (she half rises to see better), the others with disapproval. A sudden halt. On the other side of the road a private automobile is stopped with a highly visible chauffeur; inside a fat, bald man with a cigarette in his mouth and next to him a beautiful dark haired woman, bejewelled and provocative. Our ticket taker gets out, approaches the window of the car, and stands there at attention, cap in hand, to consult. We all wait docilely. Finally he comes back in and we depart.

"From now on," he declares with a serious air, "I begin to respect the boss."

"What happened?"

"What? Didn't you see? What a woman! He's her lover, and just think, he has a wife in Riccione two kilometers from here!"

Everybody seemed enchanted by the boss's heroic deed, and the young fellow returns to the earlier subject that evidently exasperated him. "You know, one day I met the Fascist who had snitched on me and had me sent to Germany. He was afraid and tried to get away; he said, 'You're making a mistake, it was someone else.' I answered him, 'Take it easy, it's over and done with. Now I see that you were right.'"

I say to myself that this is the time to fight. I ask: "But why are all these bad things now the fault of the Republic? Why don't you say it's the fault of Fascism? Wasn't it Fascism that started the war? And wasn't it the war that brought all these misfortunes?" But they don't answer to the point. "Yes," they admit, "the war was the only mistake," but they don't see any connection between the war and conditions today. They repeat obstinately, with a sort of ingenuousness, that *before* everything was fine and *now* everything is bad, that's all there is to it. Someone asks me, "Tell us, what do you think?"

I discover with horror that I almost lack the courage to say what I think, and I plunge ahead. I explain that we had always thought badly of Fascism, even at the time of the maritime colonies, the new roads, the trains running on time. We put up with it out of weakness and inertia, and because the decision to leave one's country, work, and loved ones is a terrible one to make. Then the racial business began, and we had left immediately, without waiting for the outcome. "I'm from Florence; I found many who were missing; someone was deported from almost every family, from many more than one. They tell me that eight thousand people were deported from Italy altogether. Well, to me they seem eight million because I can give a name and a face to each one." My eyes fill with tears. I say angrily, "They would never have been killed by the Republic!"

They are immediately moved. For heaven's sake, the Jews? But Mussolini liked the Jews, he saved so many of them! That was all Hitler's fault; we were allies; we couldn't have done any less. They give the names of Jew X or Y. Do you know him? A cousin of mine was his maid and saved him. Ask her about it. Eh, if you just ask Gina, you'll see what she says. When I say that giving in to a bad friend is no excuse, they drop the whole subject with a shrug of the shoulders.

At Rimini they all get out. We change our seats and finally can stretch our legs. Soon, soon, with the first twilight breeze, we're on our way to Ancona.

52 The Return

Since we had let them know we were due at eight o'clock, and here we were arriving at six-thirty, Luciana proposes to telephone from the station to avoid surprises and excitement, but I disagree. "What difference does an hour make? It's just enough to give our coming a touch of the unpredictable."

But she was right. Because, when we got out of the lift, the uncles and aunt—who were getting some fresh air at the entrance of the house with the door open—stared at us nonplused, unable to recognize us, and at our joyful exclamations "it's us!" looked even more dumbfounded. We couldn't understand why in the world, expecting us by a later bus, they couldn't guess that it was simply a matter of being a little early, but in a few minutes the mystery was cleared up. By an error in transmission, our telegram announced us as arriving on Wednesday instead of Tuesday, so that we were early not by an hour (which would have been comprehensible) but by a day (which made our appearance seem downright unreal). Besides, at first sight we had been mistaken for two rather elegant acquaintances, and the idea of their unexpected arrival had thrown my aunt into confusion, making her painfully conscious of the state of her clothing, which on that afternoon was particularly unassuming. Thus did that return to the maternal home take place—a return of which I had dreamed so often under such different skies: in France under German bombardment, in Lisbon while waiting eternally for the American visa, in New York as savings dwindled and the first job delayed its coming.

And so we had returned. We sat in a circle and looked at one another and tried to feel love for one another as we had wished for it in anticipation and in dreams. But we were also afraid. Afraid of seeing that Aunt Emma was still tinier and older and talked without stopping, that the admiral uncle (deprived of his rank by the Germans for reasons of race and restored by the Republic on the eve of his retirement) had a meek and self-absorbed look, dragged his feet, and with one hand covered and protected the other that had a continual tremor. That the lawyer uncle was old and thin and absentminded.

They talked urgently of pointless things; the most recent letters came out of purses, the latest photographs of children. Quickly to cover the fear, to stifle the questions, to evade the expectations of the years of exile.

Then finally our room with its two little cots. Luciana bursts into sobs. "Why, why did we come?"

And since in those days one of us became strong as soon as the other felt weak, I answered: "To see how things stand, to make a new beginning without the burden of memories."

But I said this only to give a lesson to my heart, which was beating desperately.

53 Lost in the Past

Slowly we retie the ancient threads. With the city sweltering under the torrid sun, with the cousins who stopped by to greet us, with the rooms that had hardly changed, with the servants joyful and welcoming.

Little by little we were initiated into the new rules which had replaced those of an earlier time in the lives of our relatives. They were rules of a rigid and complex ceremony from which it was impossible to escape. They concerned the method of using water (granted to residences only for a few hours every day) so that each member of the family had enough. Or breakfast in the morning, which would be brought to our rooms so that we wouldn't intrude upon the servants with untimely visits to the kitchen. Or the person we could receive at home and those we were supposed to visit, whether out of deference or in order to avoid an excessive coming and going of guests. Or the subjects we should be careful about, because—ignorant as we were concerning certain conflicts that had arisen in the family during the war years—we might inadvertently wound the people involved.

Soon our days were woven of a similar fabric, which enveloped us in a faint melancholy. Sometimes, to break the circle of those conversations that went on from morning to night and turned on lengthy comments about a phrase spoken by one person or another, we went off by ourselves to the lawyer uncle's library and took down this or that book from the shelves. While I was immersed in Anatole France or Maupassant, Luciana declaimed verses of Rostand or Giacosa. What I had loved once suddenly appeared flat to me; what had left me cold at twenty contained new riches. Maupassant was dead and Tolstoy sublime.

In that same room (how many years ago?) I had fought with my favorite cousin over *Anna Karenina*. I still see myself, stubborn and hostile, maintaining that Vronsky was a thief. "Whoever takes someone else's wife under any circumstances is a thief! I don't care in the least for your hero!" And this moral judgment naturally included Tolstoy's literary merits. I remember my cousin's quiet smile and indulgent tone, she only a few years older than me. "You're very young, you can't understand, you'll change. . . ." I shrugged my shoulders, certain that I would not change. How old was I? Twenty? At twenty I also thought I would kill myself if I lost the man I loved. . . . It's not without humiliation that I now admit to having accepted both adultery and loss from life.

Seeing us immersed in his books, sometimes Uncle Roberto stood up and took his favorites from the shelves, either to illustrate something or to recommend them for our reading. Then we felt moved by a sentiment of admiration and deference, aroused by this old man of seventy-seven years, impeccably dressed, who by virtue of his manners and refinement belonged to a sort of aristocracy, an aristocracy different from others, neither useless nor unjust.

Before putting a book back on the shelf, I ask Luciana, "Don't you want to read *Fort comme la mort;* I'm putting it back?" And she absentminded: "Wait, Maupassant . . . he wasn't very suitable?" "Wasn't," I say laughing. "But we're two middle-aged ladies now, don't you remember?"

How well I understand her! During these long sultry days, buried as we are in the rhythm of this immobile life, far from our children, we too have been touched by a magic wand. If we don't escape soon, we'll fall asleep forever.

54 Political Party: None

Every evening when the table is cleared, the maid brings my uncle cigarettes and playing cards. A few years ago it was cigars, but it's hard to find them now. Only from time to time one of the nephews manages to find some, and then there's a great celebration. With the cards, uncle plays solitaire. It's hard to win, and all evening he tries and tries again, while guests, interested in the game, surround the table and give advice.

Among these guests there are sometimes two, two brothers, who avoid one another, barely exchanging greetings. It seems to be an old story, from the time when they fled in a boat from Ancona (still occupied by the Germans) to the south, which was already liberated by the Allies. They were at sea for two days and two nights, six adults and eight children, I believe; they ran the risk of sinking more than once, the sea being very rough and the boat overloaded. When they landed at Bari, they thought they would go crazy with joy. They occupied a house together, two families in two rooms; the men went out to buy food, the women cooked and washed; the children had no school, they were always at home, they cried and fought. Everything started one day with an argument over washing the dishes, when one of the women didn't feel well and the other maintained that she was pretending and said she would absolutely not do the washing up herself. . . . And now the two brothers no longer speak to one another. "You're right," the younger one says to me. "We didn't suffer together; we suffered next to one another." It suddenly seems to me that not only they but all the others, all over the world, have suffered *against* one another, and it is terrible.

Corrado tells us that in the hard times, (when the fate of the war depended on the outcome of the game of solitaire) they could even stay up until four in the morning around those combinations of cards.

In private with Luciana I'm indignant. "You understand, Corrado is a forty-year-old man, an intelligent person, a lawyer. What does he do with his evenings? Read, discuss, enjoy himself? No sir, solitaire." Occasionally I take him aside and try to understand what he's thinking, what political party he belongs to. He's a Socialist, follower of Saragat, believes that the devil is less ugly than he's made out to be, that the Fascists are few and don't constitute a danger. Social reforms? There's no money; they'll come later.

When I can, I question the other cousins. They all pass lightly over these various matters, partly because every important problem is "political," and they don't talk to women much about politics; and partly because what happens in the country is the work of "the Government," and for many Italians the government is not something they have chosen and which they can in some manner influence, but only an external, hostile body everlastingly imposed on them by unfriendly chance.

In general, the better off people are, the more afraid they are of communism and they retreat fearfully toward the right. One cousin, a well-known doctor who, beyond the earnings brought him by his profession, has a handsome family inheritance, asks me about America and the "Truman Doctrine." He's very happy to think that, in its application to Italy, it means financial help as well as a war on communism. "It's absolutely right! The Americans are doing a great deal for us; we have to go along with them."

Someone says angrily, "So then once more foreigners decide what we must do in our country! Now, I want to know: why do we pretend to have freedom, a democratic government, the right to vote?"

The doctor's wife is actually a monarchist. She has no plausible reasons for her convictions; she shakes her head and says everyone is free to think what he wants to, no? Looking at her: calm, fat, and more or less superficial, I can understand again why for so many Italian women the monarchy is really a cheap substitute for fiction.

One evening a younger man who is leaving for Pescara comes to say good-bye to us. He is going to take part in an automobile race, and from there to visit his fiancée who is on vacation. At a moment when I hear him say the usual, "our poor country!" or something of the sort, I ask him: "Do you belong to a political party?" He answers proudly, "Party, none. Ideas, liberal." I hesitate, don't understand. "Liberal ideas, really? Or ideas of the Liberal Party?" Because the two things in Italy don't necessarily go together. "Ideas of the Liberal Party, of course." And he adds triumphantly, "Ideas of the right, conservative!"

I don't know what my face shows that makes him ask, with a sudden worried look: "And you?"

Once more I'm almost ashamed to disturb his peaceful security: this serene world consisting of a good job, the Pescara race track, the fiancée who will inherit a coffee shop, the "nest" that awaits him in his mother-in-law's house. I answer timidly, "Mah! I, you know, am rather on the left . . ."

From the embarrassed astonishment that comes over his face I understand that in my family certain things are not done. But more than astonishment, I'm struck by something, I don't know what, made up of irritation and disappointment, almost as if he could in the end have expressed a different opinion just as easily, but how could he have legitimately foreseen a reaction like mine?

But embarrassment and disappointment don't last long. Soon his face broadens into its habitual smile: "I told you at the beginning, no? Political parties, none!" and at peace with himself once more, he cheerfully takes his leave.

The author's grandmother, Nonna Elisa: "They used to say I was the most beautiful girl in Ancona."

Carla's grandfather, Giuseppe Ascoli (fourth from left), was born in the Jewish ghetto of Ancona, but his sons went on to become lawyers, generals, and admirals in just one generation. Here Carla's mother, Ada Coen (in white, seated on the chair), with her parents, eleven brothers and sisters at home at the turn of the century.

After the unification of Italy and the abolition of the ghettos, Carla's family lived much as any other well-off Italian family.

Carla's mother with two of her brothers.

Carla at one year old with her grandmother and mother.

Carla's family spent summers in Ancona where they were offered the
hospitality of the patriarchal villa and were surrounded by grandparents,
aunts, uncles, and thirty first cousins.
Carla's father, Dante Coen (second from right), spends a summer afternoon
playing bridge in 1921. (p. 236)

Carla with her mother, sister, and others.

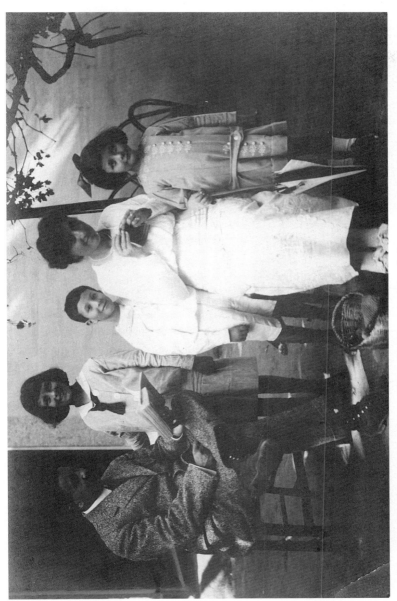

Family portrait circa 1915. Carla is second from the left, next to her father.

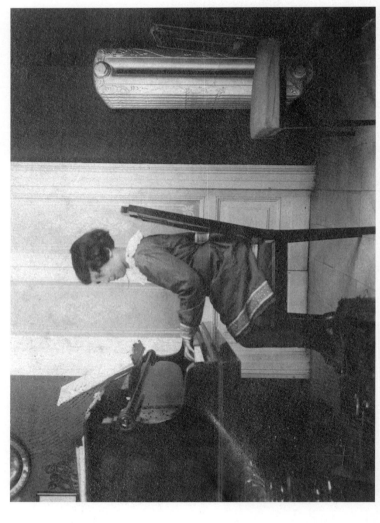

"I can still remember certain sweltering afternoons . . . in vacation resorts when I had to sit at the piano while Guido and Luciana took a nap." (p. 26)

In Russia, where Alexander Pekelis, Carla's future husband, was born in
Odessa in 1902, his Jewish identity was "an indisputable fact to him" and
central to his life. Among other things, Jewish students had to meet higher
standards for admission to school because of the quota system (p. 53). Here
Alex is shown at two stages of his education, quotas notwithstanding.

Service—and loyalty—to la patria was a given for the men in Carla's family and several distinguished themselves in Italian service in World War I. Her father's brother, Giorgio Coen (second from the right), with his comrades at the Collegio Militario, was decorated for valor in the Italian cavalry. Twenty years later, with Mussolini's "leggi raziali" in full force, their patriotism did them little good.

Playing "field hospital" and collecting funds and clothing was a way for children to support the soldiers. In 1916, Carla (at right) and a friend joined the effort. Years later, when Mussolini asked for gold for la patria, she would give her gold wedding ring.

Carla with her favorite uncle, Aldo Ascoli, who was an admiral in the Italian navy. (p. 44)

In the 1920s, Carla and her family still moved with ease in Italian society. At age nineteen, in 1927, she dressed as "Manon" for a costume ball on the tennis courts of a Catholic neighbor.

The worlds of assimilated Italian and traditional Russian Jews join in January 1930, as Carla Coen and Alexander Pekelis are married.

FOTOGRAFIA DELLO STUDENTE

Carla Gebelis

Firma dello Studente

Alex had envisioned that Carla would become his law partner (p. 66). She registered for law school in 1938 when she was pregnant with her third child.

Daniela, Rossella, and Simona (from left to right) became "Danielle, Rosselle and Simone" in France (1939).

While their father haunted consuls' offices in Lisbon, pleading for visas to leave Europe, the children still had their daily outings. Here are the girls with their maternal grandmother and their faithful French nursemaid, Anne (holding Rosselle) in September 1940. Anne ended up emigrating with the family through Spain, Portugal, and finally to the United States.

Safe at last in the U.S., the family settled in Larchmont, N.Y. Two more children—a son, Haim, and a daughter, Alexandra (Anne's "petit coco")— were born there.

After surviving the war years, Alex died in 1946 when the TWA plane carrying him home from a conference in Switzerland crashed in Shannon, Ireland. Here, in the last photograph of him, Alex prepares to board his final flight, carrying a Hebrew-language newspaper.

Throughout the years of separation during the war, Carla (right) had always imagined that the setting for her reunion with her sister would be La Selva, Luciana's in-laws' family villa outside Florence. (p. 240)

55 Back Where I Came From

Every morning around eleven Uncle Roberto goes out for a shave; half an hour later Aunt Emma goes to meet him at the barber's, and together they go back up the Viale Adriatico for a walk.

With his shoes well polished, a clean shirt, and impeccable hat, Uncle still remains at seventy-seven years the most elegant and refined gentleman I know. He criticizes sharply the new style of going about the city in shirtsleeves and open collar and prides himself on never taking off either his jacket or his tie, not even at home.

He is the oldest, she the youngest, of thirteen children. With the passage of the years and the falling away little by little of so many brothers and sisters between them, their bonds have grown closer and the difference of age weaker; but there is still a hint of devotion in her impatience, and of benevolent indulgence in his despotism.

They walk slowly, stopping from time to time to greet a friend, and then they sit down for a few minutes on a bench at the end of the avenue before going back home.

The avenue begins at the Post Office building in the heart of the city, and flanked by modern buildings and timid, young linden trees, proceeds upward as far as the cliffs. Often the names of streets and squares and avenues are changed in Italy; the name of a partisan had been substuted for that of a Fascist bigwig, a date belonging to an episode of the Liberation for one sacred to the

Empire. It also happens now and then that—in the heat of this purifying enthusiasm—the innocent are banished, and some bewhiskered dignitary of the Risorgimento, confident at having triumphed over a street forever, finds himself suddenly driven back into the oblivion of high school textbooks. Thus Viale Adriatico had been rebaptised Viale della Vittoria in the new Republic. But we continue to call it Adriatico, to follow it scrupulously step by step, and to look impatiently for the sea as soon as we arrive at its end.

Once many years ago, when the avenue was still new and the houses along it had not all been built yet, here in the open square one was alone with the sea. Now in the meadow to the left they've built an ice cream stand with tables set all around it and at the busiest hours a radio blares loudly from a terrace in the rear where there is dancing. On the stairway that leads down to the cliffs heavy, sweating men and women appear, on an outing. The Duomo, perched on the highest point above the city, used to be the first place one went to on an outing. You climbed up by lanes and alleys, here a gate, there an arch, further on a little chapel. In passing, you poked your nose into a courtyard or stopped to catch your breath in the square of the town hall where your father and mother were once married. Now all this zone no longer exists: the Duomo at the top of the hill is still intact, but on the entire slope below there are nothing but ruins. The Allied bombings have left little standing. So people avoid these parts and come instead in trucks to the end of the avenue; then they go down the cliffs, look dutifully around, and climb wearily back up.

Near the trucks are booths full of red watermelons with black seeds cared for by scruffy women who tiredly chase away the flies with feather dusters made of paper. When someone approaches, they shout, "Beautiful watermelons, beautiful; who wants some watermelon, cool, watermelon like ice cream; you eat it, drink it, and wash your face in it!"

Heavy-set men in shirtsleeves and dazed mothers of families in black smocks climb back into the trucks eating watermelon. The motors roar, the truck bodies shake, some children—spitting seeds into the air—begin to sing. Deep wheel tracks are left behind in the meadow, and here and there greasy paper bags; in their midst, as white as can be, the monument to those fallen in the First War, still surmounted by the lictor's fasces. Too high, evidently, for someone to take umbrage and climb up to destroy it.

Below the fasces a frieze runs all the way around with verses by Leopardi: "Blessed are you who offer your breast to the enemy lances . . ." I liked these verses so much when I was in school, written in honor of those fallen at Thermopylae. I also liked the pompous ending: ". . . you whom the nation honors and the world admires!" In wars nowadays the breast is not offered anymore, not always. And death does not always occur on the field of battle, not always. And danger is not before you, it's all around, everywhere, and there's no shield to protect you. A door that opens, heavy shoes, a truck that starts up . . . and even the neighbors heard the screams.

And no one can stop and pay homage to the dead, because it's too terrible, one can't live with the images of those dead, one can only forget and go on.

Luciana and I turn our backs on the monument and descend a few steps to the first balcony. We fill our eyes with the sea, greener and more radiant than the world, and we breathe the odor that bursts forth from the waves when they crash against the cliffs down below.

"Girls!" Aunt Emma calls from the bench. "We're starting our walk again. Remember that we eat at noon!"

"We're coming right away," Luciana answers in a loud voice. But we don't move.

"Remember?" I say to her. "Remember when Aunt called us like that twenty-five years ago?"

"No, not just like that. She said that we'll eat at noon, yes, but then, remember? Wash your hands, because your uncles will be getting here soon!"

A sharp, sudden, overwhelming gust of nostalgia. We came to Ancona almost every summer, not here to the city house but the house in the country, just outside the gate at the end of a short, very steep climb. If we went up in a carriage, the driver always got down to lighten the load and urged the horse on with anxious shouts. Automobiles, on the other hand, were limited to a noisy shifting of gears, and for a moment we children felt our hearts beat for fear of not making it and having to roll backward all the way down to the bottom. Our father would say laughing, "Some people go to the mountains for a vacation; some, to the hills; we vacation on a slope!"

The house was right on the main road, shielded by a small flower garden. There was a wide entrance and a stairway that divided into two, for the bedrooms, and a small dining room where there was a clock with a pendulum.

"A clock with a pendulum and ballerinas on the walls."

"And liqueur glasses on the buffet and heavy wooden doors with big iron bars that they locked at night. And in the living room, re-member? certain ladies' portraits with a languid expression and veils tied under the chin!"

"But the bathrooms were the most beautiful," says Luciana.

"Yes," I admit without hesitation. "The ones on the first floor with windows on the veranda, warmed by the sun, and the other shadowy ones on the ground floor, half buried, with barred win-dows at the level of the garden. In the evening, if you were very quiet, you could hear all the talk of the grown-ups who were get-ting some fresh air in the garden."

"When Aunt told us to wash our hands," Luciana moves away from the parapet and I follow her reluctantly, "we flew down the stairs together to see who would get to the sink first, remember? We sprayed water on one another and pulled the towel . . . until the uncles came home from the city and and we had to be quiet right away!"

I remember very well; it doesn't seem that so much time has passed.

I remember the sound of gravel under the wheels of the car, and the uncles coming into the house and going up to their rooms. I remember Grandmother at the head of the table with her two sons at her sides in the fresh jackets they wore at home. And the jokes between courses and the card game of "scopa" right after siesta outside in the garden in the straw chairs under the mulberry trees.

"Do you still remember Grandmother?" Luciana takes my arm and quickens her step.

Yes, I remember. She always had a crochet needle in her hands from which there flowed, clean and precise, the most elaborate lacework. She never stopped from morning to night, erect in her armchair, hardly raising her eyes to greet benignly her daughters-in-law, children, and grandchildren. Only on special days her hands rested in her lap and instead of a crochet needle they were folded around a little book with yellowed pages covered with strange characters, bound in leather worn by use. Her pale lips moved continually, and the children said to one another, "It must be a holiday, Grandma's praying." If they asked her, she answered with the impatience of an initiate for the profane: "Don't you know? It's Rosh Hashona, the Jewish New Year!" Or: "Don't you know? It's Yom Kippur; today all over the world the Jews fast." And we children who more or less all came from assimilated parents or "free thinkers," and had never set foot in a synagogue, repeated after Grandma those strange and mysterious words: Yom Kippur, Succoth . . . Thus the Jewish holidays of summer lighted up for a moment to our eyes, while those of winter stayed forever in the dark.

In the afternoon when we played being ladies, we too sat in the shade of the mulberrry trees pretending to have a crochet needle or prayerbook in our hands.

"Do you know," I say out loud, "that the Germans tore out the mulberry trees?"

"The mulberry trees, the Germans; the rest, the Poles; and what was left, the evacuees. . . . By now, there's nothing to do about it!"

"And the marble bust of Grandpa in the garden?"

"What do you suppose? It's gone with everything else. Aunt Emma says the walls are all stained and the windows on the veranda broken; they keep chickens there. Do you know what? Even if we go up to the cemetery, when we approach we should cover our eyes, it's better not to look. . . ."

I nod in agreement and think about what the house is good for when Uncle Vittorio, the favorite among the children, died hidden in a peasant's farmhouse. . . . And I think there's no need of a house to mourn or remember our dead. And I think why should we have the house when the others lost their lives in the ovens . . .

But while we hurry to catch up with Uncle and Aunt at the corner of the road, desire and regret burn stronger than reason.

And that evening, when the table is cleared and Aunt Emma turns on the radio, and Uncle Roberto, drawing his first puffs of smoke, slowly shuffles the cards, I sit next to him and ask with humility and devotion: "Will you teach me to play solitaire?"

56 Native Tongue

Why we should have taken it into our heads that Sunday, August 16, would be a good day to travel, God only knows! In Italy, very likely, it is the worst day of the year. All the summer vacationers were on their way home, and already at five in the morning, in the utter darkness that precedes the dawn, the station at Ancona was swarming with people.

More came aboard at every village until our compartment was full and with two small children in excess. They wanted very much to sleep, but they couldn't, and so standing in the middle of the compartment, they cried and sucked their thumbs.

From the window I looked out at the crowded little stations, and behind them at the white roads where the earliest wagons of the day were hurrying, and beyond them at the fields cultivated in a checkerboard pattern in a pale imitation of Van Gogh. Inscriptions covered one another on the walls like the strata of different geological eras. When the train slowed, one could read some of them: the Mussolini period (THE PLOW TRACES THE FURROW, THE SWORD DEFENDS IT), the Allies (GAS STATION TO YOUR RIGHT), and the German (that now escapes me).

Above a shop awning behind a small secondary station is written FRUITS AND VEGETABLES, W. CADSEY. That's a new sort of name in Italy; it looks funny. A Polish soldier, perhaps, who liked the village and stayed there? Must be an enterprising man. Maybe he fell in love with a girl, who knows, the daughter of the station master?

At Riccione a lady comes aboard, faded and ill humored, her nails painted with a very dark polish half chipped off. She puts her head into the compartment and examines us one by one like a police inspector. In Rome I would say that she's looking for trouble but doesn't know offhand where to find it. Then she asks sourly: "Have those children paid for their tickets?" The young mother moves the little one from one arm to the other, gives an impatient shake to the bigger girl standing at her knees, and smiles timidly.

"What's it to you?" we protest indignantly in chorus. "Don't you see that they're extras, on their mother's knees? They're not taking anyone's seats!"

For a moment the hag seems disconcerted and begins to take her leave. But the prospect of standing all the way to Bologna must frighten her, because she thinks better of it and returns to the fray. "These are hard times," she proclaims angrily. "Where there once used to be six, now there have to be eight . . ." It's not very clear what she's getting at: perhaps if there have to be eight, the two children are not excessive but are actually taking the places of passengers who pay. However, now I amuse myself by getting into the argument.

"Just because these are hard times," I come back at her, "we don't make a fuss over whether children have paid or not. And then, why don't you let us see your ticket?"

A blazing look. Her situation, too, must not be perfectly regular, since, instead of giving me a lesson and coming out with the proof of her rights, the lady prefers to sweep away from the field of battle. We lean back with a smile of complicity. "Brava," says an old woman in a corner. "Once in a while someone has to give them a lesson, awful bullies!"

The little girl whimpers: "Mamma, is that a bad lady?"

I go back to looking out the window, trying to identify the subtle hint of uneasiness at the bottom of my soul. I had told her what

was what. Bah, what's wrong with that? No, it's not that. I don't
think I did wrong. It's just been so many years since I argued, since
I fought like that in public. Why? And then, all of a sudden I recognize it, that hint of uneasiness. Isn't it almost fun to get into an
argument when one doesn't have a foreign accent?

Nevertheless, I have the impression of being a little foolish at
having this feeling when I think of Marion or Pearl or Herb. Don't
they always say that my way of talking is charming, that my dishes
are delicious, and that my point of view is eminently sensible? But
those are friends, they don't count or not completely.

Still, I don't know, my ideas are confused. It's only the unexpected pleasure at being part of something, one among many, a
person like all the others around me. In the United States as soon
as I open my mouth I'm classified: foreigner, probably refugee, etc.
There's nothing wrong about such a description; it is my condition, but it fixes me in a definite position. Whatever I do, say, or
write from that moment on is done to adapt me to a particular
model. If I don't like chewing gum, or if I'm a Roosevelt supporter;
if I don't have a new hat for Easter, or if I'm shocked by a loyalty
oath; if I don't enjoy myself at luncheons for women only, or if I'm
in favor of the "Stratton law" . . . all of this is somehow related to
my accent. Besides, I'm different. So much so that I'm different
from my own children. One of them, correcting a mistake of pro-
nunciation, patiently added: "I know, all foreigners make that mistake!"

I remember my vehement protest! "Excuse me," I said, and
added the word "sister" to make my assertion more convincingly
American. "Excuse me, sister. When I became a citizen, the judge
told me that I was just as American as he was."

In reality, I had always known that the judge had not been absolutely right on this point, and it did not matter very much to me:
who would have wanted to be American in so annoying, unattractive, and immodest a way as the judge! But I certainly didn't want
to admit this to my daughter, who concluded cheerfully, "You

might be an American, Mamma, but you certainly don't sound like one!"

Thinking of the people around us here in the compartment and of all the others we have casually met in the few preceding weeks in the streets, on the bus, in stores, I realize that in Italy I am decidedly like all the others; I am not different, not at all. Why, then, can't I feel as if I am part of this people, not . . . uff! Better drop it. And then I find myself laughing softly, because it occurs to me that I cannot be part of this people, I cannot be Italian, but I certainly sound like one!

"Why are you laughing?" Luciana says. "Are you hungry?"

How could I not be hungry! Since five this morning . . . we spread napkins on our knees and open with curiosity the package prepared by Aunt.

"Remember?" Luciana laughs with a gleam in her eye.

She's thinking of our returns from Ancona, those of thirty years ago at the end of vacation, and of the very same packages mysteriously prepared by the same aunt. Eating was the only distraction on the trip (comic books didn't exist then), and afterward watching the leftovers fly out the window, and emptying the thermos on one another as we smothered our convulsive laughter at Mother's scolding. What a pity that Mother didn't know then that convulsive laughter is a marvelous outlet for children: the measures she took to control it were prompt and energetic.

"You haven't told me why you were laughing," Luciana reminds me.

"It was nothing. Nonsense!" and I tell her a little of my fantasies.

As usual, she doesn't seem much impressed. "Very nice," she says. "A country where I'd feel good, one more reason to keep my mouth shut."

Luciana is in general a warm champion of silence, and I think I notice an indirect criticism of my bellicose attitude in what she says.

"On the contrary, it's too bad," I reply with some heat. "Not at all for my personal satisfaction, but for all the little causes that one fails to defend every day, like that, out of timidity or fear almost of discrediting them with weak support."

"Ah, yes, I understand that," Luciana admits, carefully gathering up the crumbs and small chicken bones. She puts them back in the bag, throws it out the window, and sits down again. She picks the last crumbs from her dress with her fingers. I like her hands so much, the fingers a bit short but slender, the nails cut short, almost square, and that mole on the middle finger that is as familiar to me as the sun and air.

"Remember," she says, "when we first came to know Sandro in those gatherings sixteen or seventeen years ago? He began to court you almost immediately, I think. Do you remember one evening in Piazza Donatello, when we were all going home in a group? He said it's lucky to be born Jewish and we laughed at him and said, 'Go on, don't exaggerate, you're joking!' But he wasn't joking, and he made us all stop at a street corner to explain it to us."

"Roughly what he said was, 'Look, a Jew has fewer temptations. Even if he achieves a comfortable life, peaceful, prosperous, there's always in his family, or in the preceding generation, or in the very air he breathes, something that reminds him of the fragility of things, and keeps him wide awake, and warns him of what's rotten. We're a sort of thermometer registering a country's degree of civilization. When the Jews suffer in a country, there's something wrong there somewhere.'"

"Yes, I remember. I heard him say that many times." I begin to follow the thread tossed out by Luciana, but I don't know yet where it will lead us. "I remember that he said: 'A Jew must be much more stupid or more scoundrelly than others not to understand certain things, to swallow a Hitler or a Mussolini. They punch us in the head; you have to understand that!'"

"And he talked," Luciana goes on, "of the *numerus clausus* in the Russian high schools when he was a boy and the special exams he had to take in order to be admitted to the gymnasium when he was ten years old. Do you remember when he said, 'We always have to make an extra effort, have a little more courage to get recognition.'"

"Yes, he often said that it's better to be the prey than the hunter! Oh, I can remember his happy laugh: aren't we lucky to be forced to behave like decent human beings?"

I'm looking out of the window now, but Luciana's voice is there again in a sort of affectionate impulse: "I don't exactly know why but it seems to me that what you were saying about your accent also refers to this. Don't you think so? It reminds me, as Alex said, of a greater effort, a bit more courage, that's all." And she adds with a smile, "You won't ever be able to avoid behaving like a decent human being!"

I return her smile, moved and grateful. "I need a little more guts," I say to myself. "That's all!"

Opposite us the mother begins to comb the children's hair. The old woman carefully puts her glasses into her black purse. From the net over my head a small suitcase almost falls on my knees. "Be patient!"

I think: it's hard to have guts; will I make it?

57 Goodbye, Luciana

I had spoken with Luciana often about her departure, which would precede mine by three or four weeks. "I don't like to leave you alone; there's no one in Florence right now. Let's call someone . . ." and she ran through the names of some common friends, Lina, Carlo. . . . But I had objected violently. "What do you expect the others to do for me? I'll cry for sure, and then what? All the more reason to keep to ourselves." Luciana resigned herself; she had not called anyone, and the last days had come and were passing peacefully, uniformly, without anything distinguishing one from the others. The hotel, shopping, dinner at the restaurant, a quick visit to a church or a museum to see an old friend, a carriage ride at sundown.

We said, "How nice!" or "We've got to do it again some other time." Or: "No one can take these hours from us." And meanwhile each of us was counting to herself: six more, five more, four more days.

And then there was only one day left, and all my self-assurance collapsed at once like a balloon punctured by a needle. It's not disappointment or heartache; these are familiar feelings and I can put up with them. *It's panic, the same elementary and irrational panic that seized me twenty years ago, before the exams.* I've got a stomach ache, I'm frightened. She is going to leave tomorrow and it's useless to deceive myself: I can't face that moment.

And it's not that I can put everything aside for when Alex comes home and shows me how silly I am. All that was finished long ago and forever; I can't talk to him and he can't answer me, and all the pain is here and my heart becomes heavier and heavier and surely one day it will burst.

And so, to fight against this panic, the only solution I can find is that of cowards: I run away. Quickly the suitcases are packed, a seat reserved on the coach, money cleared at the bank, and the last minute shopping done. We're finally ready, with nothing more to do to hide the approaching moment. A last coffee? We sit down at a table in Piazza Vittorio, which has a new name now that I can't ever remember; the usual waiter brings us the usual two espressos. One more time I help myself to Luciana's lump of sugar: she none, I two.

We say: "It's a beautiful evening; the trip will be pleasant." Softly, to ourselves: "After all, it's only a year; we'll see one another next summer."

And again: "Look at that girl with the straw-colored hair; she must be an American." That time in Paris we thought we were separating for a year and it turned into eight years.

Or: "Be careful not to forget the umbrella, it's in a corner together with the suitcases." A winter passes quickly, and in the spring it will be time already to think about a reservation on the liner.

"Do you see that woman? No, the other dressed in brown, with the red purse. Isn't it Signora Gui? No, don't look at her now. . . . Mamma mia, did you see how she's changed?" With Sandro too, we said good-bye that evening at the airport for only three weeks.

And finally this, too, is finished. The time comes to go back and get the suitcases and go to the station. Everything in order, behind the window of the bus I prayed impatiently to be gone—we had been parting for so long by now. "All right, all right, good-bye, ciao, write, I won't say anything else."

It's finished. Turn and look: it's only her back, but it's still her. The back a little bent and the step a little tired. Do you think she's crying? Ah, how I hate the ones who have done this. I hate them with the violence and irresponsibility of a child. So many times one says, life, chance. . . . But this, no. This didn't have to happen: wandering and being dispersed, each one feeling so sharply the longing for the other. Oh, somehow, I don't know how, we have to repay the hurts and make them feel it all!

The motor starts, we're leaving. Even if she turned now, I wouldn't be able to see her. I don't like to cry. To cry means to accept, and if one accepts one can't repay the hurts in the same way they were given.

We arrive in Viareggio in two hours and almost everyone gets off there. Between Viareggio and Forte dei Marmi there are not supposed to be any stops, but at every little town one of the remaining travelers approaches the driver and asks him if he would please be nice enough to stop for a minute and let him get out.

The driver swears: "My word of honor," he says, "do you take me for a tramline! All right, go ahead, help yourselves; I don't have a schedule, I don't have a boss who's checking up on everything I do!" But he stops. "Quick, run, if they catch me, I'll lose my job!"

I was the last one to get out in the main square of Forte dei Marmi. No one was waiting for me, and no one was at home. An unknown blond opens the door, leaves me standing in the entrance (me and my suitcases), and goes back through a side door.

I remember vaguely having heard talk of summer tenants, and in fact a little later my breathless cousins ask me anxiously who had come to the door and how I had been treated. They were in despair over having missed me and kept on asking: "Just imagine that rude person who never opens her mouth! And the husband? Did you see the husband? What did he say to you? Ah, what a shame!"

I reassured them, explaining that I hadn't even guessed the existence of the husband, nor had I been subjected to any ill treatment.

"Have you eaten? Oh, we're awful, at ten o'clock at night you haven't eaten yet!" And here they are in the kitchen. "An egg?

There isn't any milk. Wait, there is still a little tin of Nescafé that you sent us, if you like it without sugar. A slice of bread? It's ration card bread, will that be all right?"

The dining room is that of my childhood; the old majolica plates are on the wall. "Two are missing, that silly Marietta. . . . You know, she buried them to hide them from the Germans? She broke two when she took them out."

A couch in the corner sticks halfway into the room (so that you can have the little room beyond all to yourself).

I'm pleased to have my own room, a real room, not a hotel room. This drawer is free, this other for shoes. Will one blanket be enough for you? And one pillow? In this room twenty, twenty-five, years ago I protested against my mother's habit of rushing to unpack the suitcases as soon as we arrived. Today it's I who rush, take out my photographs, my books. Only when everything is in place and the suitcases are empty and on top of the wardrobe, I decide to go to bed with my conscience at peace. "Mamma," I seem to hear my children, "you are unquestionably a middle-aged woman!"

At this hour Luciana will surely be sleeping; tomorrow they have to leave very early. It's strange not to know anymore what she is doing at every moment, where she ate, if she saw anyone this evening.

When I turn off the light, the first mosquito buzzes annoyingly at my ear. This too is familiar. Window screens are generally not used in Italy, and in this house one of the mistresses, Lina, is firmly against the killing of any animals.

I hide my head under the sheet and fall asleep dreaming of DDT and mosquito nets and screened porches.

58 Nella

"If the genitive is *caritatis,* what will the nominative be? Think hard, you should know it. The genitive is *caritatis* . . . the nominative . . . ? Come on, try!"

The clear, shrill, methodical voice comes from the next room. I look at the clock, it's eight. Lina is already at her first lesson, and her slightly tense voice tells me that she is tired. I burrow into my bed, savoring the pleasure of not having to give or receive Latin declensions.

Lucy looks in at the door. "Are you awake? I've just come back from the market, but my boy is already waiting for me. Ciao. Are you going out for lunch? Till this evening then." She's gone already, and soon after another voice rises from the garden under my window, a boy's voice, uncertain, halting: "I . . . go . . . home."

I get up, dress, go out. We've already agreed that I must look for other friends during the day when Lucy and Lina are busy; at five o'clock the lessons end, and we can be together in peace.

At the shore, stretched out under the umbrella, I think of what these days of heat and sun must be like to them, spent entirely in this way, trying to get into children's heads at this very moment things that wouldn't enter during all the months of school and that now *must* be there before the October exams.

My invitation to lunch is for two o'clock. The villa is at the beach, among the pines and oleander, more beautiful and delightful than ever. I want to go in as I used to by the main stairway, but the stairs are no longer there, just their remains at the top and bottom, under the rubble.

"We don't go that way anymore," Aunt Livia comes to meet me holding out her arm. "The last German bomb . . . as fate would have it! I could have had it rebuilt immediately and didn't want to; the estimate seemed high. Today it would take a fortune!"

She hugs me, leads me to the terrace facing the sea where the table is set and a maid in white gloves is serving the *aperitivo*. She introduces me to the guests: "Dr. so and so, Countess someone else . . ." Dressed for the sun, sandals in the latest style, lounge chairs, impeccable table, roast chicken with mushrooms, Filomena's sweets.

"You remember Filomena, don't you? She's still here, still the same, still cordon bleu! Yes, Nella is here too, winter and summer, she remained as caretaker. But you know what happened, don't you? Husband in the war, older child by typhus, and the little boy by a fragment of a German bomb. She was unlucky, poor Nella; only the little girl was left her."

Friends from the neighboring villa come for coffee. I know almost all of them. It's strange: I know very well that the house is the same and the owners are the same. Nevertheless, it strikes me as an anomaly that they have all remained the same, even the the habits and the guests. It seems like the third act of a play, in which the scene is the same as the first, only the protagonists have somehow powdered their hair and made up their faces as best they could.

A few haven't even given themselves the trouble of putting on makeup. Nadina, for example, has truly been touched by the magic wand of Sleeping Beauty. She sits on the couch with the same ease as twenty years ago. Eighteen . . . thirty-eight? Her beauty glitters with the same cold perfection: a fairy tale with a dash of nightmare. Even the young man who talks to her and makes her animated and smiling is the same one who talked to her like that twenty years ago.

I feel like rubbing my eyes. They say that she did not want him then, when she was sure of a splendid marriage, but that failed her;

now she is regretful, but he no longer wants her. In a low voice my aunt tells me of the effort a house like hers costs her. "Just think, Ornella has been here for two weeks; Umberto arrives tomorrow, not to mention all those who turn up at lunch and dinner. I do the shopping myself, you know, early in the morning; even so I always go to mass at seven o'clock. Yes, yes, the staff is good, but there are the children with their meals, bathing, going for a walk; only one nurse for the two children, one always has to give her a hand. I assure you, it's a race from morning to night!"

She goes on at length like this; I nod my head mechanically. The times are not what they were: last year's dresses are kept, one travels in buses . . . And the worldly ritual is carried out according to the rules, with a sigh, almost in homage to a harsh and inevitable duty. Which one? And why?

On the way out I stop at Nella's, the housekeeper. Twenty years ago we came to her with patterns of summer clothes; she copied them quickly in certain inexpensive materials that we bought at the market stalls. Now, too, she's standing in front of her sewing table, intent on cutting something.

We talk of this and that, not looking at one another, a little embarrassed. And then suddenly the ice is broken. She tells me about her husband first (I was in a daze. I asked myself, And now, how will I take care of them?), and then of the girl (what do you want? it was war . . . when we finally were able to find a doctor, it was too late), then of the little one (the last German bomb, Signora mia, and the explosion was so big . . . but by then we were used to it; imagine, I thought that the baby was in the house playing, and then I heard a voice calling "oh, Nella-a!" and my blood froze).

I don't know what to say. And she asks me about Sandro and the children and says, "Poor lady." But I'm almost ashamed, because the children are healthy, and I have a house in America and friends. She shows me pictures of her wedding, her daughter on the day of her confirmation, the little one dressed in her sailor suit. All the while, Caterina, the only one remaining, her hair brushed and braided, is standing nearby with curious eyes. She doesn't listen to her mother and the stories she knows so well; she looks at me attentively, touches my scarf, my purse.

"Be still, little tease," Nella says distractedly. She gathers up the photographs, puts them away with care. "Sometimes I ask myself, is it possible you were like that once: young, happy, with a husband, children, like everyone else? No, it's not possible. That's not me, that's another person whom I don't know."

Maybe we all suffer the same way; this I have already understood a little. But maybe we torment ourselves in the same way, and approach and withdraw from the precipice with the same reasonings. Is it me, or am I someone else? Do I exist or don't I exist? What is true, yesterday's happiness or today's despair? And these human beings all around, drab, colorless, are they life? And is this flame burning inside me death?

When I leave and Nella hugs me, I think that this perhaps is the only positive outcome of suffering. That now many more people put their faith in me.

59 What People Might Say

Forte is full of automobiles, especially on the weekends when, according to the ordinances, it's supposed to be forbidden to use them in order to save gasoline. There are those who have a doctor's permit, or a farmer's, and those who do without and trust in fate, hoping not to be stopped and fined.

But even more common than automobiles in Forte are (and always have been) bicycles. The marvelous road between the sea and the Apuan Alps, white with marble, seems made for them, and the Italian bicycles are so light that I feel myself ten years younger.

I leave early in the morning and stop off to see various friends spread out along the coast; toward evening, when lessons are finished, Lina comes to meet me and we slowly go back home in the sunset. Just beyond Forte there is an area that was formerly occupied by beach homes and is now completely destroyed. Much of the rubble has been cleaned up, but here and there a house still stands with its barred windows, empty holes like eyes that can no longer see. The deserted country all around has an air of the steppes. Here and there solitary walls rise like grotesque stage sets marked with old, faded slogans: TO BELIEVE, TO OBEY, TO FIGHT or THE FUTURE OF ITALY IS ON THE SEA. The road continues for a bit, grandiose, deserted, and with blocks of marble scattered about (I'm afraid of seeing one of Dali's mad creatures suddenly spring up; I feel like whistling to give myself courage); then one suddenly runs up against a collapsed bridge. Looking carefully, one finds a path hidden in the brush which connects to a road that then descends steeply to a wooden bridge. Italy is full of such bridges, put up quickly and never replaced; they end up carrying a much greater traffic than they are strong enough for, so much so that one often reads in the papers that a car has fallen through or that a bicyclist has crashed into another, or the planks have given way.

Every day I cross that bridge, for the most part composedly as befits a woman of a certain age who knows what she's doing; I dismount, wheel the bicycle by hand, and remount only on the other side at the end of the rise. But sometimes a breath of wind whispers in my ear: "If you dismount, you're a coward," and then I have to stifle a great fear, hurl myself down through a cascade of stones, cross the bridge trying to forget how narrow it is and how uncertain its guard rails, and labor up the other side. But my conscience is satisfied; I've met the challenge and can continue on in peace.

At the Apuan Alps where my nephew lives the beach is beautiful and less crowded than at Forte. The black marketeers thin out and their place is taken by artists. Eugenio Montale, Italy's leading poet, takes the sun lying motionless on a deck chair, his chest flabby, his stomach bulging over his bathing suit, which makes him resemble a Buddha who has finally agreed to change position.

Gualtiero Volterra, ten years ago one of the best Italian pianists, exiled for racial reasons, has just returned from Australia and is buying kites for his daughter, who speaks Italian with a strong English accent. His wife, who had stopped in New York for three weeks, had the unfortunate experience of spending a lot of money at a bad hotel, losing three suitcases, and seeing only other Italian emigrés; she is completely disgusted with the United States. "Everything there is a cheat, and we had better come back to Italy permanently. And then what can be said of problems like children and their upbringing? Let's not talk about it! Just think, girls of fourteen use makeup." She got hers away from there in a hurry.

And she concludes triumphantly: "Here with the same amount of money, instead of an ordinary three-room apartment, we can afford a house in Florence for the winter and a villa in Forte for the summer. And I can send my daughter to the most fashionable school in Italy! And besides that, I can have three servants! Excuse me, my dear, I have no doubts about the final decision."

At one o'clock I go home with my nephew and his nanny. It's not far, but under the direct sun the distance seems endless. On one side the little boy talks about bicycle races; the girl on the other, about an American soldier she had come to know last year.

"You see, Aunt, I like Bartali! He's the best, no doubt about it; he showed it already in the the Tour of Switzerland."

"He was a good-looking boy; I met him by accident in my village; his family's Italian. They live near New York, he told me the name, something like Bruccolo? He said to me, 'Maddalena, you'll come to America, meet my family.' He came to see me in the evening, but I went out and left him with my father; I was afraid of gossip, you know."

"Some guys are really dumb, they think Coppi is better. He's an idiot who runs out of breath and has no style; he won once by pure luck."

"When he was transferred, I didn't want to give him my address. He said, 'Maddalena, you're not nice to me.' And then once, when I was in service in Florence, he suddenly turned up, he found me by himself and wanted me to go out with him. Just think, go out with an American; who knows what they would have said in the village!"

"Aunt, Aunt, why aren't you listening? Who do you think is better, Bartali or Coppi?" He pulls my arm insistently, but I'm caught up in the amorous adventures on my right and only give him evasive and indecisive answers of the sort with which adults hope to free themselves, at least for a while, from the nagging of children. Finally, I understand that there's no other solution: if I want peace, I have to confront the question. "I think you're right,"

I say. "Bartali seems the better man to me, and decidedly you should bet on him." I'm a little ashamed of the grateful and triumphant look with which he receives my profession of faith, but I'm finally free to turn the other way and ask, "I don't understand, Maddalena. If he was a good fellow and talked about his family and liked you, what was wrong with going out with him? Maybe he really had serious intentions."

"It's impossible, Signora, impossible," and she shakes her head, resigned and stubborn. "And what do you mean, if he was a good fellow; his mamma also wrote me from America. But you mustn't go out with an American; you could be taken for one of those. . . . I wouldn't have been able to show myself in the village." There's nothing to do about it. Maddalena may remain an old maid all her life, and her Joe will marry someone else in Brooklyn. In a few years, if he can't sleep one night because the children are teething, or if on his way out in the morning he sees a pile of dirty dishes and his wife still disheveled, he will think of that marvelous Italian summer and a beautiful girl, dark, with black, lively eyes, and legs perhaps a bit too long. And all this out of fear of what people might say in Castelnuovo di Sopra.

60 Times Have Changed

Ten years ago Poveromo was sea and pine trees, that was all. There was a hut on the beach with a kitchen inside and some tables and benches outside. In the kitchen a woman with her sleeves rolled up over her round arms made some pastries with honey that were recognized by experts as genuine strudel; on the benches at tea time the snobs of Forte affected a country simplicity.

At that time everyone said, "It would be nice to live here." But Calamandrei was the only one who had actually bought land with the idea of someday building a villa. Calamandrei was a lawyer and a scholar, professor of Law at the University of Florence, and a painter in his spare time. "It will be a house hidden in the pines," he said, "with a studio for me at its top. And the walls will be of glass, so that from my table I will be able to see through the tops of the trees the sea on one side and the mountains on the other."

After our departure in '38, we always were in touch, first from France, then from Portugal. When the American consul in Lisbon had denied us visas (unless we could show him *concrete* proof of our antifascism), we immediately thought that only Calamandrei could help us. And in fact, in a few days, disregarding the censorship, Calamandrei had sent us the articles that we needed, properly translated and notarized before the American consul in Florence, accompanying them with the wish that we would find in the New World that success and acceptance that had been refused us in Italy. Enough to get anyone fired!

But the Fascists did not always take an interest in firing men like Calamandrei. Even though his political position was well known, he was before all else a scholar, and as such—according to them— not especially dangerous. They must have made the calculation that to dismiss him would have created a sensation, and so they left him alone.

This is why nothing interfered with the building of the house. Calamandrei's last letter, just before the outbreak of war with Italy, told us that the times were more and more difficult and his personal mood more and more depressed, but that the nest among the pines had just been finished.

Six years had passed since that letter, and Sandro was not with me as we had planned so often, and not huddled with Calamandrei in a corner discussing the law. Instead, after hugging one another with heavy hearts, we sit politely in the armchairs on the terrace talking of various things. Of the house, which is beautiful but a little bare, with half the pine trees cut down; the profession, for which Calamandrei has no time any longer, being always in Rome for the Constituent Assembly; his son, who is a flaming Communist (he got married, you know, and they have a kid who's here with us for the summer); and the Action Party, of which Calamandrei is a member, and its early dissolution which is being much discussed these days.

Times have changed, and Fascism is defeated, but the sad and thoughtful expression on Calamandrei's face is the same. Perhaps there was once greater will to fight, and more hope. And he fought well in those terrible days when Florence was divided in two, the Allies in the suburbs, and the Germans and Fascists still inside, and all the population anticipated the job of cleaning up the city. The Action Party came out of it with a halo of honesty and heroism and for a certain time united around itself the flower of the country.

But now one hears it said "its time is past," that it no longer has "a reason for being," that it "ought to dissolve itself into the great mass parties."

I want to ask so many things, lift the veil of bitterness just a little, but it's impossible; a woman friend comes in with a baby boy and a letter (is the professor going to Rome this evening?); an assistant comes in with some political news (I've been told that in this evening's paper . . .). There's no way to talk. Here and there some things I know or imagine: Fascists still in important positions, the bourgeoisie more afraid of social reform than reaction, wretched political intrigues.

I understand so well. The good, the pure, are horrified by corruption, and politics is in large measure corrupt. But there's no life without politics, and you can't cultivate the earth without dirtying your hands. And then?

We make a tour of the house. In the living room a sheet of glass covers a German inscription hastily written with a piece of coal: LICHT AUS! SIE KOMMEN ZURÜCH. We climb up a spiral staircase and finally are in the glass studio between the mountains and the sea. It's so beautiful that it takes your breath away. From the terrace there is coastline as far as the eye can see, and the waves wash gently on the deserted beach.

I recall the words of that lady yesterday: "With what a small apartment costs in New York, here you can afford . . ." I'm fascinated and tempted; this isn't only a property, it's beauty itself.

Tempted and troubled. I don't know, can something be too beautiful? Or excessive? Maybe. Excessive for work and suffering and struggle? Excessive for the little Communist in his carriage down there among the pines?

I go home pedaling slowly in silence; the sun sets with a heightened display of red colors. Groups of people drift back from the beach toward home. In front of the "Capannina" the ladies are still feverishly bent over the bridge tables.

61 Death in Sant' Anna

After dinner I'm ready to go to bed. But there's Lucy who hasn't been out all day and would like to take a stroll, and there's bread to buy for tomorrow morning's breakfast. So we go out again into the dark and deserted streets.

The bread shop is empty; only a white-clad baker is left who is sliding an enormous black tray covered with soft pastries into the oven. His wife waits in a corner for him to finish, holding a half-asleep little girl in her arms. Some ado over the coupons from the ration book; the baker's face darkens when he hears bread spoken of, and he reaches out to caress the child. It's a black bread that should be eaten right away, as soon as it's made; tomorrow morning it will already be dry.

We return home slowly. The vacationers are all on the beach, seated at cafés or walking back and forth; only the local people are making the rounds of the village at this hour or stopping casually at the corners.

Leaning against a gate, in the middle of a group of women, Marietta, Lucy and Lina's elderly maid, greets us as we pass; she recognizes me and leaves the others to come and talk to me.

"It's impossible, have you come back? But you know, you've gotten so big."

For forty years Marietta has been telling me how much I have grown, so I'm not surprised. Her noisy and wet embrace also re-awakens the past.

"Tell the truth, are you all right in America? Let me introduce you to Armida, you remember her don't you, Armida? Armida, come here. She's a teacher now."

We exchange greetings and congratulations. So many years have passed, such a long time. You were smart to get away; the things that went on in this country!

"My girl, we had the front here for seven months. Always afraid, always hiding. The English shelled, and the Germans . . . better not to think about it. At first they were polite: do this, do that, learn how to organize yourselves. But when the others got closer and the firing got worse, to hell with organizing! They became bad, don't ask! They were afraid, you see, and took it out on us. At Sant' Anna, you know Sant' Anna near here? I used to take you there in a cart with a mule when you were little and no one knew what to do with you, your teeth were coming in and you cried all the time. Only going in the cart you didn't cry."

For a moment the memory of me as a child and the terrible period of my teething distracts Marietta even from the Germans. It's Armida, fat and vulgar, her hair tied on top of her head and with an annoyed look, who finishes the story.

"Yes, at Sant' Anna they killed twenty-eight people all at once, because of a German, a thief, who had stolen some chickens and been killed for it. Mamma mia, I can't even think about it! Just imagine, that evening me and a friend took it into our heads not to sleep in Forte. Who knows, it seemed so close to the sea. . . . We walked as far as Sant' Anna and were dead tired. From outside we heard the gunshots and the screams of the ones who were left . . . Our blood froze and for a minute we couldn't move we were so afraid! Then we got out of there, in the ditches . . . we slept in a farmhouse halfway back. . . . Not really slept; we leaned against one another too afraid even to talk . . . our hearts were in our mouths every time a mouse passed. I tell you if one had touched me I would have wet myself that night."

Marietta nods her head and laughs at me affectionately. "You don't know about these things, eh? You had it easy in America."

But there is neither envy nor bitterness in her words. After all, I belong to her a little, and she's not displeased to think that she too has someone in America.

"Is it true," she asks, "that there are good people there who send packages to someone in need if only they have the address? I heard it from a friend of mine who has a daughter working for some friends of an American soldier. As soon as you get back, find out if it's true, my girl, and for goodness sake give them my address, don't forget."

While talking we had started to walk again. Another pause at Marietta's door. "Don't take nine years to show yourself again, eh?" I promise that I won't, that I'll come back next summer and bring the children to see Italy. ("I bet you don't have a sea like this in America"). And I must go to see her at home, not like this in the middle of the road. And I must tell her more ("because today you made me talk about myself, you haven't even told me if there are beautiful churches in America").

We go home, to bed. All night I dream of going in a cart, but the mule is terribly slow and I get very angry because I'm in a hurry to arrive. I shake the reins, I call him, but nothing works; he stops and won't budge. And then a sudden burst of gunfire and desperate screams.

I wake up, but it's only the cats yowling in the garden.

62 Piazza Fratelli Rosselli

The bus for Rome left at seven in the morning, and Lucy had warned me that if I didn't want to miss it, I had to borrow an alarm clock from our neighbor, the engineer Cecchini. "We owe him a visit in any case," she added with concern, "he's always so polite to us! It would really be inexcusable if you left without having met him."

So we all engaged in this mission together, across the garden red with geraniums and encrusted with shells like the careful structures made by children on the beach. In the parlor we were greeted warmly by the blind wife who besieged us with attentions and questions. With our hand in hers, we tried to find something among our misfortunes that might reconcile her to hers and disappoint as little as possible the anxiety to see our visit end and our voices go back into the darkness.

On the way to the door the engineer pressed upon us two alarm clocks, one ordinary, the other . . . "You'll see, you'll see tomorrow morning! Then you'll tell me about it. . . ." The blind woman smiled indulgently and protested: "Mario, you haven't really given them the alarm clock with the waltz! You know it doesn't wake anyone up." "Be calm, I'm not being foolish at all. I've given them one to wake up with and one to put them in a good mood . . . ," and well pleased, he accompanied us to the door.

But at five-thirty the next morning, there was no good mood. Only the monotonous song in the air of a bird in pain, which seemed to fill the house, and the desperate wish to crawl back under the covers and avoid at all cost the trip that awaited.

The porter who had promised to come and take the suitcases naturally fails to show up. We load everything on bicycles and proceed at a snail's pace, stopping at every moment to pick up what falls down. Finally we're in the square; the bus is ready, an immense bus with an immense trailer. We try to pick out our seats, but it's extremely hard to know which are the right ones; no one seems to have what was promised them, and we all wait impatiently for the office to open. At last it does. Everyone rushes to get in; the clerk understands nothing and listens to no one; the driver blows his horn; we all rush out. The trailer is immediately full, the other half empty, with the best seats still free, reserved for some unknown and powerful passenger who will come aboard at the next stop, Viareggio.

At Viareggio they make us get out to exchange our provisional tickets for regular ones, but not a soul turns up for the good seats in the first coach. The CIT Agency in Viareggio maintains they have been reserved by the office in Forte; CIT in Forte (duly called on the telephone to explain its behavior) repeats that they were reserved by the agency in Viareggio. I decide to leave the group passionately following the stages of this discussion; I slip into the disputed coach and install myself quietly in the best seat in the first row, next to the window, with all the space I want to stretch my legs and enjoy the trip.

It's strange, but hardly one or two people follow my example. It's now clear that by keeping apart the better and best for someone inclined to hand over a nice tip, the agency has simply ended by not selling the seats. So what prevents the other passengers from taking them? Perhaps a residue of deference for the "big shots" who haven't shown up but who might yet put in an appearance. Perhaps a sense of embarrassment in the face of the lack of a fixed rule that assigns them a task, a function, even—as in this case— just a numbered seat in a bus. Many adults (and almost all children) like to know what they may do, what's permitted them and what's forbidden; in this way they feel safe and sound and at ease. Finding out for themselves can be a terribly exhausting business.

It's already nine o'clock; we've lost two hours. But this time we really leave. We climb up the coast alongside a sea of incredible colors: sometimes the blue of an oleograph, sometimes a dark green almost gray. The trailer holds us back; it swings behind us like a serpent's tail, and we have to slow down almost to stopping at every curve. Thinking about it, travel like this can be rather dangerous. Narrow roads in bad condition; the usual temporary bridges made of planks, often being repaired; heavy truck traffic, and, alongside the road, sheltered in the ditches, an uninterrupted flow of bicycles.

At first the pines are thick near the sea; then the cypresses of Bolgheri (which an old lady behind me dressed in black doesn't fail to recall in all-knowing tones); then mulberries. Again pines, this time shorter and alternating with cheerful oleander bushes. Poplars stirring at the edges of streams. Trembling silver poplars. When I was little, I didn't very much like to hear poplars always described in the same banal way. I thought they were not silver but green, albeit of a very special green; and they didn't tremble because trembling suggests cold or fear, and the poplar is far beyond those earthly feelings. Rather it speaks, or sings, high above, and it moves because it feels the wind when the other trees and the humans down below don't even notice it.

"Here in Italy," an American friend had said to me a few days earlier, "they never know the names of the trees."

But I do know them, in fact; and what difference does it make?

I think of my little boy, who said to me one day, "Mamma, I want the birds to take their nest away from that corner." Surprised, I asked him why; I always saw him ecstatic at the sight of nests. "Because," he explained, "every morning when we go out with the class, the teacher makes us stop underneath and tells us, 'Look, children, that's such and such a nest, and the birds make it so and so, and that tree is a maple, and the other is a cherry.' You see, she won't be able to do that anymore."

We stop at Grosseto for lunch, in a large, round square all white under the burning sun, with immense colonnaded buildings that still smell of the Empire. I search for the street sign, expecting to still read there PIAZZA OF THE FASCES or OF THE LICTORIAN; instead my heart skips a beat because the sign reads PIAZZA FRA-TELLI ROSSELLI.

The restaurant is packed: traveling salesmen, local profession-als, and the entire busload. Two well-dressed gentlemen complain that we have gone back to the days of the stage coaches. "Want to bet we won't be in Rome before seven?" A woman seated aslant eats with one hand and with the other holds and soothes a tiny child completely befuddled by the journey. Next to me an elegant lady comments on the imminent departure of the American occu-pation forces: "They're going, too bad, they were nice." Her neigh-bor, a young man with a knowing air, tells her that important con-tracts for barracks furnishings were signed yesterday between the American army and the Italian government, and adds in bad, pre-tentious English, "We are overplaying the Russians, my dear!"

We eat spaghetti and chicken and fruit and cheese, and naturally we drink, a good red wine in straw-covered flasks. When we go back, it's hard to keep one's eyes open. The heat, the food, and the long, white road under the sun. We doze counting the kilometers on the little white stones at the side of the road.

The sound of traffic on the flagstones of Rome wakes me up. My God! here we are and I didn't hear a thing, haven't understood a thing, and haven't gotten ready. I rub my eyes. While the lady in black identifies in a loud voice the monuments we pass, I lean out of the window and can't take my eyes from that pavement made of little hexagonal tiles next to one another. They speed under the fenders and stop at crossings and then disappear, blurred by the tears that fill my eyes.

63 Piazza Navona

That first morning was bitter. Because I was born in Rome; I went to school there and lived there until I was eighteen, and—in the long years that had elapsed—I had called to mind those streets and those buildings so many times. The streets especially, and the bridges. But rarely when I was awake. If I thought of Italy and the past, I saw Florence and my adult life. But in my dreams I was always in Rome and on the way to the Villa Borghese, walking, which seemed interminable to my childish legs. Or on the way to school, across the wide bridge and then through the dark streets and imposing buildings. Or on the way to see my favorite cousins and the porch and immense door (but at night a smaller door opened inside of it) and the elevator and service door and the shouts of children welcoming me behind the door.

And now I passed through these streets, and it was not a dream but reality. It was not that the streets seemed smaller to me, or the bridges narrower, or the people poorer, or the city more confusing or dirtier. It was just that nothing seemed real to me. The dream, that yes, that was real, but all this was vague, unreal, apart from me; I could not live it.

That is how I spent the first day, at lunch with the aunts and uncles, then greeting the others, then running to the hotel, almost without daring to stop for air. In my room, with the shutters closed, stretched out on the bed, I ask myself, "Who am I? Where am I?" thinking that perhaps far, far away I really have children of my own, but now I have carelessly broken the circle of familiar things, and I surely will never again be able to go back inside it.

But in the evening Paolo Milano, an old friend, comes looking for me to have dinner, and we go out into the lighted city. "Where do you want to go?" and he names two or three typical quarters where, I have to admit, I never set foot in my life. "What kind of Roman are you?" "What's that got to do with it?" I protest. "At fifteen, sixteen years, you go to school, you study. You don't eat in restaurants, you don't walk around like a tourist. And then, I thought I had the rest of my life for that!"

Paolo laughs. He, too, comes from America after an absence of nine years. But he wasn't only born in Rome; he didn't only spend—like me—his adolescence there; he went to the university and became a professor, a drama critic, and lived the Bohemian life; he knows writers and artists, monuments and restaurants, and if there is a dash of intellectual snobbism in his experience, his love for the city is warm and genuine.

He takes the lead now and I follow docilely past the lighted "Tritone" fountain, across Piazza Colonna, and then down winding little streets and unexpected little squares. The squares open suddenly as though a curtain had been raised, and they remain half in shadow and half in a light that seems to come from invisible footlights. At the focus of the light are the tables of a restaurant and people intent on eating, with plants set all around to mark off an enclosure, and waiters with napkins on their arms. I don't know if it's the dark immobility of the surrounding buildings, or the alleyways on the sides, which seem to lose themselves behind the scenes: I want to hurry my steps as fast as I can before my turn comes to speak and the audience discovers that I don't know my lines.

The restaurant "Ai Tre Scalini" on Piazza Navona is closed; the proprietor stands in the door with his arms crossed. "What's going on?" we ask. "Beh, the usual story; they slapped a fine on me again." He gives us no details, but we can imagine them; they've served meat on Friday or something of the sort.

"When will you open again?"

"Mah, in four days." It's clear from his tone that they'll go ahead just as before. He points with a tired gesture to the opposite sidewalk. "Go on over to zi' Peppe, the food's good; whatcha wanna go running around so late for?"

I'm surprised at this generous behavior, but Paolo points out that probably in a few days it will be zi' Peppe's turn to stay closed, and the Tre Scalini will inherit his disappointed clients. We have dinner on the sidewalk opposite, under the stars.

I've heard Piazza Navona compared so many times to a living room, perhaps because it's so quiet in spite of its size, and there is almost no traffic. But there's nothing about it of a living room, or the artificial and chatty intimacy that word suggests. This immense oval made of austere buildings, and the two majestic, overflowing fountains in the dark, are part of us and at the same time high above us like inaccessible pagan divinities. In one corner a man and a boy may well play with a ball, and on the benches near ours coarse laughter and dirty words may be exchanged: still, the atmosphere remains that of a temple.

While we eat, two guitar players arrive, an old man with a sly air and a fat, likable woman, disheveled, in a black smock, who seems to have just left her stove. One sings with difficulty, plays the guitar, and accompanies the music with slow speech almost to himself. The other has a hoarse voice that goes straight to the heart. When we ask for a song, they don't go through with it in the perfunctory manner of the elegant establishments; but with the gusto of people who abandon themselves to their pleasure. Maybe the old man knows that he's doing it for money, but the woman has surely forgotten that: one leg propped on a chair, her swollen belly touching her knee, hands on her instrument, and her rapt face looking up into the night.

When they leave, we do too. "St. Peter's?" Paolo asks. I don't even nod; I know nevertheless that everything is magical, even if the carriage and coachman have little resemblance to fairy vehicles. Paolo is telling me an anecdote of the time of Fascism and the war, one of those rich stories in which the hero, naturally, is a coachman. Spirited and philosophical witticisms are always put into the mouths of coachmen; but so far as I'm concerned, every time I've tried—as Paolo says—to "probe" one of them, I've found myself face-to-face with one of the most banal creatures in the world.

Ours drops us off in St. Peter's Square and goes on his way. For a few moments the tired trotting of the horse on the pavement is the only sound in the night. Then this, too, disappears, and nothing is left but the sound of the fountains. We cross the square in a religious mood; instinctively we lower our voices and deaden our steps. When the water of the fountains sprays our faces, I feel like bowing, as when I was a child and passed near a holy water stoup.

At the other end of the square, on the steps going up to the church, an old man is huddled: a beggar or a philosopher? What does he do on other evenings? Does he always come here? And what is he looking for?

We're silent, or we speak of various things, Moravia's last book and contemporary Italian literature. We climb the steps slowly, slowly. I wish it were finished already; I wish I were at home. It's like when one is very young and someone has spoken marvelously sweet words, words that presage love but aren't yet the certainty of love. And, of course, one wants to stay and hear them again but also wants to go away. Because one's eyes and ears are wide open and one's whole soul is taut, it's impossible to grasp them completely, impossible to live so completely in the present. So it's perhaps better to have them already behind one and to savor them with the minuteness and intensity only granted to the past.

"And now?" asks Paolo. "Now let's go home, I'm very tired." We go back across the square; a group of cheerful vistors arrives in a noisy automobile; their laughter echoes in the night. We run to catch the last bus. When we separate, I feel almost relieved that Paolo doesn't suggest another meeting. It would be naive to try to repeat an evening like this.

64 Blank Ballots

I had told Carlo that this time I would have to forget completely about sightseeing. "I've been away for so long, and there are so many people I haven't seen yet, and I'm so tired. Let's put them off until next summer when I come back."

But Carlo, one of my cousins and one of my best friends, has the stubbornness and lack of consideration for the opinions of others that brothers generally feel it their duty to exhibit. So he continued to insist on his plan for spending an afternoon viewing the Villa Celimontana.

"It's not as if I were asking you to go to an art gallery or something like that," he said. "It's just a garden, that's all! If there's someone you *have* to see," the emphasis on "have" was supposed to express his disapproval for my whole attitude, "we can take them with us, and if you feel tired, no one will prevent you from sitting down on a bench and resting."

So I accepted, I would go; but the idea of taking someone with us was out of the question, naturally. At the right moment, however, I also gave in on this point. After all, I had had a great deal of practice taking part in Carlo's favorite projects in my younger years, so that I could easily do so again. I wasn't in the least surprised when we began our expedition that Saturday afternoon; the three young people who joined us weren't my friends, it's true, they were Carlo's; but from the moment that I met them and liked them, everything went well.

The trolley-bus is crowded as usual, and arrives, as usual, shuddering and at top speed, weaving from one side of the road to the other and trying to stay attached to the electric cable above by means of a thin wire. We quickly reach the Coliseum and begin to climb the hill at its back.

"This type of exercise," Carlo announces proudly, "keeps the body and spirit of a person alive. But that coming and going back and forth looking for work is a mental torture, I would say . . ."

"Yes, tell us about it," Luigi says. "How far have you gotten?"

"Beh, I'd rather not talk about it, I think. You know how these things are, everyone tells you that you're damned right, that the law must be applied, and you should get your teaching job back. I go on signing applications, with documents, publications and dates included. But once you've lost something, it's useless to fool yourself; it's lost forever! No one will give anything back to me. . . . Maybe it's different in other fields, I don't know, where there's less competition."

His wife watches him apprehensively and says, "Tell them how the secretary greeted you on the very first day." Probably she wants to relieve his bitterness, and she succeeds because his face lights up and he laughs quietly. "Oh, that guy is marvelous! I went to see him seven years ago, before leaving for South America, you remember, Luigi?" Luigi nods; he also has an administrative job or something of the kind at the University. "I wanted the documents in my file; he kept raising objections, said they were important, that I would be better off leaving them in a safe place. Nevertheless, I decided to tell him the truth; I knew, after all, that he was a respectable person: 'Mala tempora currunt, Signor Giannini,' I said, 'I'm a Jew, you know that, and I'm thinking of going to South America; I need my papers, they could help me find a new job, at least I hope so!' He answered that I was crazy. . . . Are you tired, Carla?"

I didn't expect this sudden interest. "No, I'm not tired, not very much anyway. Do we have a lot more to climb?" "No, we just have to get to the top, up there, and please, don't play the helpless woman." "I'm not playing the helpless woman; you asked me . . . OK, go on with your story!"

"Yes, Giannini said that I was crazy; anti-Semitism never existed in Italy before, and these questions of race were completely sense-less anyway and nothing would come of them. 'Just remember my words,' and pointing kindly at me, 'Nothing will happen!' I was in-sistent, naturally, took my precious documents, and left. . . . OK, when I came back last spring and had to get some forms for my ap-plication, naturally I went to look him up. He received me with open arms, kissed me on both cheeks, remembered me very well, and finally, pointing his finger at me again, said with an air of re-proach, 'All right, what did I tell you? Nothing happened!'"

We all laugh heartily and agree that it's one of the best stories to come out of the war, but I don't think its disturbing implications escape any one of us. In fact, apparently nothing else matters so long as the little world of each one is safe, and for this little indi-vidual the war, the bombings, and the deportations never really happened. And the worst of it is he's a decent fellow, cheerful and good-natured.

The climb ends, and we are going through the gate of the Villa Celimontana.

"For heaven's sake!" says Luigi, "keep away from the University if you want to remain optimists. It's entirely in the hands of the priests. Look at the cafeteria, for example. God knows we've tried to organize something to feed those good kids who don't have much money. But no matter how we tried, we didn't succeed: everything is expensive. We either didn't give them enough or made them spend too much. Beh, the Christian Democrats, now, have managed it to perfection, a good meal for a few lire. How they've done it, God only knows!"

"How they've done it?" Vito laughs ironically. "By a way that you know too! Who do the Americans help out? You, or me, or the Italian people who are suffering? They give to the priests, no? And these can then pass themselves off as generous; big deal!" He begins to kick a pine cone fallen from a nearby tree and falls behind distractedly.

"Beh, you have to understand the Americans a little," Tornello interrupts with the thoughtful and preoccupied air of someone who would like to be impartial. "General Alexander said that too, remember? I can only deal with governments that exist!"

"Good old idiot!" Vito has now moved on to more picturesque language. "Good old idiot!" he repeats with conviction. "The war was fought to defeat them. And then there weren't any priests; the Allies brought them . . ."

"Don't get mad. Alexander wasn't the first, and there are plenty of others who think like him. Look at Max Ascoli, a longtime anti-Fascist, went to America years and years ago just because of this. He's the head of that Italian American organization that seems to be a fine thing; they say it gives work to lots of Italian artisans. Well, someone asked him the other day why he put an ex-Fascist in an important position. Do you know what he said? He chose him because he knew the business, and giving work to a Fascist didn't matter to him if that way he could give a thousand workers something to eat!"

Now it's Luigi who rebels. "But that's not to say there aren't any anti-Fascists who know the business," he protests angrily. "It will take a little more time to tell them apart and get them started producing. They've been out of circulation for so long. And then, listen, you can talk until tomorrow. No one can make me give up the idea that there must be a value, a value in an absolute sense, in not putting a Fascist in an important position, *on principle*. And believe me, the effects on people of the application of such a principle are profound. Neither you nor your Ascoli can measure it!"

The villa is closed, but the garden—open to the public—is a wonder. The avenues are swarming with children and the marble benches with ordinary people, knitting and gossiping. The people of Rome are at their ease among the pines, cypresses, and marble ruins. We look down from a crooked stone wall overhanging the road. The Roman countryside stretches as far as the eye can see, one hill after another, with pines on their crests clearly outlined against the reddish sky.

But we hardly pay any attention to the sunset, each one following the thread of his own thoughts. Tonello pulls a leaf from a laurel bush and chews it impatiently.

"You know what's what," he asks Luigi with irritation, "will you tell me whom you'll vote for at the next election?"

"What do I know? One makes you more angry than the next. I'll end by voting for the Communists. Let them come to power in time to put a stop to this tide of conservatism."

"Now you're exaggerating," says Vito goodnaturedly. "You'll do it to spite Tonello."

"Exaggerate? He's crazy, I swear!" Tonello stops and takes Luigi's sleeve. "Have you already forgotten what the totalitarian regimes are? Keep in mind that no good dictatorship exists; only dictatorships exist. Period!"

"Ah, and the priests are not a dictatorship?" Carlo laughs ironically. "Do you know that you're naive also?"

"More than naive," declares Luigi, sitting down on a bench, while Lida and I hasten to follow his example. He goes on playing with his pine cone while the others remain standing, intensely engaged in the discussion. "More than naive! Have you read the speech the Pope gave yesterday? What do you have to say about his propaganda plan? 'Don't hesitate, my children' (and his voice takes on a sugary tone) 'don't hesitate to borrow, if necessary, the methods of your adversaries.' And that religious convention on the eve of the elections. Home, family, work! Can you believe that sometimes it enrages me to be a Catholic? Tonello believes it, right Tonello?"

"I don't say I believe you," and Tonello spits out the chewed-up leaf. "You know what I'm looking for: a good center party that will let me live democratically."

"But so far you haven't found it. So what do you do then?"

"Vote a blank ballot."

"You're right," Vito admits. "There's nothing else to do."

Now Carlo and Luigi become really angry; Luigi stands up excitedly, and Lida looks at her watch and makes a sign to me.

"Blank ballot?" they ask in chorus, as we resume our walk. "That's out!" and they stop in the middle of the path, gesticulating. "What, are we going to start over from the beginning? The best people in the country, with the best cultural and moral background, just drop out?"

"I'm not dropping out," Tonello protests wearily. "It's that I don't know which way to turn, can you understand that?"

"After all, it's the same old story. Nothing pleases us and so we abstain. Meanwhile a new world takes shape without us, and one day we'll be called upon to suffer the consequences of our abstention."

"Nothing to be afraid of," says Luigi comfortingly, putting a hand on his shoulder. "We'll adopt the usual surprised air. Mah, it's not our business, we want nothing to do with it, don't blame us!"

Carlo's indignant voice becomes persuasive: "Come on, Tonello, in the end you also know that a blank ballot is a refusal to get involved. Enroll in the party that seems least bad to you, that comes closest to your point of view, and fight to change it, to bring it closer to your ideas."

We're approaching the exit. Tonello shakes his head. "I've tried," he says, "we tried, didn't we, Vito?"

"Sure," Vito answers with a shrug of his shoulders. "They know as well as we do that we tried, and with all our hearts, in the Liberal Party. What came of it? Nothing! It's perfectly useless."

"It's not useless," Carlo insists, but his voice is tired. He stops at the foot of a statue without a head and leans against the pedestal.

"Try again," Luigi comes back. "Keep trying. As long as you try something you stay alive. Victories are won in hopeless struggles."

Now all of us are around the statue.

"Do you know why it's so beautiful?" Carlo asks us sternly.

No, we don't know. Why?

"Beh, Corrado Cagli explained it to me one day when we were up here together. First of all, a perfect body . . ." Corrado Cagli is an important painter, and we look with more attention, reverently. But all we see is a nude boy with one arm stretched along his side, a knee slightly forward. There's no longer much light, but it's still hot. I'm dead tired. I want to say, so what?

65 Under Fascism, I had No Politics

Renata had told me over the telephone that it was pointless for me to exhaust myself running after trams and transfer connections; her husband would come and pick me up by car on his way home from the office. I tried to fend her off, more out of embarrassment than anything else; I hadn't seen Renata since our years at the liceo and did not know her husband. To meet like that in the lobby of the hotel seemed to me odd. But when I saw him, big and hearty, already slightly bald, he seemed likeable and I was convinced there were no reasons for embarrassment.

"I'm sorry," he excused himself as we got into the car, "but I can't go straight home; a problem came up at the last minute . . ." and leaning forward he gave an address to the chauffeur.

"Tomorrow we have to deliver twenty trucks," he explained leaning back. He lighted a cigarette, and throwing the match out of the open window, lightly scratched his eyebrows. "The customers arrive from Naples tomorrow by private plane, and at the last minute there are headaches of every kind."

"Trucks?" I ask. "You make trucks?"

"Make? Oh no, dear lady! What do you think we make in times like these? It's obvious that you come from America! These trucks are used, left behind by the Allied armies. We refurbish them, clean them up. Hard work, let me tell you! There's no regular schedule or definite job. One minute I'm a salesman, the next a diplomat, the next a mechanic. This afternoon at one o'clock, in all that heat, you know where I was? Testing a car outside of Porta S. Giovanni: a sweat! And until I've delivered it and put the money in my pocket, I can't take it easy."

"Why?" I ask innocently. "Don't they run well? Aren't they in good shape?"

He looks at me suspiciously for a moment, and I seem to read in his eyes the Roman doubt whether I am what I seem to be. In English we would say: "Are you really stupid or only pretending to be?" But the Italian way of saying this is much more concise and picturesque. However, he must have reached the conclusion that I'm stupid and don't mean to offend him, because he explains, not without a certain gentle irony: "Dear lady, if I had to deliver them in the condition my customers require, do you know how much I would have to make them pay? A million each!"

He flicks the cigarette stub from the window and repeats irritably, "A million each!"

It seems to me a good idea to change the subject, and I ask about Renata. Renata is well. "You'll see, she hasn't aged in the least, she's always elegant." But he thinks of something else. "At this rate," he shouts impatiently at the chauffeur, "we'll get there tomorrow morning!" The other mutters something in reply to the effect that going faster at this hour is a way of getting oneself killed, but he speeds up and I start to get nervous. What the devil am I doing here outside the walls, instead of gossiping more or less comfortably with my friend?

We turn into a dark little street and then pass through an iron gate into a murky courtyard. In a corner, sheltered by a canopy, three men in overalls are talking under a pale light bulb hanging on a wire.

"Stop on the side," orders Arrigo (Renata calls him Ricky in her letters). And flinging open the door of the automobile with a hasty "Be back right away," he joins the three under the canopy.

The chauffeur turns to me and politely offers his newspaper. I take it without much enthusiasm, but before I can look at it, he launches into speech: "The signora comes from America, right? A great country, America, and the Americans are good people! *Smart* that's what they say, right?" and he laughs a big, self-satisfied laugh. I understand that I have to give up the modest pretense of looking through the newspaper in peace and peer hopefully toward the canopy, but the four are still gesticulating. Arrigo has separated from the group and goes to the telephone. I can't distinguish his voice from the talk of the others, but they must have given him an answer, for he throws his cigarette to the ground, stamps on it, and then puts the receiver to his mouth and his lips move excitedly.

"America is a great country," the chauffeur resumes, not letting himself be discouraged by my earlier indifference. "They ought to send us a few more soldiers to clean up this country of ours!"

I gather that we're going to engage in a bit of conversation, so first of all I must try to find out who he is. Is he Arrigo's personal driver, or does he work for the company? Neither one nor the other, he tells me with a sort of pride. "I work for myself: I rent! By the day. Only the car or, like today, car and driver. I also used to deal in automobiles, one or two years ago. Those were golden times! Take this car here, f'example, how did I get it? I had a doorman who used to work with me and he got a good percentage, you can be sure. He always knew who had cars. This one here belonged to someone who couldn't decide to sell it, who knows why; I asked him about it at least three times! Beh, finally that doorman friend of mine goes to see him one evening and they're talking and he tells him, there's a law, or ordinance, God knows what he cooked up, that tomorrow—he says—they're gonna requisition all the private cars in Rome. Are you sure? the guy says. Really? Absolutely! Beh, so I let him think about it all night, and early in the morning I go look him up. He gave it to me f'nothing, what a deal . . ."

Here's Arrigo hurrying back. "I'm infinitely sorry, Signora; I had to call Milan. Go ahead, Renata expects you. And excuse me. Antonio, take the lady to my house and come back and get me."

And he's gone again. Antonio starts the car. I imagine that he's not interested in talking anymore; in any case, at so much an hour the money keeps going into his pockets. We pass in front of the pyramid of Caius Cestus, barely visible in the dark. "It's beautiful, Italy," he says to me. "Too bad that every now and then someone has to come from outside to clean her out."

"Not only from outside," I answer pretty much out of habit. "From inside too, no?"

Oh, yeah! She's had it from all sides: mines, bombings. "But if they leave her alone for a little while, you'll see how she'll get back up. If only there weren't any Communists! Those should be wiped off the face of the earth. Nenni, Togliatti, you know what I would do to them? I would hang them. And that's why I say America should send us more soldiers; not take them away, put them back here."

My friend was getting so heated, he began to interest me. "Excuse me, how about you, what party do you belong to?"

"Party? None of them!" I've already learned that whoever answers like that actually has very strong ideas, and I wait patiently for what's to follow.

"Under Fascism I had no politics; I worked. But then, at least, a lira was a lira. Nowadays, let's not talk about it. Beh, I work now, too, and I don't ask for anything. But one thing I know: that whoever rents and buys automobiles are the big shots, and you can't live without big shots, and that's the side I'm on!" I ask if he has a family. "Yeah, a wife and two kids. And that's the trouble, y'see, Signora. That I'm an economic man. . . ." The mistaken adjective gives the phrase a flavor of scientific definition: *Homo economicus.* "You work, you earn, you save something, and someone comes along who's been watching you all the time and doing nothing, and he says, 'Now we share!' Nossir. I'm against the Communists, that's for sure. And in Italy they won't stick, I'm telling you! Because the people are intelligent in Italy, and when someone's intelligent, he wants to climb up, get ahead of the others, and he won't let himself be put down to the level of an idiot! If those workers don't have enough to eat, why don't they make the best of it, like I do!"

He's so absorbed in the expression of his ideas that he keeps turning around to look at me; a sharp swerve saves us just in time from knocking down a pedestrian, and then I don't dare interrupt him or ask him any questions for fear of something worse.

"You gotta make the best of it: one day steak, one day onions. But not on your life! If ya go to the restaurant, who's there drinking and enjoying themselves? All Communists. Soldiers, troops, that's what America ought to send us! And wipe out all them . . ."

By God's will, we've finally arrived. I thank him, go into the house, and as soon as the first hugs are over I want to discuss what I've heard with Renata.

"Yes," Renata says distractedly, "Arrigo also thinks it won't work in Italy, because the Italians will never stand for the Communists' iron discipline, like they didn't stand for Fascism."

The idea makes me laugh. What does it mean, they didn't stand for Fascism? She explains that they put up with it in a manner of speaking, all the time taking care of themselves. When Fascism started to use strongarm methods, it collapsed in fact.

This reasoning persuaded me only partly. "And then," I object, "there's a difference between the two dictatorships in spite of everything. Because the Communists appeal to an idea and ideas are very effective means of propaganda; if you believe, making sacrifices is easy."

I have to find some Communists and talk to them directly. It's too silly; I've been here for two months; I hear about them from all sides like a terrible menace weighing down everyone's life. Where are they?

"Talk to my doorman," Renata says. "Every now and then they strike and get higher pay. I think he has more money even than the ones who trade in gasoline! He's got a beautiful apartment for free, just like ours, and every night there's a crowd there talking nonstop and bad-mouthing the bosses . . ."

But the doorman, I decide, is not enough. I have to find another source of information.

66 Mimmo, Enzo, and Alex

To tell the truth, when I say that I want to talk to a Communist, there's one that I always think of. It's Mimmo Sereni, formerly Minister of Public Works, now representative to the Constituent Assembly. The last time I saw him we were both in the lower gymnasium and were how old? eleven? twelve? He was a small boy with dark, lively eyes that made one feel at peace. Then he changed schools, I don't know why, and I lost sight of him. But some years later I heard him spoken of in low voices by common relatives, as having fled. "It seems that Mimmo is a Communist . . ." and "They say that Mimmo is all involved in anti-Fascist propaganda . . ." and later, "They've caught him and given him ten years in prison . . ."

Phrases like that were repeated just for something to say, and they reflected both a fear of having such a dangerous person in the family and pride in having given birth, against the background of our weakness with respect to fascism, to someone who had put into action what all of us had felt in our hearts.

At that time I was going to the liceo, then to the university. I knew little about politics, but whenever I heard the word "Communist," I thought of Mimmo. And many years later, when circumstances had already made me leave—unwillingly—my shell of peaceful well-being, if I happened to be aroused against communism by a book or article in the press, there was always a corner of my mind where that dark little boy peeped out with his calm, intelligent look . . . and troubled me.

In Paris, in the terrible winter of 1939 to 1940, during the months of that "phony war," I came to know Mimmo's brother, Enzo. He was the only man I ever likened to Alex, because both of them were able to make life seem truly worth living. Enzo was not a Communist, he was a socialist, and when I once asked him, "Beh, aren't they just about the same thing?" he had taken me to task, teasingly. "A whole education to start over! Don't you know that there are no worse enemies than those who seem close to one another in theory, but not at all in fact? For goodness sake, Mimmo and I are polar opposites!"

They were polar opposites, but they loved one another. Enzo was in Paris on a mission from Palestine and before returning, when the Germans had already invaded France, he was worried about Mimmo, whom he knew to be in France, but whose address he did not know. What would he do if the Germans caught him? And did he at least have enough money to make his escape?

I always remember a last evening in our house on Avenue Victor Hugo. The Germans were not far from Paris, but Sandro persisted in not wanting to leave: who knows, leaving must have seemed to him an admission of that frightening and terrible thing, the defeat of France. I was afraid that it would suddenly be too late to get away as we were, with two old ladies and three little children, and I turned to Enzo for comfort. "What do you think? How will it end?"

"It will end well, you'll see," he promised. "We'll fight on the Loire, on the Garonne; we'll retreat to Africa if we have to. But we'll win!" And he laughed his generous laugh, trusting and honest.

"They'll win," I thought. "Meanwhile, we will have been swept away." But I was ashamed to say this, and then Enzo's laugh, his vitality, were contagious.

That winter is distant now, and I don't want to call it terrible anymore; I want to call it a dear, infinitely sweet winter. Enzo is dead. In '43 he left his kibbutz in Palestine to serve in the war; he had himself parachuted into Northern Italy, the occupied zone, and the Germans took him prisoner. When they told me that he had been caught and that he had to be considered lost, I didn't want to believe it. I remembered a phrase Enzo always used: "Only he who wants to die, dies!" and I repeated it to Sandro and said stubbornly, "It's impossible that they've killed him, he didn't want to die, he would have defended himself." Instead he died in Dachau. There's no doubt of it; his name was found clearly written in the registry there.

And Sandro, too, is dead.

And when I think of Mimmo, it's not only an interview with a Communist I'm after, but a little of their vitality and their strength in these turbulent times.

67 A Real Communist

One evening I was speaking of him to Paolo, Mimmo's cousin. I said, "I would really like to meet him." "Very easy," he answers, "but I don't see why you make so much of it. He's like all the others, you know. Follows the line of his party! It's no fun; they're all alike!"

"They all may be alike," I replied, "but I don't know even one . . ." and the subject was dropped there. Very easy, he said, but he hadn't offered to introduce me and I hadn't insisted.

A few evenings later I talked about it to Carlo, he too being a second cousin or something like it. This time I found myself facing a display of reluctance. "I haven't seen him for so long; he's a representative; I'd feel embarrassed . . ."

And so I decided to use what is called the American approach, that is, confront the problem directly. In this case it meant finding a telephone, calling Mimmo, introducing myself, and making an appointment with him for the next day. It was a matter of five minutes. I don't know if all Americans have the same familiarity with the American approach, but they should: it saves time, worry, and it gets you right to your goal.

All of this doesn't prevent me from being overcome by an attack of timidity when—the next day—I approach Montecitorio and ask the sentry, "Excuse me, is it here that one talks with the representatives?" But the sentry is extremely kind, he's almost not even dressed like a sentry. This matter of uniforms is a comic affair in Italy nowadays. Evidently there's no money to invest in such things, *maiora premunt*. On the other hand, how does one suddenly break free from an international and age-old convention like that? In Italy they have resolved it as children do, by means of symbols. To make a child feel like a general a braided cap is enough, and on Halloween night a hood of black paper is more than enough to change her into a witch. Thus in Italy today a sign (a hat of some sort, or epaulettes, or something else) indicates a function, and sometimes the material of certain uniforms is as thin as a sheet of paper and looks as if it will fall apart at a touch.

However, what has been lost in display has been made up for in courtesy. My sentry is less decorative than he used to be some years ago when he wore a black shirt, but in recompense he gives me directions with a smile. In the waiting room I give my name to certain clerks with an air of importance, behind a grate. Then I sit down with other people who have asked to talk with a representative and who, like me, seem more worried by the imminent meeting than proud of it. Four women come in as a group, whisper among themselves, take some forms, and sit down around a table to fill them out with an important and happy air. "Where it says reason for meeting," one of them says with a mysterious smile, "I put family mission." "Family mission?" another questions, uncertain. "Is that the right word?"

A pause in the happiness: they look at one another, suddenly a bit fearful. "Oh, yes," the first one replies; she is evidently the leader of the group. "He knows well enough who we are and what we want." She signs boldly and goes to the window to hand over the form.

Communists, I ask myself, or Christian Democrats? The leader returns, they all sit down on a couch against the wall, and each one opens a copy of "Osservatore Romano" on her lap.

They call my name, mangled, two or three times. I finally recognize it and go up the stairs. On the threshhold of the reception room I immediately recognize Mimmo, short, thickset, older than thirty, but with the same look—what to call it—of certainty? From the first words I look for the bright, aggressive smile of Enzo. It's not there. Still, I'm moved to speak to him simply and frankly; I trust him immediately.

While we go downstairs and he leads us through a narrow alley toward a caffè behind Piazza Colonna, I explain my difficulties in orienting myself in the midst of the political atmosphere in Italy today. "It's not only that I've lost so much time," I confess with a certain embarrassment, "but I was used to getting the news well digested and interpreted by Sandro, without any effort on my part."

"Convenient, but rather dangerous," and he looks at me a little ironically. Dangerous, I have to admit, and all of a sudden my daily struggle to understand things without Sandro seems important to me and worthy of him.

In the crowded little caffè we take the only free table, right in the middle, and go on chatting little by little and in bits, all the while disturbed by people coming and going, sitting and standing up, hastily downing an ice cream or a coffee.

First of all, about Enzo. "You know that we were very far apart in our political ideas?" he says quickly with an almost ostentatious claim for honesty. Then about the Italian political situation, which we necessarily examine rapidly, from left to right. Naturally, he calls Saragat and his followers a plague (the right wing socialists who abandoned the Socialist Party because it followed the Communist line too closely). I ask him if it's true that the other (Nenni) socialists always vote along with the Communists, without ever having their own line.

"But it's only natural," he answers. "Every Socialist Party, in the true sense of the word, has to go along with us!"

What then of Enzo's socialism? Hadn't he just said that they were polar opposites? But when it occurs to me to bring that up, we're already far beyond the subject. And how can I argue, with my uncertain background in politics, against his logic and his certainties.

Timidly I mention an article or a book I know, like *Darkness at Noon* by Koestler. Or I say something about totalitarian regimes or dictatorship. Or I say that yes, many things are bad about America, but in America, after all, I learned how to take notice of them.

Mimmo dismisses the book with a shrug, and as for the words "dictatorship" and "freedom," he says they're nothing but words. Because what sort of freedom do we have in the so-called democratic regimes? Who decides peace and war? Freedom to be killed, that's all. As for my having learned to think in America, he has a good laugh over that. "Poor us!" he teases me cheerfully. "Not only have they regimented you worse than in any totalitarian regime, but they've left you with the illusion that you're thinking."

But the arguments don't amount to much. After all, I talk only so that he not be silent, and between one phrase and another events of long ago show through almost against my will. I ask him about his children and he shows me photographs; one is almost a woman, another a girl, the third a child a year old. "One every time I got out of prison," he says laughing.

He speaks with restraint of the years in prison, almost reluctantly: his arrest in Nice, and months passed in the hands of the Fascists, then of the Gestapo, until finally the liberation. When I observe, I don't remember in what connection, that one of the terrible conseqences of totalitarian regimes is the atrophy of thought, he objects that it's not true. No one can take freedom of thought away; he never lost his, not even in prison, not even under torture.

"What did you think when you were tortured?" and I'm afraid of my own question, as if it were lifting a veil before a vision I did not have the strength to bear. But the answer comes hesitantly and with a great deal of modesty.

"Well, I don't really know; it's hard to describe. But it was thought, I'm sure of that, the whole time. Almost a dialogue with myself. Something like, 'All right, now we'll see . . . if you can live up to your big ideas. . . .'"

He doesn't look at me; his eyes follow a memory, a memory too deep for me and for this noisy caffè.

I know that unfortunately Mimmo is not the only one to have suffered like that. But for me at this moment it's as if he were; I don't know any of the others; they are many, too many, and they don't have—like him—a name, a face. Suddenly he personifies all of them, the millions of helpless victims, and the others who knowingly faced the evil and who were wounded and killed for me and for you. If they drank the hemlock and died on the cross . . . it's pointless to hide it from oneself, it was for us. And we have to do something in return, although I still don't know exactly what: fight as they fought, or perhaps simply be happy? One of these probably, or maybe both, but surely not just brood and shake our heads and say it's too awful.

Another minute and (God help me!) I would have hugged a Communist, if he hadn't stood up and begun to shout: "Giorgio!" at the top of his lungs. So I met instead Giorgio Amendola, a tall, blond, powerful man, very much more like the young fellow he had been than Mimmo is. But naturally, when I had last seen Amendola, he was not—like Mimmo—a boy in his first year at the gymnasium, but an adolescent just a couple of years behind me at the liceo. Since then I had heard of his father's death after a beating by the Fascists.

We didn't discuss politics with Amendola. Standing behind him at the counter where he was cheerfully putting away an ice cream, I reminded him of his great, unhappy love for a girl with blue eyes; he reminded me of my attachment to a handsome fellow with dark eyes. Then Mimmo said that they had to go back to the Assembly and we went out to the street and said "good-bye" and "maybe we'll see one another again" and "thanks for everything."

I walked back home, slowly passing through narrow streets and crossing the Umberto Bridge, letting the afternoon breeze ruffle my hair.

When I told my aunt and cousins where I had been, they found it very interesting. "How long did your meeting last?" my aunt asked. I didn't know, maybe an hour. I explained that Mimmo had to go back to take part in a session of the Assembly.

"Stupid girl," Carlo scolded me. "Haven't you been saying for days that you wanted to see Parliament in session? Why didn't you ask him? It would have been a perfect opportunity!"

He was right, of course, but I had simply not thought of it. My usual habit of slipping away when something really matters to me, of thinking it beyond my strength. And naturally, what can I expect but to lose the opportunity at hand?

So everyone shook their heads affectionately, saying it was lucky I was not a journalist. Trying not to regret the lost experience too much, but unable to divert my thoughts from the encounters of the afternoon, I went to the open window in Carlo's study. Below, the Tiber was thick with mud, and beyond it the domes stood up against the leaden sky. On the tops of the hills the pine trees sketched that eternal Roman motif of which I could never tire. How would I be able to live again without these windows and this river?

The sun was gone, but in setting it had illuminated with a strange light the churches and baroque palaces; now they seemed to shine with their own glow, cold but intense, on the gray storm clouds.

68 Last Day in Rome

The ship for the return voyage to the United States was supposed to leave from Genoa, and for some reason the trip from Rome to Genoa frightened me to death. If I made use of my favorite means of transportation, the bus, it would take an eternity, and the trains—after our experience during the August vacation period—did not attract me very much. Besides, I think that I was worried by the idea of leaving all alone and having to confront by myself the consequences of all those good-byes.

So I was overwhelmed with joy when Ramy, a childhood friend of Alex, called one evening and offered his company and that of his automobile. In fact, I felt so relieved that I agreed immediately to leave two days before the date I had previously set. It's true that this way I would have only a few hours to take my leave, but perhaps it was better like that!

I had made that decision without my aunts. In Rome there were only six, a small number in view of the total of seventeen scattered about Italy. And all of them, to tell the truth, had behaved very well and had allowed me complete freedom of movement; but, poor things, they were counting on the last days to make up for lost time. When they suddenly saw themselves deprived, they decided to take the situation in hand and organize according to their own lights at least the final twenty-four hours.

Of course, it wasn't a matter of personal interest; they were too generous for such mean feelings. They were concerned only for their favorites among the family and especially for certain imaginary obligations which I threatened to leave unsatisfied.

"My child," one of them said to me, "are you going back without seeing Anna?" Anna was the mother of an aunt in the United States.

"You're free to do as you like," said another, "but I think if you go back to the United States without having said hello to Cesare, your mother will be very upset. Good heavens, he was a friend of your father before you were born!"

"Listen," a third one chided me over the telephone at dawn on the last day, "I understand that you're tired and confused. I'll try to make it as easy for you as possible; I'll call her myself and have her here for tea in the late afternoon. You must see her! She asked about you from the moment you arrived, and I can't disappoint her so."

All right, do what you want! And I plunged into my craziest day in Italy, the most completely crammed.

So far as I can remember, one person or another was with me all day long. Thus one came to get me early in the morning, and another brought me back home in the evening. In between was a precipitous dash from one section of Rome to another, from one house to another. I don't remember very well where I was or who I saw that day; here or there a face, a phrase, a smile.

Next to a window, the curious old grandmother. It's enough to name someone for her to intervene querulously: "What name was that? Wait, wait. Guido? Not the Guido son of Sabatino, that good soul?" She waits anxiously for confirmation, and then continues happily with a string of details about Sabatino, his family, the scandals of fifty years ago.

Around a circular table, an Italian coffee, black and burning, in tiny, flowered cups. Boys and girls come and go in the room.

Exams, lessons; the mothers complain. One had to come back from vacation because of her son's schoolwork; another, on the telephone, refuses an invitation. "No, I'm sorry, what a shame! But how can I? If I go out, he won't study anymore."

At lunch, in an apartment full of workmen, we eat on a little table in a corner of the living room. Under the sheets that cover them, spacious divans are suggested, pictures with immense frames; below are the rolled-up carpets. My hosts have just moved and are profoundly embittered by the million in key money they had to pay as well as by the effrontery of the old proprietors, who continue to pass through in order to get to their apartment. Intolerable! The maid (she must have come with the house or something of the sort) serves us with a tired and disdainful air. The door, the telephone rings without interruption. And always for the former owners of the house, who don't have a phone yet. The maid calls. My hostess gets up from the table (she can't leave everything up to the maid) and then one hears her voice tense with the effort to hide her indignation: "Signor Rossi, it's for you, Signor Rossi!"

At two o'clock, I don't know how, there must be some misunderstanding, I find myself alone in the street. Alone, and I'm almost certain I don't have any other appointments until four. I struggle with a temptation that's been dormant in me for two or three days, since I went to a bookstore to exchange some books I had been given for my children and came out instead with an album of Corrado Cagli's drawings. They are drawings from the war years, when Cagli was in the American army, dated '44 to '45 and created in Texas and Germany. They seemed very fine to me, and when I heard that Cagli was in Rome just then, I thought it would be interesting to talk to him and see what he had done in the meantime.

But to go today is madness, with all this dashing from one visit to another. But if I don't go today, I'll never go; tomorrow I leave! How is it that when I was twenty, if I wanted to do something but thought it prudent not to do it, I refrained, but now instead . . .

isn't a mature person supposed to be more staid and possessed of self-control? Apparently not, since I don't use my blessed breathing space to go home and rest, but jump into a beat-up taxicab at Largo Goldoni and give the driver Cagli's address.

The taxi gets me there in a flash, and as he leaves, the driver, smiling and deferential, comments that many journalists live in this neighborhood. I don't know why he seems to have such a high opinion of journalists, but I don't want to disappoint him so I confine myself to answering with a cordial smile.

When the door of the apartment opens I have a moment of uncertainty. I haven't seen Cagli for eight years, since Paris, but the image I have of him is different from the dark and disheveled young man who opens the door to me. "Corrado is shaving," he reassures me, seeing my hesitation. "I'm Mirko." He invites me in and to sit down, and meanwhile I observe him with curiosity because I already know many things about him. That he's a sculptor, that he's a Communist, and that he's good. An exceptional sculptor, they say, but nowadays that's not enough to make ends meet, so Mirko designs jewelry in order to live. Last year he even had a show in New York, but couldn't take part in it personally because he was refused an American visa. He's a Communist.

We talk about Uncle Giacomo and Aunt Annina whom Mirko hid during the worst period of the German occupation. They had been arrested one evening, had spent the night under guard, and then had been unexpectedly released the next morning. But they hadn't dared go back home, and Mirko had taken them in. He is "Aryan," but his wife is Jewish, and they had every reason to want to go unnoticed. To take in two Jews, and, what is more, two Jews who were already under suspicion, was simply risking their lives. I think that it must be acts like this (here and there in the world) that redeem it and keep it from falling into the abyss.

And Abraham said: "Oh do not let the Lord be angry if I speak just once more. Suppose ten righteous are to be found in Sodom?" and the Lord said, "For the sake of these ten I will not destroy it."

Fortunately Mirko does not know that I am comparing him to one of the righteous, and he tells me about those times very simply and naturally.

"Your uncle," he says, "was a great guy. He got bored and asked me for heaven's sake to let him go outside. But I refused; you must also know he had distinctly Jewish features, it wasn't a good idea. One morning, I remember, he asked me to let him go out for just a minute, to buy a paper at the corner. I was the cruel one who said no! After all, it was a matter of life or death, there was nothing to joke about. Beh, it's unbelievable; I go to my studio to do some work; an hour later—I don't know why—I go out and look down the stairway. I see your uncle come in, not exactly inconspicuous there in our working-class block, with his well-cut overcoat and his hat with its stiff brim and his handsome gray hair. And what was more, he was holding a marvelous branch of a flowering almond tree intended for my wife. What can you do with someone like that? Yell at him?"

Cagli arrives, we sit down and have a coffee. It must be the fifth I've drunk today; what do we do in America without espresso? He's interested by my enthusiasm for his drawings, but not excessively; he says he's doing completely different things now, he'll show them to me. In the meantime we talk about Italy and America and the Italians in America and the Americans in Italy. And we take note of how difficult it is for the ones to understand the others. Cagli, who emigrated to America before the war as a result of the racial campaign, had then fought in the American army. He talks about his companions in arms, good, ordinary people; of the invasion of France and the days of anguish during the German counterattack. The American soldier who emerges from his stories is a simple, serious being, enthusiastic, curious, and nostalgic. And yet it's this same American whom the Romans describe as tricky, arrogant, and drunken.

It's plain that we're both in love with Italy. And that we both want to return to America is more or less evident. I think we'd both be rather embarrassed if we had to explain the reason why. We don't really know, but it's pleasant, somehow or other, to feel that we share certain loves, certain loyalties, and certain yearnings.

We go to look at the pictures. They are few, hung on the walls or piled up against a chair or standing on easels. I feel angry, as if I had been cheated. They are all more or less inspired by the same subject: a group of musical instruments on the floor in a corner. They are shown in various ways and with various tonalities, but always obsessively rectilinear, angular. Surrealist? Who knows what the right word is? I'm so disappointed that I don't even pretend to understand. After all, Cagli is still the father of those drawings that I like so much. So I tell him in confusion all the heresies that come to my mind: that a thing of beauty doesn't need an explanation; it must speak for itself; that I like all of his drawings because they seem to resolve so many problems through their art, philosophical, even political. . . .

He doesn't seem annoyed by my impassioned peroration, and he doesn't completely reject it. He tells me what my problem is: "You're not used to the kind of interpretation in all this. It's a matter of training. Not only do you see everything mistakenly, that is, looking for all the tangible, familiar items that give you pleasure, but generations and generations before you have taken the same model for granted, so that it's more or less in your blood. You could only get rid of it little by little." And he adds in order to pacify me: "Just sit quietly, look around, and let it sink in. That's the only way, you know."

I sit down in silence. Mirko is mixing colors on a table nearby. Cagli goes out of the room, then comes back, now and then changing the pictures on the easel in the corner. My eyes turn to them almost involuntarily. There is one on the wall to my right that I like very much. But why? It's impossible; I wouldn't want any of them, I know that. Nevertheless, didn't I say before that beauty doesn't require explanation? If I like that picture, I don't need to ask myself the reason why. I should say, it's beautiful to me, that's all.

Now Cagli is talking on the telephone. The instruments standing on the floor seem shabby, colorless, and unreal. On the easel there is a musical symphony of brown, fractured by a red trumpet.

"It's almost five," Mirko says, putting his implements away.

"Almost five?" Generations of people who have thought mistakenly cause me to wake from my magic spell and rush downstairs to the first taxi I see. At five I'm dutifully drinking tea in the midst of a group of lady friends. I'm a little out of breath and feel as though I've left something behind, a sort of symbolic slipper, somewhere in a fairy tale country.

69 Without Alex

Three months ago, in the noisy crowd of the port of New York, I already seemed to breathe a bit of Italy. This morning, in the hotel in Genoa, I can already sense America.

Handsome leather suitcases, from big, roomy rectangular ones, to middle-sized, graceful, round ones, to little, cute ones. Three-quarter-length coats in unusual colors: dark green, red, wine. Flowers on hats. A very well-groomed lady, high heels, tight-fitting black coat, short, pointed nose, flaunts a white gardenia and an amiable husband.

We watch disconsolately as our suitcases leave on a truck and are surprised to find them all at the port station in the middle of a fearful crowd of breathless people, carefree porters, weary functionaries. We can't go in, no one knows why. Everyone is crowded behind an immense glass door; now and then the mass sways frighteningly under pressure. Behind the door some sort of guard makes determined and unyielding gestures. Finally, we find another door with another guard; we pass through with a confident air. The end of another, more disciplined line, in ranks of four, contained by a wall on one side and a rope on the other. People find one another, hug, smile, talk.

"Next year I come back no matter what; it's great here. At my town we've already harvested the grapes, and what a harvest! Fewer grapes than last year, but the wine will be better, a lot better."

"So you liked it, eh?"

"Did I like it? As soon as I saw it, I told her, my wife: if she doesn't want to, she can stay in America; I'm coming back here."

"You don't mind leaving your job?"

"My job isn't worth a damn! You know what I do in America? I'm ashamed to tell you, I'm a waiter!"

The line makes another step forward; next to me a little girl lifts up a tiny suitcase, moves it a few centimeters, and sits down on it again, holding a fat, broken doll tightly to her chest. But the door of the office toward which we're moving doesn't seem to get any closer at all.

"I don't know what's so good about them, after all. The only thing I saw is that they've got their eye out for every penny they can grab. I told my relatives: 'Sorry, it's not for me. Any time you'd like to make a trip and come to the United States, you'll be more than welcome.' I'm telling you, it's simply disgusting."

"I'd like to do like the Jews, the country where I'm well off is mine. And if my wife doesn't get it, so much the worse for her."

"They lost their damned war and they think they own the world. What cheek, I tell you!"

Thank God, we're almost at the door; another minute and we'll be inside. Tickets, passports in hand. At customs, there are our suitcases! Finally the ship. Up the gangplank, through the gilded salons, down the impressive stairway to my cabin with six beds, big, airy, beautiful. I'm the first one there; I stretch out on a bed and fall asleep.

Murmuring voices wake me up, the sound of a contraption. I open one eye. Seated opposite me on a lower bed, mother and son are intent on opening an accordion case, and they smile at me. I return the smile and try to fall asleep again, but soon the notes of an Italian song wake me completely. The boy is playing his brand new instrument conscientiously; he stumbles, gets angry, shakes his head. The mother doesn't take her eyes from him and smiles a sad and hopeful smile. "That's all Mamma, I don't know anything else. Now I'm going back up, all right?"

The boy has gone; the mother puts the accordion away and lies down; she turns around and meeting my look of sympathy, she whispers, "I've never been so lonely in my life . . ."

I ask if I can do anything. No, nothing, it's just that she's left her husband in Italy, and probably he won't be able to rejoin her for two or three months. The boy? Yes, he's a good boy; she's going back out of love for him, his school and everything else. "You see, I lost two before he was born, and I don't know what I would do if something happened to him!"

"Hello, girls!" Our third comrade is wearing an ugly and showy suit, a matching green hat complete with feathers and veil, which she places carefully on her bed, eyeglasses, freshly curled hair, and a cheerful look. I give up trying to rest and begin to busy myself instead with my suitcases.

"Oh, you really bought an accordion," says the lady in the green suit. "I promised my husband that I would bring one back, but I just can't remember those things. He'll never forgive me . . ."

A little later they discover they have friends in common, and in time they go off arm in arm waving good-bye to me. "See you later!"

I ask myself. Did I feel lonely when I had to leave Alex for such a short time? Oh, yes. Only that it was always Alex who left. Sometimes just to Cleveland, or Washington, or Chicago, but I usually cried, yes, I remember. And sometimes he telephoned me from the city: he had an unexpected meeting and wouldn't be home before eleven or midnight. I would say coldly, "Very well," and go directly to my bedroom to cry. Oh, God, I would like to take back those tears, those vain, useless tears! I wish this was the first time in my life that I had cried. If I could see him just once a week, or perhaps once a month, or once a year! Once a year, compassionate and all-powerful God, God of Abraham and Isaac and Jacob, and I promise I will never feel lonely again.

70 Leaving Italy, Again

We arrive in Naples on a gray, foggy morning, and the city reveals itself little by little, as if slowly lifting a curtain. As we drop anchor, a sudden gust of rain sweeps the landing area. While passengers who embarked in Genoa hurry off to enjoy an hour in Naples, others climb the gangplank to come aboard. The ship swarms with porters; the cranes squeal as they lift the trunks piled on the dock. In the bow they're loading chestnuts; the barrels swing up twenty at a time from some lazy, fat barges that never seem to grow empty. I'm one of the few people remaining on board; I wander here and there. A man with a band on his arm proclaiming the name of some agency I no longer remember invites me to visit Pompei. Another with a wooden box with many little drawers hanging around his neck offers me cameos, filigrees, Venetian enamels. It seems that he has tirelessly searched every shop in Italy for all the things he could find in the worst possible taste. In a corner two men with little books in hand check the loading of the barrels.

Conversation. Work, earnings, family. Times are not good in Italy; everyone wants to emigrate. One of them has a son, yes, only one, all he needs is another! The other is very young and declares that he's absolutely not going to start a family now. It would be crazy! He asks about America. Eh, in America they must be well off, for sure. More and more stowaways leaving on these steamers. . . . Do they ever find them? Well, yes, sometimes, unfortunately. But lots of them get through! Even two boys a month ago, ten or twelve years old. What they do when they get off without knowing the language, God only knows!

One talks, the other writes in the notebook. Every now and then they interrupt themselves, check their numbers, then go back to their conversation.

The American army. As far as likeable is concerned, they were likeable, of course, goes without saying: cheerful and good-natured, they were like children who enjoyed playing. But rogues, mamma mia! Drunkards, first of all, and when they were drunk they didn't know what they were doing. And then, what kind of discipline! Soldiers and officers talked to one another like we do. The Germans, yes. You have to tell the truth: it was a pleasure to see them, correct, stiff, always at attention in front of superiors.

It's the younger one who says that, eighteen years old, I don't even know how he manages to remember the Germans. The other gives him a nudge sometimes, trying to soften his too cocksure opinions; he's probably a little suspicious of me. Faced with this childish way of thinking, I too have childish reactions.

"It's strange," I chime in, annoyed, "they're so great, so well disciplined, they know everything, foresee everything, and then they always lose. They lost the other war, and they lost this one. And the Americans, big kids, not serious, undisciplined, think of that combination! they always end up winning."

"That's true," the young one looks at me with a serious air. "Who knows why. There must be something that drives them. Because they come from different countries, right? And yet they fight together."

"Certainly, there's something that drives them. I can tell you; I got there six years ago from a France in flames. It was hard to get in, but then we found work, friends, good schools for the children."

"Yes," he says with satisfaction, "that must be it: they don't fight for the country, they fight for a way of life."

I would like to explain that the way of life is part of the country, but he's already shaking his head thoughtfully, his pencil in the air. "Nevertheless," he says by way of conclusion, "it was really bad luck; this time they deserved to win."

Down below the barge is almost empty. Little by little the deck fills up with passengers. We were supposed to leave at five, but it's already six, and we're still on the lookout for stowaways. Four or five incompetent soldiers, dressed in strange uniforms, ragged and mismatched, make their way across the deck, taking quick and embarrassed looks under the cranes and inside the lifeboats. It is like a scene in a play, with sets and actors. The only thing missing is the muffled and dramatic accompaniment of drums behind the scenes.

The sun is setting; I give a last look at the coast, which is still Italy. I've told everyone that I want to live in America, but that I'll come back, I'll bring the children. Mah! What was that remark (of Stendhal, I think)? Who has seen Rome once will never again be perfectly happy! I shrug my shoulders. "Pazienza!" It means that I'm adding nostalgia to my other sad thoughts. Does it matter?

I suddenly seem to understand that leaving is the price you have to pay for rediscovering, that you can't have joy without some suffering. It's all far from being clear. And yet, for a moment, I seem to understand, I seem to be ready to pay the price for my share of joy.

The sun is down; we're leaving. Below us, in a ferry on its way back to port, a woman raises her eyes to look at us and makes the sign of the cross.

71 The Count, the Baritone, and the Tenor

The next morning I'm seasick. I get dressed slowly, little by little, collapsing onto the bed every five minutes; if I can make it to the chair on deck, I'm saved. Finally, I stretch out in the fresh air with a terrible sensation gripping my viscera, almost like a hand that seizes me and flings me back and forth along with the movements of the ship. I lie back with my eyes closed, not going down even to eat. People pass back and forth and begin to acquire identities. That one is this one's mother; this one is that one's husband. Voices come to me in the polite tones of first acquaintance or tense with the irritation of small family disagreements. When they go to dinner, the deck is empty except for two or three chairs occupied by listless persons like me.

But the next day the sea is calm and the sun comes out. We sit down in our chairs and look one another in the face. I can't shake off a feeling of bliss of which I'm ashamed; it's not noble to be happy just because one isn't sick to one's stomach. At table, as a result of a fortunate series of circumstances and not my own merit, I find myself among the cream of society. "I congratulate you," says the nobleman to the majordomo, "you haven't seated any peasants at this table." The majordomo assures him, "Who do you take me for? Peasants, here with you?"

I almost feel myself a little uneasy, but I notice with relief that the count attacks his first course with the avidity and conviction of an ordinary mortal.

In the afternoon, lying down again on the deck, we all pretend to read as we wait for tea: a page, a little nap, another page, a bit of chat. The hours slip through one's fingers. Three or four seats from mine children are playing with scissors and paper, filling the deck with odd little colored bits. A blond couple, in love and happy, carry up and down a varicolored straw basket with a baby inside it, blond and happy like them. One of my roommates, a washed-out blond who spends the night with her light on reading, doesn't raise her eyes from her detective story even during the day; someone told me she is an employee of the State Department on her way to a new post. Three nuns go about looking stern, never leaving one another; they drink coffee in the lounge, and at the sound of the orchestra, they make a sign to one another and stand up. Sometimes they stop in a corner of the deck, all three together against the railing, absorbed in their magical and mysterious rite. They don't see that their black veils flutter in the wind like the wings of majestic birds.

The tenor walks back and forth, chest out and hat over his eyes. He's the genuine article, from the long white hair that distinguishes him as "una testa," to the pointless anecdotes, which he laughs at himself with so much gusto.

The baritone, bundled up in a swathe of sweaters, vests, and scarves, is intensely preoccupied with arranging them according to the changes of temperature. He gets up, he sits down, taking off one or another garment, always preserving a diffident and solemn manner. He often has a sheet of music in his hand, which contrasts strangely with his aspect of a preoccupied bourgeois. One would describe it as a surrealist touch slipped by chance into a mild nineteenth-century portrait.

The ship's doctor complains: "I'm sad this evening, I don't know why. I have a position that many on land envy, and yet I feel uneasy . . ."

The countess comments languidly on the passengers: "This one is badly dressed, that one looks unhappy, this one is a Jew. Oh, is that so? You're Jewish too? For that matter, some of my best friends . . ."

An attractive young man with a busy, energetic air protests: "There's something wrong on this ship; I can't arrange anything entertaining. The women are too sophisticated."

The lady from the hotel in Genoa still has the same embalmed gardenia on her head, day, night, and midnight. It's become an indivisble part of her personality, an almost hideous excrescence.

A gentleman comes out of the bar and stretches out on a chair next to mine, irritated. He says, "To hell with those cards and drinks! I'm bored, I don't know why; I've never been so bored on a ship."

From an open window of the deserted lounge comes a barely comprehensible murmur: "I like you so much. . . . You're a very dear person, you know? I think that you must be a marvelous instrument . . ." After all, the technique doesn't change, nor even the childish indignation toward women who don't take seriously the part assigned to them. As if by not going to bed with someone before the end of the voyage, they're not good sports.

72 Pre-emptive War

One by one I peel off my coverings. First the coat, then the wool sweater. I roll up the sleeves of my blouse, turn down my stockings to my knees. Now there is very little between me and the sun. My glasses are still on, away with the glasses. Now the sun floods me, penetrates me, cancels all thought, makes me happy.

I'm at the top of the ship, on the sundeck; near me two masculine voices discuss politics. It was Roosevelt who wanted the war with Japan. Just a minute, please, think about what you're saying, think of Pearl Harbor. Pearl Harbor is an incident; come on, be honest, you know the Japanese were provoked; listen, I don't say that Roosevelt didn't have the right to carry out his policy, but it's clear that he wanted war. Impossible. Roosevelt wanted to help England, that's all, and he would have been happy to stay out of war.

Now they talk about Danzig and the war in Poland. "At least that was aggression, wasn't it?" one voice protests. "Aggression, we have to agree on what that word means," replies the other, "because if one country pushes another to its limit so that it takes a desperate action, it's not at all clear who is the real aggressor."

I open both my eyes. It's an Italian engineer from "Radio Marelli" going for training to General Electric plants, a man of forty, healthy, energetic, able to reason logically and convincingly. I close my eyes and wait for more. He regularly comes to his con-

clusions in a predictable order and form, as if they issued from a
newspaper or Italian textbook of ten years ago.

The necessary living space for Germany; the injustice of the
Treaty of Versailles; the sacred right of Italy to its colonies. The
other speaker, a naturalized American, whose mother was deported by the Germans, fights back as best he can, choked as he is
by passion. "Wait a minute, the mistakes of the Treaty of Versailles
were in large part corrected afterward. . . . Excuse me, but do you
honestly think that if the Allies had continued on in the attitude
of Munich, the war wouldn't have spread? That after Poland, they
wouldn't have gone into France? . . . No, listen, there has to be a
way of singling out the aggressor, it's not possible. . . ."

His voice trembles with indignation, with things not said, with
years of suffering held in, but he is dashing himself against that
smiling, self-satisfied wall that has an answer to everything, a
seraphic certainty.

The attack on France? Ah, were you in France in 1940? Yes, it
wasn't very nice, but to compare it to kicking the lion when he's
down seems to me an exaggeration. Go on, France has done plenty
in past centuries, and now look at Briga, Tenda . . . what hog-
wash. . . . We're even."

I move in my chair, open my eyes again. I encounter a friendly
smile: "The lady thinks like me, isn't that so?" I shake my head violently and stammer: "Even, even with six million dead in the concentration camps?" He answers, "Yes, it's sad. But at bottom even
there we're even. Think of Hiroshima! You know there are sick
people, dying people, from the atomic bomb?" I protest again,
"But it's not right to put Hiroshima and the concentration camps
on the same level. You can't possibly in good faith see acts of refined cruelty, sadistic and systematic, which began and inflamed
the conflict, in the same light as the single, terrible but decisive act
that ended it."

He asks me what passport I carry. American? Well, then, it's
natural, I couldn't say anything else.

"What does that have to do with it? The Americans think in a hundred different ways. And then, I became an American by way of fascism, not an anti-Fascist because I was American."

He laughs good-naturedly. "Aren't you hungry? It's time for an aperitif; let's go down to the bar!"

When he has gone, I stretch out again and close my eyes, trying to find my earlier well-being and relaxation. But the sun is not strong enough.

73 Flashback

For several hours already we had encountered seagulls. I didn't see them arrive; one never sees them. Suddenly, there they are. And they don't even seem to be flying; Their rigid, motionless wings beat rarely, from time to time. And they take their places with us without ever leaving.

Someone told me that seagulls are not white but gray if you look closely, and they love to follow the ships because they feed on the refuse thrown out of the kitchen windows. I'm sure that's just gossip. I've never seen a seagull come to rest on the surface of the water. They're certainly not here to eat; they are a strange and splendid delegation that the earth sends to arriving guests.

They make me recall another pure, azure morning like this one, more than six years ago. Oh, I remember the year and the month and the day; I've had to write that date so many times on official forms!

Date of arrival: January 9, 1941.
Port: New York, N.Y.
Vessel: SS *Serpa Pinto*.

It was a beautiful morning like this one after ten days of hellish weather. We were almost all refugees on the boat and we were on deck to drink in, as if in a dream, that miraculous sun. But we could not abandon ourselves to the warmth or the joy of finally being in port because we were still afraid.

We had already forgotten many things, it's true. The air-raid sirens and the long, cold, monotonous nights in the cellars; the French roads all black with cars pointed in the same direction, mattresses and bicycles on their roofs; the German airplanes swooping low and fast; the sudden emptying of the cars into ditches; the merciless, metallic rat-tat-tat of machine guns; the screams of terror.

It's surprising how quickly one forgets these things. At the first plate of beefsteak in Lisbon we forgot our hunger; at the first sheet we forgot the nights in the fields; and none of us woke anymore with a start in fear of airplanes.

But there were other things that were now in our blood like a sort of poison. They were called "work permits" and "residence permits," "identity cards" and "driving permits," "temporary safe conduct and gasoline ration cards," "exit visas," and "transit visas," and "entry visas." As Italians (since Italy was at war with France), it was assumed that we could not travel; as Jews, that we could not stay; as civilians, that we had no right to gasoline; as anti-Fascists, that we could not hope for a transit visa through Spain.

Despite all that, for some absurd reason we wanted to go on living, and so we set ourselves in motion and learned about many things. How to wait in the prefectures of various cities until we found the right man, the one who was a little more good-hearted or a little more corruptible than the average. How to get gasoline from some run down garage in the outskirts of the city, and stand guard at the end of the street to watch for the police while the garage man filled our tank at five times the normal price. How to get friendly with the secretaries at the consulate, and dine with them, and send them flowers. How to pay enormous sums for a Haitian visa, which got us nowhere, but actually gave us the right to ask for a Portuguese transit visa.

The lie became our only weapon, and we didn't worry ourselves with any fanciful notions concerning our right to use it.

But when we finally reached Lisbon, and when—after weeks of frenzied telegrams to relatives, friends, and various officials—we finally obtained a Brazilian visa, then we noticed in a corner of the last page that we were required to declare that we were not Jews. Suddenly we felt utterly exhausted, and God knows why we didn't have the strength to tell just one more little lie. The Brazilian consul was very patient and politely took the time to explain to us that it was only a formality and it would be best for us to accept it; by then the Germans could arrive at any moment; it was assumed they could cross through Spain any day, and we would be taken prisoner. But we just could not bring ourselves to follow his advice; somehow it made no sense to run away from the Germans if we had to begin a new life in a new country still disguising ourselves. Besides, we were so tired; couldn't the consul take note of that? So we said thank you, excuse us, but we prefer not to take the visa if you don't mind. And our relatives in Brazil, who had done all they could for weeks to obtain it, were terribly angry. And, to be sure, everything in Lisbon was terribly dear and we had little money left, and as for the American consul, it seemed that he never intended to grant the American visa, not trusting us enough or something of the sort. Because if we had really been anti-Fascists, blablabla, we would have been in prison, isn't that so? Certainly not wandering about the world as we were.

And so the ships left one after another, and each one said that probably it would be the last, and some of our friends managed somehow to get aboard them, while we, we went back to our hotel and began waiting again.

These, strangely enough, are the things that can't be forgotten, not even right there before the very entrance to New York.

I'm not afraid of bombs anymore, but I still am of paper. I think that maybe a stamp could be lacking and they could send me back. And I don't look at the sun or the seagulls or the shipping traffic that is becoming more and more dense. And I don't see the land, first vague on the horizon, then magnificently clear, or the skyscrapers that shoot up unexpectedly, or the cars going back and forth along the shore like busy ants. Or the Statue of Liberty holding up her torch.

All I do is clutch my purse (where has Alex gone? where are the children?) to make sure the documents are still there, that everything is in order.

But all there is in my purse is a small, modest green booklet. Don't you remember? This is 1947, not 1941. Sss! Don't look for Alex. And don't be afraid. You have an American passport.

Yes, I can relax. I have an American passport, and all the officials on board down in the lounge are very polite. In truth, they smile continually during the entire procedure, and it doesn't take more than five minutes.

Here I am again on the deck, with New York rising up before us in all its exciting magnificence. Why does one say of an Italian city that it "stretches out," and of New York only that it "rises up"?

A fat man of dark complexion, with a cigar in his mouth and his hat pushed back on his head, stammers in admiration: "What a sight!" Two young men discuss the kinds of automobiles speeding along the highway. One of them has a telescope and shouts excitedly, "I'll bet anything that's a Studebaker!" The other pulls impatiently at his friend's sleeve, claiming his turn.

A lady whom I had greeted during the past ten days with a nod of the head looks at me with new respect. "It's magnificent," she says, and I'm aware of being radiant, full of an absurd pride.

A friend said to me the other day that we, who were uprooted, are not capable of being happy anywhere. Wherever we may be, we will continually feel the absence of someone or something. Maybe it's true. I strongly felt the absence of America when I was in Italy, and probably I'll begin to feel the absence of Italy again as soon as I disembark. But perhaps our problem is not that we love too many countries, but that we still love too few. Perhaps this is the only good thing to have come from so much suffering: that some of us were forced to abandon our nationalism, to look around ourselves, to understand and to love. And we have to try very hard not to return to our shells or to find another one in which we can comfortably hide.

We get closer and closer, almost touching the tip of Manhattan. Then we turn and begin to move up slowly: piers 42, 43. The one we're aiming for is pier 83; it seems impossible that we'll ever get there, so slowly are we moving. Sometimes it seems that we're not moving at all.

By now the cabins are all empty, and suitcases are piled on the stairway landings. People, dressed up from head to foot, walk back and forth on the deck, or wait leaning against the rail. Everyone wears a hat that changes their faces, almost their characters. The free and easy air that Basque berets had dispensed so freely among the most conservative types during the crossing now gives way to the casual style of soft felt, or the more serious looking stiff felt, or the distinguished, aristocratic look of top hats. Kerchiefs, scarves, and turbans have been changed for sporty blouses or have given way to feathers, half veils, and birds. Even the small girls almost all have hats, giving them a well-bred, busy, and gossipy air of little women.

In the corridors the staff talk among themselves. They are still wearing their white jackets, now wrinkled and dirty from their work of the last hours. Being already, in a certain sense, on vacation, gives them a tired and indifferent air. It's as if they have collapsed upon themselves and at the same time are assuming their true appearances as separate individuals.

We are all gathered on the side that looks at New York; it's strange that we don't all tip over.

Piers 56, 57.

"Where are you going when we land?" a girl asks a young man who is going to teach (and study) in a college in Missouri. "Maybe we can still spend an evening together."

"Where am I going? The YMCA no less! They've found out that I'm a minor and won't let me leave the ship if I'm not chaperoned, think of that! I wonder if they're just going to keep me as a ward in New York or accompany me as far as the college. Can you imagine it, the professor who goes to class under the wing of guardian angels?" He laughs, but isn't able to hide his annoyance.

Piers 60, 61.

The baritone waves a letter from Chicago: "Your presence indispensable for the performance Monday evening." He pretends not to understand the spelling very well, in order to have a pretext for showing it around in search of clarification. He repeats to himself the word "indispensable" with childish complacency.

Piers 64, 65.

An elegant blond lady shouts into the ears of an old woman whose wrinkles are heightened by rouge. "We can't land yet," she says, pronouncing each word distinctly. "They say there's still a ship in our pier, and it has to be pulled out before we can go in. That's why we're going so slowly." The old woman nods with the timid, disarming smile of the deaf.

Piers 68, 69.

"What will my husband think?" a lady exclaims with so much harshness that one can't do less than suspect that her husband's thoughts are probably the last of her concerns. "I telegraphed him: three-thirty; weren't we supposed to arrive at three-thirty? The quarantine ended at two! We're just wasting time, and God knows why!"

Piers 72, 73.

"Mamma," whimpers a tired, disheveled little girl. "Mamma, listen to me. I want a glass of water. Mamma, can you see if that boat is leaving now? Can we go in now?"

"Shh, be good, dear." And then, nervously, "I'm telling you to be good. Don't start to cry now, be a good girl. Here's Papà, he'll tell you." Papà is the least upset of the three. Actually, he's smiling as if this were a day like any other. "Don't you worry, my dear," he says gently, "it's only the customs men. It seems that they were telegraphed yesterday that we would dock at seven; the captain didn't expect such good weather. We have to wait until they're ready, that's all! What do you want, my love? A glass of water? Of course, come with Papà; I'll get you a nice, cool drink."

Now we're perfectly still.

Down below it looks as though the dock is overflowing with people. We're tired of waiting and walking back and forth restlessly. On the other bank of the Hudson River the coast of New Jersey becomes more and more indistinct. Here and there lights begin to come on. The water becomes darker. I feel good being at home. Nevertheless, I'm not in a hurry to land; there's no reason for me to rush. I lean against the rail and go on looking down at the river below.

The people around me continue talking; their voices still have the warmth that comes from ten days spent together. Can it be that, in a few minutes, they will be strangers again?

Someone, somewhere, is passionately defending the cause of Italian women. "Our immorality came from hunger," her voice trembles with resentment. "Otherwise, Italian women would have been able to give the others a lesson. For one thing, they don't drink!"

Now the river is completely black beneath the noisy ferryboats glittering with lights, making their crossings.

Historical Background and Personal Chronology

1555/6: Papal Bull strengthens medieval principles of segregation of the Jews. Ghetto of Rome established. Other major cities of Italian peninsula follow.

1804: Napoleon I crowned Emperor of the French.

1806: Napoleon makes himself King of Italy. Ghettos are abolished.

1814–1815: Fall of Napoleon and the Congress of Vienna. Subsequently ghettos are reinstituted.

1815–1848: States of Italian peninsula reconstituted under domination of Austria

1844: Giuseppe Ascoli, author's grandfather, is born in the ghetto of Ancona.

1848–1849: Failed revolutionary movements by Italian states against Austria. Only state to retain its liberal constitution, Piedmont emerges as hope of liberal Italy.

1851–1861: Emergence of Cavour as leader of Piedmont and of Italian unification movement (with Garibaldi in the South).

1861: The Kingdom of Italy is proclaimed. It incorporates all of the territories of the peninsula with the exception of the province of Lazio, including Rome, which is still under the dominion of the

Pope. Ghettos throughout Italy are abolished with exception of Rome.

1870: Italian troops enter Rome. Rome and all of Lazio annexed by Italy. Ghetto of Rome is abolished.

1902: Alexander Pekelis is born in Odessa, Russia.

1907: Author (Carla Coen [Pekelis]) is born in Rome.

1917: Beginning of Russian Revolution.

1920: Alexander flees Odessa alone on the last ship to leave the city before the Bolsheviks take it over. Crosses Turkey and the Balkans to Germany, studying at universities of Leipzig and Vienna, and ultimately arriving in Italy.

1922: Mussolini and the Fascists "March on Rome." Mussolini subsequently granted dictatorial powers.

1924: Murder of the Socialist Deputy Giacomo Matteotti, who had denounced illegal acts of violence carried out by Fascists.

1927: New electoral law abolishes universal suffrage.

1928: Alexander receives law degree from University of Florence.

1929: Alexander receives fellowship from Ministry of Education to study at London School of Economics and Political Science.

1930: Carla Coen meets Alexander Pekelis and they marry soon after.

1932–1936: Italy invades and occupies Ethiopia. Germany recognizes conquest. League of Nations declares Italy aggressor and applies economic sanctions. Beginning of Rome-Berlin Axis.

1932: Fascist Party of Florence prevents Alexander from teaching at University of Florence.

1933: Daniela, Carla's first daughter, is born.

1935: Alexander appointed full professor of jurisprudence at University of Rome.

1936: Simona, Carla's second daughter, is born.

June 1937: The Rosselli brothers, exiled leaders of antifascist movement and **friends of the Pekelis family,** are assassinated in France by Italian Fascists.

September 1937: Carla enters law school.

March 1938: German annexation of Austria brings German power to the Italian border and makes Mussolini more than ever dependant on Germany.

July 1938: Rossella, Carla and Alexander's third daughter, is born.

September 1938: German invasion of Czechoslovakia.

August 1938: "Leggi Razziali." Despite past policies and assurances, Italian government institutes laws directed against Jews. Revokes citizenship of all foreign Jews who had taken up residence in Italy since 1919 and orders them to leave the country within six months **(directly affecting Russian-born Alexander).** Discharges all Jewish teachers and students from universities, prohibits marriage between Italians and non-Aryans and the latter from employing Italians.

September 1938: Alexander leaves Italy for France.

December 1938: Carla and three small daughters join Alexander. Couple's Russian and Italian mothers join the family a few months later.

May 1939: Conclusion of political and military alliance between Italy and Germany.

August 1939: The German-Russian pact is signed.

September 1939: Germany attacks Poland from the west, Russia from the east. England and France declare war on Germany. (Italy had declared neutrality.)

April, May 1940: Germany occupies Denmark, invades Norway, the Netherlands, and Belgium.

May 28, 1940: The Pekelis family leaves Paris by car and begins their flight to the South of France.

June 10, 1940: Italy enters the war on the German side. In France, the Pekelis family suddenly becomes the "enemy."

June 13, 1940: Germany occupies Paris. Petain becomes head of French administration, replacing Reynaud. His first official act is to sue for peace.

August 1940: The Pekelis family crosses border to Spain and proceeds across peninsula to Portugal.

December 28, 1940: The Pekelis family leaves Lisbon aboard the *Serpa Pinto* after six-month wait for visas.

January 1941: The Pekelis family arrives in the United States. Shortly after, Alexander is appointed professor of graduate faculty of the New School for Social Research.

September 1941: Haim, Carla's fourth child, is born.

December 1941: The United States enters the war.

September 1942: Alexander begins Columbia Law School.

1943: Alexander is named editor-in-chief of the Columbia Law Review. Upon graduation, a new position is created for him — graduate editor-in-chief.

1945: Alexander becomes chief consultant to the Commission on Law and Social Action of the American Jewish Congress.

August 1945: Alexandra (Coco), Carla's fifth child, is born.

December 1946: Alex dies in a plane crash returning from Switzerland where he had attended the World Zionist Congress (which approved the partition plan that created the state of Israel) as a delegate of the American Labor Zionists.

Summer 1947: Carla returns to Italy for the summer. Subsequently writes "Back Where I Came From," which is Part Two of the English edition.

1953: At the urging of her eldest daughter, Danielle, who is attending Sarah Lawrence College, Carla approaches President Harold Taylor with the proposal of starting an Italian Department at Sarah Lawrence. The first Italian class is launched that fall.

1969: Carla retires from Sarah Lawrence College.

1970s: Carla writes "Memories (1907–1941)," which is Part One of the English edition.

1985: Carla dies in New York City.

1992: Daughter Simona goes to Italy and meets Arianna Ascoli, Carla's first cousin. Arianna later translates "Memories" and sends it to Casa Editrice Sellerio, in Palermo.

1996: Sellerio publishes both parts as *La mia versione dei fatti.*

2004: Northwestern University Press publishes English edition, *My Version of the Facts.*

About the Author

Carla Coen Pekelis, born in Rome in 1907, was the oldest child in a family of upper-middle-class Jews. The family moved to Florence when she was eighteen, and Carla appeared destined for a comfortable life. Instead, she married Alexander Pekelis, a brilliant Jewish refugee who had fled his war-torn homeland in 1919. Settling in Italy, he became a lawyer, taught law at the University of Florence, and eventually became Professor of Jurisprudence at the University of Rome. During this period they had three daughters together. Carla started law school with visions of their practicing law together, but their plans were cut short when the Fascist racial laws, enacted in 1938, forced Alexander to flee to Paris. Carla joined him shortly thereafter with their daughters and two mothers-in-law. Less than two years later, they were again forced to flee—this time through the south of France, Spain, and Portugal to avoid the advancing German army. After a Kafka-like wait in Lisbon, they arrived in the U.S. in December 1940, settled in Larchmont, New York, and had two more children. In 1941, Alex was appointed Professor for the Graduate Faculty of the New School for Social Research, and later graduated from Columbia Law School. Alex's most significant professional contribution during his tragically short career was the *amicus curiae* brief he wrote in the 1940s challenging the segregated school system in California on behalf of Mexican-American children. His daring and brilliant argument against the "separate but equal" doctrine was finally adopted by the United States Supreme Court in *Brown* v. *Board of Education* a decade later. Alex died in a TWA plane crash in Ireland in 1946, as he was returning from a Zionist conference in Switzerland. After her husband's sudden death in 1946, Carla went on to start and head the Italian department at Sarah Lawrence College. Carla died in New York in 1985. She kept a diary her entire life.